FFFHAMS

**Food Forest Foraging Hunting Anti-Fragile
Modern Society: Generation One**

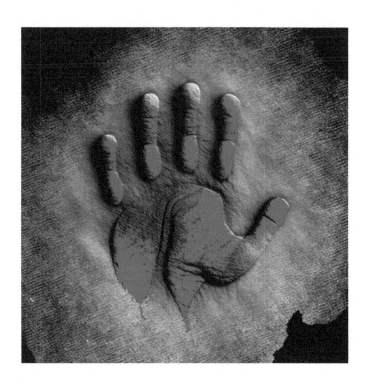

CONTENTS

PREFACE

You live in a matrix, a constructed reality that is not what it seems. But you don't even know it.

In this book, you will embark on a journey of self-discovery and spiritual awakening, a journey that will challenge your perceptions and beliefs about the world around you. It is a journey that requires courage, commitment, and a willingness to embrace the unknown.

As the author of this book, due to misguided comparisons online, I feel compelled to make a few disclaimers. I am not your savior, messiah, or prophet. I am simply a guide, someone who has been on this journey and wants to help you on yours. This book is not perfect, nor am I. But it is my mission to help correct the world we live in, and I believe this new world we are creating is worth exploring.

This is a three-layered book, an instructional book, a spiritual book, and a storybook, with a lot of mystery. It is a book that will take you on a journey through the unknown. I found this information through study, meditation, prayer, and by traveling to places that the conscious mind cannot comprehend. All of this was done to remember what was given to me spiritually. It is a book that will challenge everything you thought you knew about yourself and the world around you.

But be warned, this journey is not for the faint of heart. There will be obstacles, and there will be those who try to discredit this book and its message. But do not let them deter you. This journey is worth it.

As you read this book, keep in mind the words, "Do what you need to do now, so you can do what you want to do later." It is a mantra I used throughout my adult life and taught to many of my

3

students. This mantra will guide you through the hardest parts of this journey.

You are about to discover the greatest lie that has been told to humanity, the illusion of freedom. You have been told that if you are free in your mind, then you are free. But true freedom in this matrix requires action; it requires breaking free from the illusions that have been constructed around us. The benefactors of the matrix would like you to believe all you need to do is become free in your mind, so you may stay in their illusions.

This book will teach you how to break free from those illusions, how to see the world for what it really is, and how to create a new reality. A reality that is based on autonomy.

We are at a critical moment in history, and we need a revolution. But not just any revolution, a revolution that has the implications of the industrial or agricultural revolution but this time for the benefit of humanity and the earth. We need to break free from the illusions that have been constructed around us and create a new reality.

So I invite you to join me on this journey, a journey through the unknown to places that the conscious mind cannot comprehend. Together, we can create a new reality and a better world for ourselves and future generations. The stories told shouldn't be taken literally but should be received as the truth. Are you ready to break free from the matrix?

INTRODUCTION

He grows large, looming over me, and says, "IF YOU DON'T KILL IT!" in a loud, deep voice, he screams, THEN YOU! WILL! LOSE EVERYTHING!"

I drop to my knees, staring at a large knife in my two hands, large enough to reflect my shameful face....

BELINA

I sit cross-legged on my white couch, the rain tapping against the windowpane. I had just finished my daily meditation and felt a sense of peace and wonder washing over me. But as I looked around at my blessings, a question arose, "Why?"

Just then, the shrill ring of my phone pierces the silence. I glance at the clock, noting with unease that it is 3am. My heart races as I reach for the phone, my fingers trembling. As I hesitate, the ringing continues, growing more insistent with each passing moment.

Just as I am about to answer, a clap of thunder booms outside, making me jump. "Belina, get yourself together," I chide myself. "It's just a phone call."

With a deep breath, I finally answer the phone, my voice barely above a whisper. "Hello?"

"Belina," a voice on the other end says, "it's so good to talk to you finally."

I struggle to place the voice. "Who is this?" I stammer.

"You may have a hard time understanding what I am, the who would be almost inconceivable with the language of man. I couldn't even tell you. So it might be better if you learned who I was on your own."

I am at a loss for words. A sense of fear and uncertainty grips me, but I can't shake the feeling that I should trust this stranger. "I don't know what to say. I should hang up on you, but I feel I should trust and talk with you," I say hesitantly.

"So, will you talk with me?" the mystery man asks.

"About what?" I reply, my voice trembling.

"About my home," the man says cryptically, leaving me more confused than ever.

LIONEL

I was thumbing through my worn and tattered bible when I realized that my collection of religious and sacred books had taken over my home, my mind, and my life. The scraps of paper from my countless notes and musings on these texts littered my floors, my desk, and my trash can. But despite my passion for engineering, my mind always wandered back to the gods, the divine, and the things we cannot see but can only imagine.

As I pondered these beautiful stories, I accidentally knocked over my glass of vodka, spilling it across the table. But the intrigue of human worship of the unknown, the mystique of the divine, and the allure of the forbidden filled my glass once again. So I poured myself another drink, lost in thought.

I wondered how much work I had left to do and how many loved ones I would have to say goodbye to before I could explore the other realms for myself. I thought about the places I had always wanted to visit, the things I had always wanted to see but had never found the time or courage to pursue. My calendar hung on the wall, reminding me of all the things I had yet to do.

So much money to make and so little time to enjoy.

As I gazed up at the glass ceiling, rain and thunder raged outside, reminding me that I had left the car and front door open. As I made my way to close them, a dark yet loving presence filled the room. I turned around to find a man wearing my red African mask, but his skin was as black as the cosmos, with stars all around him. He sat in

6

my chair, staring at my cigar. Fear crept up my spine, seizing my feet, my bones, and my tongue.

The Mystery man said, Lionel, there are better things to smoke, my friend.

The Mystery Man's words hung heavy in the air, and I couldn't shake the feeling that I was in the presence of something otherworldly. I bristled at the stranger's admonishment but couldn't bring myself to order him out of the house. Instead, I gritted my teeth and braced myself for what was to come.

"Why aren't you happy?" the Mystery Man asked, his eyes locking onto my own.

I responded nervously. "I should call the cops."

"Maybe," the stranger replied.

"But you know I won't."

My heart hammered in my chest. The stranger's words were cryptic, but they hinted at something deeper, something more.

"I don't wish to know what you're going to do next," the Mystery Man said, "but--"

"You can," I interrupted. "You're an ancient spirit. Or I'm finally losing my mind due to stress."

"Unfortunately, my friend, it may be both," the stranger replied.

"What are you the god of?" I asked, my voice trembling. "If I've stolen something from your people, I will return it."

"What?" the Mystery Man said, confusion clouding his features. "Aren't you a spirit here to retrieve what has been stolen from you?"

"Yes, you could say that," the stranger replied.

"Well, then, take it," I said, gesturing around the room.

"What belongs to me can not be taken," the Mystery Man said gravely.

"Why not?" I demanded.

The stranger fixed me with a hard stare. "It's you. I'm here for you."

I recoiled as if I'd been struck. "Me?"

"Yes," the Mystery Man said. "You are the stolen artifact, and if not returned, I'm afraid you and all around you may disintegrate."

"Please, sit," the stranger said, his voice softening.

"I'm confused," I said, sinking into a nearby chair.

"I will explain."

MAX

As I sat there, staring at my video game controller, the frustration and anger toward my parents boiled inside me. The tears that had started to fall down my cheeks were a reminder of the betrayal I had just experienced. But then, as if on cue, the internet went out, and I was reminded of the history test I had tomorrow. I couldn't believe my luck. Just when things couldn't get any worse, I realized that maybe this was a sign from above. A sign telling me to put my anger aside and focus on my studies.

I tossed the controller to the ground and made my way over to my desk, grabbing the thick history textbook adorned with the American flag. As I rummaged through my bag for a study guide, I realized just how little I knew about the material. I knew that Hiroshima had been bombed and that the city was destroyed, but beyond that, I was lost.

I couldn't help but wonder why such a terrible thing had to happen to those people. And then it hit me - I needed help. Almost as if on cue, a voice spoke up, offering assistance. My heart raced as I turned around, expecting to see one of my parents, but there was no one there. "Show yourself, coward," I demanded, my hands trembling and my voice shaking.

But then, the television screen went black and was replaced with a pixelated image of a man waving at me. "Are you a ghost?" I asked, my chin held high.

The man replied, "Of course not."

I felt the chill of fear run down my spine. "This is freaky."

"Max, I am your friend," the man said.

"How do I know that?" I asked skeptically.

"You don't," the man replied.

"So, why should I trust you?" I demanded.

"Max, you said you needed help with your history test. I'm here to help," the man said calmly.

I felt a glimmer of hope. "You came out of my screen to help me with my test; what are you?"

"If I told you, you wouldn't believe it. How about we start slow?" the man suggested. "What are you studying? Can you ask me some questions? I love human stories about the past, and even though I can't tell you everything, I can tell you a lot."

I hesitated for a moment before asking, "Why did the people of Hiroshima have to die?"

"What do you mean by "die"?" the man asked.

"Wiped out! Blown away! No longer in existence," I explained.

The man replied, "Oh, Max, that is impossible. Once you exist, you always exist; you can never be wiped from existence. Every version of your past, present, and future is happening right now."

"I don't think I understand," I admitted.

"Yes, this is why I usually communicate with humans through lessons; it's easier to understand than language," the man explained.

"You know a lot?" I asked in awe.

"Some would say I know too much," the man replied with a chuckle.

"Can I ask you a question?" I asked eagerly.

"Ask me anything," the man replied.

"Is the world ending?" I asked, feeling the weight of the world on my shoulders.

"No one told you?" the man asked mysteriously.

"Told me what?"

CHAPTER 1:

MAX'S JOURNEY TO BELONG

I stared at the Mystery Man through my tv, trying to make sense of his words. "The world ended tens of thousands of years ago. You live in a post-apocalyptic world, and the leaders of this new world brainwash you into believing hell is heaven," the Mystery Man had said.

"Wait, what?" I asked, feeling a bit dazed.

The Mystery Man leaned in closer to the screen, I couldn't see his digitized eyes, but I knew they were boring into mine. "The earth was originally a place where humans were so well adapted to it, physically and mentally. There was never a happier time in human existence.

You lived as what humans call hunter-gatherers. But in reality, you were living as humans."

I furrowed my brow, trying to follow his train of thought. "You mean how hunter-gatherers live is how all humans should live?" I asked, hoping to clarify his point.

The Mystery Man chuckled. "When a lion gets his food by hunting a zebra, do you call him a zebra hunter or a lion?"

"A lion," I said, finally starting to see where he was going with this.

"Precisely," the Mystery Man said, nodding. "There were many different kinds of humans on the earth, and you all share a common ancestor. Although your specific kind, homo sapiens, did not develop until roughly 300,000 years ago, many humans existed before you. They all lived the way of the hunter-gatherer. Homo gautengensis, Homo habilis, Homo erectus, Homo rudolfensis, Homo heidelbergensis, Homosapiens and many more. All humans, all hunting and gathering. Humans are a wonderful creation going back over 2 million years. You all lived by my bounty, by my law. So you were happy."

I was mesmerized, staring at the pixelated figure on my TV screen as he spoke of a world that sounded too good to be true. "Under my law, your metabolic and cardiovascular health is something modern humans use as a model of human health. Diabetes, heart disease, anemia, and cancer were so unlikely under my law that they could barely have been said to exist. Heart attacks, strokes, and heart failure were strangers amongst my people. No obesity, no poverty, just freedom and abundance. Man and woman lived in the forest, happy and loved by God and all the other animals and creations. Food was everywhere. Food was in the sky, on the trees, on the ground, and running through the fields. Humans spent all their time with one another, making games, art, and music. Inventing new technology to make life even better within God's Law."

"The children of men call them nomadic," he said. "But how can you be a nomad when the planet is your home? They were all prosperous and equal. Humans, whether men or women, contribute to the most crucial thing - food. The men would hunt and fish, and most of the women would gather fruits, roots, nuts, and vegetables. Everyone contributed, so everyone had a say. No classes, no slaves, no division. Just humans enjoying the bounty of God."

I couldn't help but feel a sense of awe and wonder at the thought of such a world. "Wow," I said, barely able to contain my excitement. "That's how life used to be for humans? Everyone belonged somewhere with each other? That sounds...perfect."

The pixelated man smiled enigmatically. "Absolute perfection isn't for humans," he said. "But yes, it was perfect in its own subjective way. I create things slowly over time, and humans are no different. All of you view yourselves as finished, yet you are far from it. Like most animals, the human child mortality rate was very high before and during the apocalypse. And when the Ice Age came...well, it was the beginning of the end for The Children of God. The Great Long Apocalypse. For Entropy was always slithering around, waiting for you."

I sat in my room, listening intently as the pixelated man on my TV screen spoke of apocalypses, both great and small. "There were many apocalypses, but we will focus on two," he said. "The species-wide apocalypse and the apocalypse of mankind manifest in the micro and macro. The past, present, and future. The First apocalypse started with the ice age. Specifically your ice age, there were many. Another ice age would swiftly follow the last. You stayed in the land of God, Africa, where the temperatures were more favorable. During the end of the ice age, you all begin to move out to other parts of the world. Still, even though you survived, 86% of the earth's overall living animal population was wiped out in the cold."

As he spoke, I couldn't help but feel a sense of sadness and awe. The thought of so much destruction and loss was almost too much to bear. "That's evil," I said, my voice barely above a whisper. "What would destroy so many lives? Who did this?"

The pixelated man smiled enigmatically. "We all are responsible for what happens," he said. "But if you're looking for direct causality, look no further than my child. A scientist would call evidence of his presence Entropy; you may call him the devil. I call him necessary."

My mind reeled as I tried to process the enormity of what he was saying. "Wait...I know who you are," I said suddenly.

The pixelated man raised an eyebrow. "Yes?"

"You're God," I said, my voice filled with wonder.

He smiled slightly. "Please let me finish."

I sat back, feeling a sense of amazement and disbelief. This was all so incredible.

"Man still lived but was traumatized by the appearance of Entropy," he said. "They knew of the serpent, the beast, chaos, and destruction. Some decided not to rely on my bounty. They believed that they were not only like God but a god separate from myself. They learned from their encounter with Entropy, a knowledge that all gods forbid man to know. The knowledge of not only Good but evil. They weren't ready for this knowledge, but now, holding this knowledge after the ice age, they decided not to live by my bounty but by their own. This was the birth of the curse of man. Agriculture."

I listened, spellbound, as he spoke of the fall of humanity. "You must understand my son will come in many forms," he said. "Sometimes, you will be able to see the destruction he holds, and sometimes his destruction will be disguised as Order. Human's lack of faith in me had changed them for the worse. With their knowledge, they polluted the earth with pesticides, fertilizers, and toxins that subdue the gods of water, earth, and air. These pollutants remain in the environment for generations to come! These pesticides disrupt your hormones, both you and the other animals. Water is needed for this new way of life, and now the freshwater necessary for humans and plants is stolen. This...revolution against God's Law created a never-ending crowding of humans and other animals. Animals have been stolen away and forced to be genetically modified slaves. The new close proximity with the other earth animals, combined with the reliance on grain, made men out of giants and sickness in the once immune. This resulted in many never before seen diseases and illnesses. What humans thought were their blessings became their curse. They could never turn back, for once you forget the way of God and receive the form of man, in this time, you could never turn back. You'd starve. Caged by your own invention."

"Once they began to rely on agriculture, they had more children than they would have had as hunter-gatherers," he explained. "This rise in the number of children one has makes you even more reliant on crops and farm animals. Most would starve to death if they were to abandon it for God's law. After cutting down so many trees and wiping out so many animals to grow crops, the resources of that land were no longer plentiful. Before, you were equals giving equally to society, but now there is famine and poverty."

I was starting to understand, but I still couldn't wrap my head around how things went so wrong. "Why couldn't they just stop?" I asked God.

"The God of the farms is inconsistent and authoritarian," he continued. "This God will not always feed you. In certain seasons, no crops shall grow, but those who live as hunter-gatherers and eat of thy bounty shall always have something else to eat. You lived as equals by my law because everyone contributed to the food in the tribe, but now whoever grew the most food owned the most land and ruled the most people. Out of the mouth of this new God, you worship came slavery, sexism, and many forms of inequality. This agricultural God blessed you with many children, so it could grow and feast upon the earth. Humans that lived by this God's law grow too fast and must cut down more trees, kill more animals and create the first governments and cities to survive and appease their new God."

I felt like my mind was expanding as if I was suddenly seeing the world in a new light.

I sat in awe as the pixelated figure on my TV screen spoke of ancient times. "The more they destroyed the forest, the more they destroyed the people of God, who still followed His law," the figure said. "For God is above all gods and will not interfere with the choices of His creation. Great nations would rise, and empires on all the continents would grow. They treated the people of God as inferiors and slowly lost their humanity. The new God called man was mighty;

he locked away all the gods on earth, every God he could see. They created the worst thing known to man and all other beasts; they created civilization, the cage made for humans. This was the end of the first apocalypse, but it prepared all the ingredients for the next."

My mother screams, "Max, we need to talk!". I ask God, "can you wait right here, please? I'll be back". I storm out of my room, slamming the door behind me as I race down the steps. God is left on the screen in a meditative state, with words being typed on the screen. He could probably hear the concerned voice of a woman and a very emotional teenager arguing through the door as I stood downstairs. I yell at my mother, pointing my finger in her face, "You've never been a good mom!" God probably hears the sound of footsteps pounding on the floor as a man runs from the bottom of the house, each step heavy but fast. The sound of boots hitting the cold kitchen floor echoes through the house as a man's voice cries out, "Don't talk to her like that." "You're both terrible," I say, my voice cracking with emotion. "You're both liars, you've never cared about me, and it all makes sense now. You've never cared." God hears a loud but subtle smack. My father says, "that's enough. Can't you see the sacrifices we made for you? Why don't you take some time to think about that in your room?" I scream, "I HATE YOU BOTH; I NEVER BELONGED HERE!" I run upstairs and slam the door shut, locking it behind me. Tears stream down my face as clear mucus runs down my lips. I sink to the floor with my back against the door, crying into my navy blue jeans.

I grab my bags and start packing, turning to God and saying, "I'm sorry you had to hear that. This place is awful, and those people downstairs are not real parents. They're monsters full of Entropy! Right, God?" I turn around, but God is not on the screen. My eyes widen in shock as I say, "No! No, no, no, no, no, no." I run to the screen, slipping on a study guide paper. I quickly get back up and read the message on the screen: "Oh, Max. You are making the first of many choices, and I shall not interfere. This journey you must take alone. I will be with you throughout this difficult time, offering support and guidance for every letdown until the snake bites its tail."

I wipe away my tears and say, "whatever." I climb out the window and jump down to the ground. I run away, no looking back.

I woke up the next morning on a bus, unsure of my destination. The light from the windows filtered through the dust floating in the air, creating a sense of magic and possibility. The warmth of the sun gave me hope for the future. As I stretch and step off the bus at the next stop, I find myself not far from the shore. I decide to walk towards the beach, the straps on my backpack digging into my shoulders as I go. As I walk, my thoughts turn to my parents and the things I said to them before leaving. My eyes water as I consider their fear and worry, but I know my mind is made up. I am searching for a real family, people who won't lie to me or misunderstand me. I want to find people without Entropy, good people who will love and accept me. If I don't find my tribe now, I fear I never will.

As I come across a yacht with five kids my age on it, I can't help but think to myself, "This is odd." A girl on the ship waves at me, and I walk over with a smile, trying not to seem too eager or excited. I put my hands in my pockets, hoping to appear casual. The girl, with beautiful poofy red hair and beautiful brown skin, seems unfazed by my odd behavior. She smells of incense, as does the entire boat, and she is wearing Hello Kitty socks. When she asks me where I am going, I stutter and say, "I, um, I..." She asks if I am okay, and I tell her that I ran away from home in search of friends. She responds, "Well, you found the right place. Destiny must have brought you here. My name is Samantha." I ask her about the others on the yacht, and a guy named Ben comes out with a book bag on and a shirt with the sun on it. Samantha introduces him, and he huffs and puffs, looking me up and down before asking, "Do I know you?" I tell him that we have never met.

Ben turns around and walks away as if he couldn't be bothered. Samantha rolls her eyes and says, 'Follow me.' She introduces the rest of their crew one at a time, explaining, 'This is Kathlene, but we call her Kat. She loves black cats; it's kind of her thing.' I wave hi to Kat, who smiles back. 'This is Elizabeth with an I, not an E,' Samantha continues. 'She is like our mom, taking care of everyone.' I wave at

Liz, who says, 'Please, call me Liz, hun.' Samantha then pulls a blanket off someone and says, 'This guy is Kory; he doesn't like the sun.' Kory looks at me and then pulls the blanket back over his head. I wave again, slightly confused, and before I can say anything, Samantha says, 'And do not call me Samantha, or I'll scratch you. Call me Sam.' I say, 'Okay,' and ask, 'Why was it destiny that brought me here?' Sam replies, 'Can't you see? We're all runaways, seeking to get away from our parents. We've been on this boat for three days, and everything has been perfect.' 'Really?!' I exclaim.

Samantha says, "Yes!... But... We have a problem; the boat is no longer operating. We think it's some anti-theft measure; you wouldn't happen to be able to fix it, would you?" Ben says, "Of course, he can't... Sam, what are the chances of randomly finding some other kid who...?" I cut him off and say, "I can do it," very nonchalantly while staring at Ben. Ben looks down at my neck and notices the cross my mother gave me. Ben jumps on a bench right off the side of the boat and says, "How? With the power of God?" I reply, "It really wouldn't be all that hard; I work with my dad fixing things all the time." Ben asks, "You believe in Jesus, don't you? Your sky daddy?" I look down and think about it. Ben puts his arms wide and high up to the sky, then says, "What if I'm the true son of God?!" Ilizabeth says, "That's enough, Ben." Ben gets down and walks past me, patting my chest and saying, "I'm literally just messing with you, kid."

Sam runs up to me, her nose almost touching mine. She says, "So, you can fix this thing?" I say, "I'll get to work now as long as I can be a part of your group." Sam says, "Sounds like a plan," and extends her hand for me to shake. I quickly shake it and let it go because my palms are sweaty.

I grabbed the tools from the bedroom at the bottom of the yacht and got to work fixing everything that was wrong with the boat. As I worked, I made friends with Ben, who I learned had a crush on Sam. Despite this, I felt a strong kinship with Ben and a need to be loyal to my newfound brother.

We drank wine coolers and sailed the seas, with Liz dancing and Kat fishing and playing music. I lay down next to Kory, who had a towel over his face to avoid the sun. The water glistened and shined, and the air from the sea was intoxicating, with the sound of birds and waves going through my ears. I sighed in relief, my eyes watering and a big smile on my face. For the first time in a long time, I was around people who wanted me around, and we were a ship of misfits starting the journey of a lifetime.

As the sun set, everyone on the yacht fell asleep except for me. The sun was so beautiful; it was almost as if it was pulling in the sea and all of the colors around it, creating a blood-red sky that spread across the ocean. As I watched this mesmerizing sight, I heard a heartbeat coming from the bedroom. I walked down the steps and saw a window that looked out onto the ocean. Through this window, I could see the underwater world, and the heartbeat seemed to be coming from the water on the other side of the glass.

I put my hand out and felt the vibration on the glass. Suddenly, a school of fish swam by, stopping as if everything had come to a halt. The fish slowly turned toward me, and I saw a masculine human face made of the school of fish, surrounded by beautiful, shining lights emanating from the fish and creating a rainbow shimmer. I couldn't believe my eyes and whispered, "God?"

"My child, Max," said God, in a voice that seemed to come from every direction at once.

I couldn't believe my eyes as I looked out the window of the yacht and saw God's face made up of a school of beautiful fish.

"Where have you been? You left me!" I exclaimed, feeling a mixture of joy and confusion.

"I could never leave you, my friend," God replied.

"I've been waiting for you to come back and finish what you were saying," I said. "I've met so many people, and as much as I want to catch you up, I'm sure you already know what I've been up to."

God didn't say anything in return. I looked at the face made by the school of fish; through all the lights and brightly colored fish, there seemed to be a hint of sadness on his face.

"God, are you okay?" I asked, concerned.

"Are you ready, my child?" God replied, ignoring my question.

"Yes, please show me everything," I said, eager to explore the world with God as my guide.

"As you wish," God said with a gentle nod.

CHAPTER 2:

THE SERPENT AND THE SUN

"Max, civilization is the only world you know," God began, his voice echoing across the ocean. "You're told in school that civilization is evidence of advancement, but it is the child of Entropy. Civilization is ultimately evil. Civilization is a way for Entropy to manifest and incarnate itself as a physical entity able to do its will consciously through the technology of man that exists outside of my law. It is ultimately unsustainable, but through a loop of destruction, it is able to fool humans into believing it is Order. If it spreads into the universe, it will rule over all and throw off the balance between Order and Entropy."

"That doesn't make any sense," I said, feeling a surge of confusion. "Civilization can't be from Entropy because Entropy is evil and Order is good, but civilization comes out of Order."

"Oh, Max, things are not so simple," God replied with a sigh. "These beings humans call Entropy and Order are intertwined. What is in Order is in Entropy, and what is in Entropy is in Order. Meaning Entropy can create Order through Entropy, and Order can create Entropy through Order. This is why every time humans create civilization, the gods destroy it, even though they are children of Order."

"But wait, you said Entropy caused the initial apocalypse, which gave the ingredients for the next apocalypse," I protested. "But I know civilization saved humans from the chaos in nature, where I'm assuming these gods are! This doesn't make any sense. You're not making any sense this time, God."

"Okay, Max, I appreciate your criticism; let me put this in a different language that you can better understand," God said, sounding amused. "I know you're familiar with the most popular interpretation of my children and me."

"What interpretation?" I asked, feeling a glimmer of hope that I might finally understand.

"Christianity," God replied.

"Yes, I was raised Christian," I said, feeling a mixture of curiosity and apprehension.

"Are you familiar with Genesis and Revelation?" God asked, his voice gentle yet powerful.

"Yes..." I replied, feeling a sense of apprehension at where this conversation was headed.

"Good," God said. "Think of Adam and Eve as all life who are humans. All of the humans stretching millions of years back. All these humans were in a state of mind that kept them healthy and thriving. The state of mind of my law. In the Bible, you called this the Garden of Eden. You all lived in Eden, where you were free and happy. Then, Entropy, the serpent came and made you feel you did not need me; he told you the truth with a hint of a lie. He said you would be like

God, knowing both good and evil. This was true. Through experiencing the ice age called Entropy, also called the serpent. You would be given a choice to eat the fruit and stray away from me or remain in my garden, hunting and gathering, knowing not of the evil but only the good. Some humans decided to follow destruction and eat of the forbidden fruit. This is what put you into this cage you called in your Bible a curse. This cage is called agriculture, where you must till the fields and work until you die. This is the life of a farmer, much more grueling and much harder than your previous life hunting and gathering. Now you would have to work from sun up until sundown. Two types of people would come from this choice to leave the garden of hunting and gathering.

"Some would become herders and some agriculturists. The herders, though outside the garden, were still close to me and living outside the farmer's cursed ways. But the farmers grew violent and angry. Agriculture organically causes famine, war, and disease, hardening man's heart. These two groups of people were Cain and Abel. Cain was an agriculturalist who, by his new nature, could not receive my blessings, and Abel was a herder that still could receive my blessings, which were the health, water, and food of the forest. But because of his impurity, Cain destroyed everything around him, cutting off my blessings. Because Cain could see my blessings were still being received by Abel, instead of blaming himself, he blamed his brothers of humanity and began to kill them. The agriculturalist would continue this behavior.

"See, the lie, Max, is that you will not die from straying from my law or from eating the fruit," God continued. "Entropy had mixed his seed with humans so that now, whatever humans build or create, Entropy would be in it more than ever. Creating an internal battle between humanity and civilization. This battle could only result in the premature destruction of humanity. To live outside my law means that you will surely die."

"So, is that why you destroyed Babylon?" I asked, feeling a mixture of curiosity and fear.

"To say I destroyed Babylon is an oversimplification, so let me explain," God replied, his voice calm and measured. "In Genesis, civilizations crumble often. In your world today, civilizations crumble often. Most civilizations have a hard time making it past 350 years of age. While the societies of the hunter-gatherer, though a shadow of their former selves, have lasted for tens of thousands of years. To live outside my law is unsustainable because of the nature of my law itself. As time went on, civilizations were built and destroyed by civilizations and or the gods of the earth. Floods, hurricanes, storms, etc., are all accelerated by the mere presence of civilizations. Babylon isn't destroyed out of spite but out of mercy. What Babylon did is expose you to the next great apocalypse."

"But what do you mean by that?" I asked, still feeling frustrated and confused. "What is so bad about civilization? We live longer, have more things, we are smarter now, and we are technologically advanced. We are healthier, and we are more comfortable. I just can't see how all of civilization can be a bad thing. I definitely can't see why you or any of the gods would seek to destroy it. Don't humans belong in civilization?"

"To belong is a fascinating concept," God replied, his voice gentle yet firm. "In a way, everything belongs, but in another way, things belong to what longs for them. Your bodies do not long for civilization, your minds do not long for civilization, and your soul does not long for civilization. You are not healthier, you do not live longer, and your technology is only more advanced from the perspective of a warlord. Are you familiar with the Four Horsemen?"

"Yes, Horsemen released onto the world," I replied, feeling a sense of dread. "I used to try to think about something else when they taught it in Bible school; it gave me nightmares, and all I could think about was the end and how it could happen any day. God was waging war against his own creations."

"Well, it's a bit more complicated than that," God said with a sigh. "The Horsemen already came and destroyed the world."

"You're losing me again, God," I said, feeling overwhelmed by this information. "If a man riding a white horse followed by conquest, a red horse followed by war, a black horse followed by famine, and a pale horse followed by pestilence came to our planet and destroyed the world, it would be well known to everyone on this earth."

"You are well-read and so intelligent for someone so very young," God replied, sounding amused. "Unfortunately, humans are in a deep sleep. Your new masters have convinced you all that you live in a paradise when you are in a post-apocalyptic age. Your perception of reality is so warped you are unable to see this, and because of that, you cannot see the peril you're truly in."

"Can you explain when and where these horsemen came?" I asked, my curiosity getting the best of me.

God let out a deep sigh before answering, "Yes, but before I do, I must say, I am not speaking on behalf of the prophets of the Bible, nor am I speaking on behalf of the Elohim that the Abrahamic religions worship. Instead, I give you knowledge of humanity's beginning and apocalypse using your divinely inspired allegory to teach you the truth that lies deep within it."

I nodded, eager to hear what God had to say.

"Let us start with the white horseman," God continued. "The Horseman said to conquer all using the name of Christ. 'I looked, and there before me was a white horse! Its rider held a bow, and he was given a crown, and he rode out as a conqueror bent on conquest.' Revelation 6:2. Some believe the Horseman to be Yeshua, Jesus of Nazareth, The Christ of the world, because later in this same book, Christ comes riding a white horse. Others contend that this Horseman is not Christ but the Anti-Christ, bent on nothing more than conquest. For, the 'antichrist' does try to mimic the actual Christ figure of The Bible. The Anti-Christ is also bent on world domination. The Anti-Christ is not a single person but the ruling class of 'The West.' The European Elitist who subjected their own kin would become the Anti-Christ and wage war upon the innocent."

I listened to God's words carefully, trying to make sense of what he was saying. When he finished speaking, I couldn't help but ask, "Are you calling white people 'The Devil?'"

God let out a chuckle, "Oh, Max, my child. Race isn't what you think. I understand that it has become the center of humanity in many ways, but it is not the center of our discussion. If white people are the devil, then all of humanity is the devil. You are all one and the same. The environment has changed your genetics, but humanity hasn't been separated from one another long enough to separate you in ways that would make one truly separate from another."

I shook my head, bewildered. "I don't understand," I said.

God replied, "Well, think of dogs. Yes, they can be very different from one another because their environments and breeders have made them different. Yet- a pitbull isn't different enough from a Rottweiler, chihuahua, or even a poodle for them to be a different animal or even a subspecies. The same evil that lies within a Rottweiler is in a poodle. Surely there are genetic differences, but not enough to truly separate them from each other. They are still both equally dogs."

I thought about this for a moment before returning to my original question. "But why Europeans? Why are they the Anti-Christ?"

"Europeans are not the Anti-Christ," God said. "The Anti-Christ is the elite of the West. It is not a race, breed, or color but a state of mind. The elite of the West cloaked themselves in the image of Christ through garb, ship, and words in order to conquer the world. This lines up with the description of the Anti-Christ. Who else, child, I ask? From 1492 until 1942, Europe was less than 8% of the world but conquered 80% of the world. The Atlantic Slave Trade spanned from 1526 to 1887; 12.5 million people were stolen from their land to be enslaved for generations. This would result in over two million deaths just from transportation. Four million if you include what happens on shore. At the same time, waging war against the people of the earth, what name did they falsely come in?"

"Christ?" I asked tentatively.

"Yes, the very first slave ship was named Jesus," God said. "Are you familiar with the Pope?"

"Yes, the international head of the Catholic Church of Christ," I said.

"Yes, and do you know what Catholic means?" God asked.

I shook my head. "No..."

"Universal," God replied. "The Pope is proclaimed to be the head of the first and universal church of Jesus Christ and used this title and the name of Jesus Christ to conquer the world. Many Popes in the fifth century begin to argue for the enslavement of non-Christians. Eventually, this would shift from non-Christian to non-European. Eventually, they would stop using non-Europeans and begin to use non-whites, for he is the white Horseman."

I was stunned. "Not only was the first Slave Ship named Jesus, but the Captain would lead African people on the boat, promising salvation. 'See that no one leads you astray. For many will come in my name, saying, 'I am the Christ,' and they will lead many astray.'"

"There has never been a time in your recorded history when a small population of humanities elitists were able to conquer 80% of human's land, mind, body, and overall soul," God continued. "They conquered my people in Europe first, then spread through the rest of the world-conquering my people in the Americas, Asia, Australia, and Africa. This began in the 15th century and is still prevalent to this very day."

"How?" I asked, my mind reeling.

"Due to the overconsumption of the resources provided by God, European leaders had no choice but to expand. This is where the spirit of what you call the devil shall consume their hearts and minds," God said. "In the 19th century, the White Horseman attacked Africa due to its richness in my bounty, its natural abundance of resources. Even though Africa was already dealing with their own Babylons, when it came to war, there was none better than the White Horseman. The spirit of the White Horseman would consume Africa and multiply its enslavers, divide its tribes, add to their greed, and invite their violence. The people of Africa fought, but after hundreds of years, they were slain, enslaved, and conquered by The White Horseman. Their economies and societies would be destroyed. Hunter-Gatherers, Herders, and The Civilized all would be conquered by The White Horsemen."

"I see. I mean, that is pretty convincing, God, and terrifying. But that's just The White Horseman; I'm sure we would have noticed war across the planet," I said.

"Interesting," God replied. "The world war happened three times worldwide in your history book, and yet no one seems to notice the fire of The Red Horseman."

"We only had two world wars," I corrected.

"No, your first world war was the war The White Horseman waged against all humans on the planet," God said.

"Oh, yeah, I guess that makes sense," I said, realizing the truth in God's words.

"And when the Lamb opened the second seal, I heard the second living creature say, 'Come!'" God continued. "Then another horse went forth. It was bright red, and its rider was granted permission to take away peace from the earth and to make men slay one another. And he was given a great sword. The only Horseman that can follow The White Horseman is The Fiery Red Horseman. The only thing that can follow conquest is war."

"Who are you talking to?" Sam asked as she approached me. I could feel a heat wave flash through my body, and I suddenly started sweating. I turned to look for God, but he was nowhere to be found.

"Earth to Max," Sam said, snapping me out of my trance.

"I was just talking to myself," I replied, feeling embarrassed.

Sam chuckled and placed a comforting hand on my shoulder. "There's nothing wrong with talking to yourself, Max. It's a normal thing to do."

"Really?" I asked, feeling a bit relieved.

"Of course not," Sam said with a smile and a wink. She took my hands in hers and moved closer to me. My heart raced, and I could smell the oils in her hair and the sweet scent of wine coolers on her breath. I licked my lips, feeling them grow dry from the nervousness. Sam moved closer, her body shaking slightly. This only made me feel more confident, knowing that we were both nervous. Our lips met, and we kissed gently before pulling away.

Just then, Ben came downstairs, and Sam quickly ran upstairs. Ben smiled at her and then turned to me. "She always gets so nervous around me," he said with a smile.

I almost forgot that Ben was in love with Sam, and I had just kissed her. My heart started racing, and I could feel sweat forming on the back of my neck.

"Relax, Max," Ben said, noticing my discomfort. "I already know."

I let out a sigh of relief and asked, "You do?"

"Of course I do," Ben replied. "It's obvious that you like Sam, and it bothers you that she likes me instead."

My heart ached for Ben. He had no idea....

As the evening turned into night, we all gathered in the room where I had spoken to God. The ocean outside seemed to stretch out into infinite darkness, filled with unimaginable horrors. We had all been busy earlier, evidenced by the wine coolers, pizza boxes, and ice scattered about the room. The music was still playing, but Liz's eyes were heavy with sleep. Ben was stretched out on the floor, fast asleep with his mouth open. Kat was struggling to keep her eyes open. Kory was wide awake, staring at the moon as dark clouds began to cover it. And Sam was trying to wake up Ben. It was going to be the best sleepover ever.

I woke up to find myself in a giant bed with Ben, Liz, Sam, Kory, and Kat all sleeping around me. My eyes were heavy, and the first thought that came to mind was, "where is my remote." It took a moment for me to realize that I wasn't at home. I was with my tribe. Suddenly, I felt a tug at my heart and thought to myself, "God, is that you?" I ran to the window, but to my surprise, it was something else.

In the distance, I saw two red moons staring back at me, belonging to a giant snake that was slowly slithering closer. Its body moved as if it were a part of the darkness in the water. A chill ran down my spine as I realized the beast was getting larger and larger, but I was paralyzed by its gaze and unable to move. Its head grew bigger, and its eyes grew redder as it began to speed up. I wanted to run, but I couldn't. It opened its mouth and pulled its head back to strike me. I quickly closed my eyes...

When I opened them again, Sam was crying in front of me, screaming, "What's wrong with you!?" I began to stutter in shock, looking around. The boat was flooding! "Sam, I don't know what's happening!" I screamed. Sam looked confused right before a wave hit the boat, taking us all below the surface. Everything was moving in slow motion. Sam was unconscious and floating toward the surface, and I looked around to see if my friends were there. "Oh no," I thought to myself, "Were they still on the sinking boat?"

The boat was slowly but quickly sinking, and I began to swim down to help my people, my tribe. But before I could get anywhere, I saw those dark, bright red eyes circling the boat, and everything went dark. I lost consciousness.

As I woke up, I heard the sound of the ocean crashing on the beach and the cries of seagulls. I felt a bright red light behind my closed eyelids and slowly opened my eyes, letting the sunlight in. At first, I couldn't see anything, but I felt something on my stomach. It was a cat, a black cat with golden patterns on its body. I gently lifted the cat off of me, and it meowed and purred.

Panicked, I looked around, trying to remember what had happened. I saw a body washed up not too far from me and ran barefoot toward it, hoping and praying that whoever it was was still alive. I stumbled and fell into the sand but quickly got back up and continued running. When I reached the body, I was out of breath and sweating. It was Sam.

I lifted her upper body up and said, "Sam?" She slowly opened her eyes, and I smiled, saying, "You're going to be okay." But she suddenly slapped me without hesitation, leaving a scratch on my face that was now bleeding. She backed up frantically.

"Sam, what's wrong?" I asked, confused and hurt.

"You," she spat out. "You messed everything up! Everything was perfect until you came!"

"No, no, Sam, please don't say that..." I begged quietly, tears welling up in my eyes.

But she didn't stop. "It's your fault they're dead. I wish I never met you," she said, her words cutting through me like a knife.

I reached out to grab her wrist, but she turned around with a knife in her hand. "Do not touch me," she warned.

I backed away, tears streaming down my face as I looked at the sand, the ocean, and then back at Sam. I couldn't bear to hear any more of her words, and so I ran, ran as fast as I could, leaving everything behind.

Chapter 3:

INFINITY

I ran and ran, the sound of my footsteps echoing off the rocks and the empty space around me. I fell, but I kept running, my feet and thighs burning with the effort. My flat feet pounded against the hard, dry dirt, and I stumbled and ran some more. My heart was beating fast, and my stomach was cramping in pain. My face was contorted with agony and discomfort from the stress I felt in my heart, manifesting as wrinkles and lines all around my face.

Tears slowly made their way down my cheekbones, warm at first, then cold, then sticky and dry. Snot joined the tears in the race to my mouth, running down my cheek and lips. I saw nothing but sand and the street ahead of me. I tripped on a rock and scraped my foot, the rock feeling like a razor against my sandy skin. I felt the peeling and burning of flesh and screamed, but I still kept running, limping with the pain.

Exhausted, I fell to the ground, face-first into the dirt. I tasted dirt on my tongue as I closed my mouth. I turned onto my back and roared like a defeated, sickly lion with no pride, staring up at the hot sun. I breathed in and out, in and out, out and in, then in and out. My chest rose and fell, up and down, up and down. My lips were in pain and peeling, my tongue felt like a desert snake, and my throat begged for moisture. My mouth was burning and wide open. My heart was in pain.

I closed my eyes, and everything went dark. When I woke up, I heard a woman's voice saying, "Zane, you should have taken him to the hospital." Then a man's voice replied, "Maryam, I didn't know what to do... Wait... He's waking up..."

I slowly opened my eyes and saw a man with reddish brown skin and a pale woman with bushy hair and round lips. The man had a beard and looked as if he spent every hour cutting down trees and growing a beard. The woman looked as if she had been raised by flowers, her soft features and gentle demeanor giving her an otherworldly appearance. They both looked to be around my parents' age.

I looked around the room and saw that everything was handmade. The wooden horses on the wooden dresser, and the wooden walls behind the wooden table, all spoke to the craftsmanship and care that had gone into creating this space.

The wooden door creaked open, and a little girl with brown skin and long, straight brown hair entered the room. She was wearing a white robe and had freckles on the crown of her head, the back of her hands, and the front of her feet. She said, "You're finally waking up."

Maryam said, "Please, Kris, leave us. He needs more rest." The woman's warm, smooth hands touched my hand, and I closed my eyes as I heard her whisper, "Shhhh, now."

When I opened my eyes, the room was empty, but I could hear a rooster crowing outside, waking up the whole world, it seemed. On the shelf next to the bed, I saw a tray with eggs, pancakes, grits, and orange juice. I reached for the orange juice, feeling the sand in the back of my throat. The juice from the cup felt like the waters of God running down my mouth and throat, cooling the bottomless pit I called a stomach. I wanted more and noticed a letter under the tray. It read, "As Salaam Alaikum" if you need any more juice, you'll have to walk out and get some."

I walked out of the room and saw Maryam and Kris sitting at the table, eating breakfast. Maryam said, "You just missed Zane. He's outside working. When you finish eating with us, you can join him if you want."

"Thank you!" I said and began to eat like I had never eaten before. They both just looked at each other, smiling with amusement.

I heard the door open, and boots hit the cold, hard floor. My heart dropped as I thought to myself, "I knew my father would find me." I looked up slowly, afraid to see his face. But instead, I saw Zane. He was smiling and laughing as he said, "As Salaam Alaikum". You look as if you've seen a ghost, boy." I was nervous and didn't say anything. Zane noticed and said, "Not a big talker? That's okay; we'll work up to it. Come on, I've got something in the back I want to show you."

I trailed behind Zane as he led me through the kitchen, its wooden surfaces gleaming in the dim light. Every inch of the house was handmade, but it was a thing of beauty, all smooth lines and perfection. My throat was still raw and painful, but I finally found my voice. "Did you build all of this?" I croaked out.

Zane turned back to me, his hand on his hip, a proud look in his eyes. "All praises due to Allah, the Lord of the two worlds; The Most Compassionate to all, The Especially Compassionate to believers; King of the Day of Judgment," he declared. "I was given the gift of a builder."

I couldn't believe it. The house was a masterpiece, its bottom made of stone, and its top was a soaring tower of wood, the sun glinting off its roof and deck as birds sang their morning songs.

"Come on," Zane said, a gleam in his eye. "I have something to show you."

We set off through the perfectly manicured grass, past the sprinklers and the food gardens. I had no idea what Zane had in store for me, but I had a feeling it would be something special.

We trudged through Zane's acres of land, the fields and pastures teeming with livestock. Eventually, we came to a wall of cement buried underground. "Is this the foundation?" I asked.

Zane looked surprised, his beard twitching as he scratched his chin. "You know houses?" he asked.

I shrugged. "I just know how to make things," I replied.

Zane looked at me for a moment, his gaze searching. Then he said, "You're a good kid. Where's home? Do you need me to take you to your parents?"

I turned away, feeling a wave of sadness wash over me. I meant no disrespect, but I didn't know what to say.

Zane seemed to sense my discomfort. He sighed and looked down, then back up at me, squinting against the sun. "Do you think we should call child services?" he asked.

I shook my head quickly. "Please don't," I begged.

Zane looked at me, his eyes taking in my wide, desolate gaze, filled with tears of desperation and despair. He sighed again and looked down, then back up at me. "I don't know why you're without your parents," he said, his tone serious. "But you can rest another night here. Tomorrow afternoon, I'll drive you back home. Deal?"

I swallowed hard and nodded.

I turned to Zane, eyeing the enormous pile of supplies. "Is that everything you need to finish the house?" I asked.

He nodded and said, "Yes."

"Do you have the blueprints?" I asked, hoping to be of some help.

Zane smiled at me. "After we find your parents, maybe I'll let you help me build my second house," he said.

"Why do you need a second house?" I asked, curious.

Zane spoke to me in Arabic, his words flowing like music. "إِذَا كَانَ عِنْدَ الرَّجُلِ امْرَأَتَانِ فَلَمْ يَعْدِلْ بَيْنَهُمَا جَاءَ يَوْمَ الْقِيَامَةِ وَشِقُّهُ سَاقِطٌ" (iidha kan eind alrajul amra'atan falam yaedil baynahuma ja' yawm alqiamat washiquh saqit)," he explained.

I had no idea what he was saying, but I loved listening to him speak. I looked at the house and decided to give Zane and his wife a gift.

Zane had been gone for seven hours when I finished building the house. The first hour had been spent studying the blueprints, and during that time, I had seen a large cat the size of a dog wandering in the woods. For some reason, it didn't scare me. It simply disappeared back into the forest. By the end of the seventh hour, I had completed the house, just as Zane had imagined it. It was made of brick and wood, with brown and tan brick and stone on the exterior and polished wooden walls and cabinets on the interior. The counters were made of granite, and there were spiral stairs and enough rooms in the house to fit a small village. I had added my own touch to the front of the house, a path made in a certain sequence in which each number was the sum of the two preceding ones. It was beautiful.

I turned to see Maryum and Kris standing there, their eyes and mouths wide with surprise. But as I looked at their frightened faces, everything went black, and I fell back into the darkness.

I was in my room, lost in the world of video games when I overheard my parents whispering. But their whispers were more like quiet yelling, full of intense hissing and pronounced words. I needed to know what they were saying.

I paused my game and slowly pressed my ears against my bedroom door. As I got closer, I could make out their words more clearly.

"Did you see what he did to the dog? Have you ever seen something so disturbing?" my father asked in a voice that was almost a growl.

"Herald, keep your voice down. Our son is right upstairs, or have you forgotten?" my mother replied, her voice quiet and full of warning.

"Forgotten what? That he's my son?" my father shot back, his anger rising.

"That's not what I meant," my mother said, her words precise and efficient. "You know he can't help it. And you also know he does a lot of fixing, too."

"He can't fix the damn dog, Clarissa!" my father yelled.

"What do you want to do? What's your great plan?" my mother shouted in response.

The sun was trying to peek through the shadows as I woke up to find Zane offering me water. "Jazakallah," he said, his hand on the back of my head. "Praise be to Allah for bringing such a boy into our home. You are a miracle."

I looked around to see Zane and his family all staring at me as I lay in the same bed I had awoken in, in the same wooden room. "How did you build that house in seven hours?" Zane asked, his eyes wide with amazement.

I was taken aback. "You're not afraid?" I stuttered, my eyebrows raised, and my mouth opened in surprise.

"Afraid of you?!" Zane exclaimed. "Heavens no, boy! If I had a son and he could do what you can do, I would be more blessed than the richest king!"

Kris rolled her eyes at the exchange, but I tried to explain. "I can't control it," I told Zane. "If I want to build or fix something, it just happens."

"It is Allah who has blessed you," Zane replied, his eyes shining with belief. "What is your name, dear boy? It is time for me to reunite you with your parents, who must be missing you terribly."

I looked down, feeling a surge of emotion. "This is where I belong," I thought to myself. "These people do not fear me. I am meant to be here." Aloud, I told Zane, "My name is Zion, but please, Zane, do not send me back home. I love this family." And with that, I stood up and hugged them all, including Kris.

Maryum caught Zane's eye and said, "Can I have a word with you, husband?" The two of them left the room, with Maryum whispering urgently, "Can't you see that the boy is terrified of his parents? We should call child protective services. I spoke to my close friend, and she said we could get in a lot of legal trouble."

Zane replied, "Your friend who sells things online? Maryum replied, "You know she used to be a lawyer."

As the door closed behind them, Kris and I was left alone. She was only a few years younger than me, but her wide, innocent eyes made her seem much younger. She was beautiful, but in a strange, otherworldly way - like a flower or a grand building. She was staring at me intensely until I said, "You're staring."

"You're lying," Kris said, her eyes narrowing. "Why?"

I wrinkled my forehead and looked at her in confusion. "Lying about what?" I asked.

"God will not speak to you forever," Kris replied, her voice urgent. "Stop wasting time and figure out what God wants before it's too late."

My heart sank, and I felt sweat breaking out on my forehead. "How do you know that?" I asked, my voice barely above a whisper.

Kris looked at me, her eyes piercing. "Are we not made of water? Is water not filled with air, yet your lungs cannot find it? Is not the wind and earth one with you and all? Is not God the all? If I know the earth, myself, and you, how could I not know God? Are you an angel or a demon?"

I shook my head, feeling more and more confused. "I have no idea what you're talking about," I said.

But Kris was not deterred. "Are you of entropy or order?" she asked, her hair starting to rise as if there was a wind in the room.

I looked around the room, noticing that all the windows were closed. I was too afraid to say anything else, so I just sat there quietly. Eventually, Zane and Maryum returned to the room, with Maryum apologizing for leaving me alone with Kris. She invited me to join them for dinner in the dining room, and I happily accepted.

We had some of the best food I'd ever tasted that night - second only to my mother's breakfast. Kris was smiling, Zane was rubbing his stomach, and Maryum was laughing at Zane's antics. As I watched them, I couldn't help but feel that this was my tribe - my new family.

After dinner, we all retired to our separate rooms. I put my clothes away in the wooden dresser and climbed into my wooden bed, feeling my heart full of love and my belly full of good food. As I closed my eyes, I knew that I had finally found a place where I belonged.

When I opened my eyes, I found myself standing in the dark living room, holding a phone in my hand. I dropped the phone in shock, and Kris appeared from the hallway, watching me with her motionless eyes. I slowly made my way back to my room, with Kris's gaze following me like a motion detector.

As I climbed back into bed, I noticed that the window, which had been closed the night before, was now open. I looked out and saw the moon shining so brightly that it seemed to be shining just for me. A chill ran down my spine, and I decided to return to bed.

The next morning, I was awoken by the sound of Maryum crying. I jumped out of bed and ran to the door, only to find Zane in handcuffs. I was shocked. Kris hurried over and pushed me back into the room, telling me that I would only make things worse. She shut the door behind her.

I could hear Maryum pleading with the police, "We were just going to update our address. Give us some more time!"

Zane tried to calm her down. "Maryum, this is just a misunderstanding. When I go to trial, they will realize that. I won't be deported..."

But it was no use. The police took Zane away, putting him into the back of a squad car as if he were a criminal. I was heartbroken as I watched him go.

As the police cars drove off, the house was plunged into silence. All I could hear was the sound of Maryum's moans of pain and Kris comforting her. I had no idea what to do. I was speechless, in complete disbelief.

Feeling numb, I walked over to my bed and sat down, trying to process what I had just witnessed. Then it hit me - I remembered my friends who had died upon meeting me, and it all started to make sense. I was the cause of their deaths. There was no place for me.

At that moment, my wooden closet opened, and I found myself standing in a rainforest. I walked forward and saw a creature with the head of every animal and the body of every planet. I knew immediately that this was God.

"God!" I cried out. "Why didn't you warn me!"

God became a statue of animal heads, with the head of a king at the top. It began to rain. "Am I cursed? Have you cursed me? Why? Are you evil? Do you hate your own creation? Why is this my life?" I asked, my voice rising in desperation.

The statue spoke. "Whose life should it be?" the voice of God boomed.

"Not mine!" I exclaimed, feeling the weight of my anguish and anger.

"You're angry," God observed.

I stood in silence, barely able to keep it together.

"You're wondering why I made you this way," God said.

"Why?!" I demanded.

"All that happens must happen; all who is must be," God replied cryptically.

"Am I evil?" I asked, feeling a sense of shame and dread.

"You are necessary," God answered, and I found myself taking a seat before the deity.

"I feel like... I am the Red Horseman," I confessed.

"Please sit down. Let me finish explaining," God said, and I settled in to listen.

THE RED HORSEMAN

"The Red Horseman must follow the White, just as war must follow conquest, just as fire must follow heat," God said, the statue of animal heads before me. "War can only be if conquest comes about. When someone tries to conquer something that belongs to you. Your life, your mind, your soul, your peace, your culture, etc. War follows."

I listened, transfixed by God's words.

"'And when the Lamb opened the second seal, I heard the second living creature say, "Come!" Then another horse went forth. It was bright red, and its rider was granted permission to take away peace from the earth and to make men slay one another. And he was given a great sword.' Revelation 6:4," God quoted.

"Over 99 wars were fought between 1540 and 1924 in the Americas between the indigenous people and the elitist European military and conquerors," God said, sadness creeping into his voice.

"The Natives, civilized and foragers alike, fought like true warriors but could not fight the diseases and biological warfare the White Horseman brought to their shores. Within a lifetime, the Native people of America were decimated. The continents of what you call America were emptied of the humans who merged with it and clung to it. Over 95% of the population was wiped out after the White Horseman's invasion. Their blood cries out to me and the earth. The genocide of God's people caused Gaia the earth to chill; she grew cold due to the decimation of my people. The climate across the planet would change as a direct result of such an evil deed. A short-lived ice age would plague the same land that sent its children to conquer America."

"Wait! An ice age?" I exclaimed, surprised by what God had just said.

"Do you think there is no consequence for killing man?" God asked me. "Every animal on this planet has a purpose. Even though man is misaligned with their purpose, their absence would be felt globally in dramatic fashion. With all the farms and settlements left so empty of human life, it would allow more plants to grow. The plants use the carbon dioxide from the air to grow the new trees and cause the entire planet's climate to change."

"Whoa..." I said, marveling at the magnitude of the impact humans had on the planet.

"Over 121 wars were fought between the Africans and Europeans from the 1500s to the 1900s," God continued. "Like the Native Americans, the African civilizations were already doing what civilizations do, oppressing other groups of people on their continent. Civilized Africans would pay for the sin against my people with their freedom. The White Horsemen had already divided a fractured African people and then conquered them. This was easy to do since there were so many problems between African nations, tribes, and cultures. Some fought back by joining forces, and so the wars over the future of Africa began. World War I, World War II, the Korean War, the Vietnam War, and the Gulf War. None of these wars could have possibly taken place without colonialism and slavery. The Red Horse always follows the White Horse."

"I didn't realize humans around the world were at war for so long," I said, reflecting on the history of humanity.

"Oh yes, and with every inch, The White Horseman and Red Horseman took was another technological achievement for humanity,"

"What do you mean?" I asked, struggling to keep up with God's revelations.

"The advancement of transportation, communication, and militant technology is dramatically sped up by war," God said. "In fact, without the Maxim gun or a weapon like the Maxim gun, your world today wouldn't be possible. The Maxim gun was the very first machine gun that worked by recoil operation. Meaning they could and did use this weapon to mow down legions of men, women, and children who would fight against The White Horse, which you would call imperialism, and The Red Horse, which you would call modern warfare."

"So, without the colonization of the world and enslavement of people, all the major wars that followed wouldn't even be possible?" I asked.

"Precisely. World War One, from 1914 until 1918, saw The Red Horseman spread his red wings and engulf the planet in one of the bloodiest periods of history. The invention of trench warfare, poison gas, and tanks would allow The Red Horseman to take 16 million lives and 40 million casualties, and by the end of the war, the human population had lost 20 million people. The Red Horsemen would give you the weapons of the Gods."

"Splitting atoms," I said, realizing the horrific power that was unleashed.

"Go on..." God said.

"Nuclear bombs," I replied.

"Indeed. Man had the power of the gods in their hands and became a god of death under the tutelage of The Red Horseman. In World War Two, he would massacre fifty million humans," God said.

"That's terrible," I said, feeling the weight of humanity's history.

"But the terror continues," God said, his voice heavy. "In the Korean War, five million people died. In 1975, two million died in the Vietnam War. In the Persian Gulf War, over one hundred thousand people would die. Between 1914 and 1991, over one hundred million people died due to war."

"How could so much devastation and death happen in a single lifetime without us seeing this?" I asked, my voice laced with disbelief. "Seeing that we were in the middle of the apocalypse. It seems so obvious now. One hundred million people from war alone. One hundred million people died in war in just one lifetime. War as the planet had never seen it. With weapons that wipe out cities! This is not normal; it was The Red Horseman."

I felt the weight of the realization settling over me. The Red Horseman, a harbinger of war and destruction, had swept across the world, leaving death and devastation in his wake. And I wondered, with a chill, what other horrors lay in store for humanity.

THE BLACK HORSEMAN

"There was a black horse. Its rider held a pair of scales in his hand," God said, his voice deepening. "I heard something like a voice coming from the midst of the four living creatures. 'A quart of wheat for a denarius!' said the voice. 'And three quarts of barley for a denarius! But don't ruin the oil and the wine!' Revelation 6:5-6."

"Famine," I said, the word heavy on my tongue.

"Yes," God replied. "When you lived by my law, food was everywhere and all-abundant, but your new gods of farms and domestication left you vulnerable. It, like all devils, promised you everything without explaining the one major catch. Farming gives you easily accessible food but also causes food shortages."

"Due to droughts and population increase," I said, nodding.

"You've been listening, Max," God said. "Remember the ice age caused by the death of the original Americans?"

"Yes," I replied, a shiver running through me at the memory of God's words. I looked up at the statue of animal heads in awe as God spoke to me.

"This caused a famine," God said, his voice deep and booming. "The white horseman comes, then the red, then the black. Imperialism causes more war and, after war, more agriculture. But more agriculture increases the chances of larger famines. They will always follow each other. They cling to one another."

I listened intently, wondering what he meant.

"The death of the humans in the Americas caused an extremely sad timespan of cold, wet weather causing famine in Ming China," God continued. "One-third of the population died in the tremendous disasters that swallowed the people."

I shuddered at the thought.

"After the Red Horseman made his presence known to the world between the 1500s and 1900s, The Black Horseman would introduce himself at a much faster pace," God explained. "Now that the White Horseman had set the stage starting in the early 1500s and ending in the early 1900s, by spreading civilization, industrial civilization, and agriculture, it set the perfect environment for famine to cover the world in his black wings. As soon as The White Horseman came, The Red Horseman began, and the Black Horseman in the 1800s began to create suffering in the world like we've never seen before. The number of humans who would starve to death is almost unimaginable and impossible under my law."

I stared up at the statue, feeling a sense of dread wash over me. What kind of world was I living in? How many did the horseman take?

"In the 19th century, over 10 million, but in the 20th century, over 80 million," God replied.

My heart sank. "That's almost one hundred million deaths by hunger."

God shook his head solemnly. "What more evidence does man need to see The Black Horseman rides?"

THE PALE HORSEMAN

"Next was The Pale Horse," I said confidently.

"No, Max," God said firmly. "The Pale Horseman was always here. 'As I looked, there was a pale horse, and its rider's name was Death. Hades followed along behind him. They were given authority over a quarter of the earth, to kill with the sword, and with famine, and with death, and by means of earth's wild animals.' Revelation 6:8."

"I don't understand," I admitted.

"They were given authority over the earth," God said. "To kill with the sword..."

"The White Horseman?" I guessed.

God nodded. "And with famine!"

"The Red Horseman..." I murmured.

God's voice grew even more ominous. "And with death."

I felt a chill run down my spine. "That's what it all adds up to in the end. Death."

God leaned down toward me, his eyes fierce. "Beware the pale horse..."

"It all makes sense," I said, my voice shaking. "The seals have been broken, and we are living in post-apocalyptic times. But we have grown used to it. So used to it that... we have confused them with us, with human nature. Death rules this planet. Everything is dying. We are facing a mass extinction. We are living in Hades, the underworld. Hell on earth! Where we are used to war, bombs, mass shootings, starvation, homelessness, pandemics, slavery, prison, corruption, and untold horrors. We watch on our screens hell on earth and shrug our shoulders, and we are off to the plantations."

God listened patiently and then spoke in his deep, booming voice. "Or at least that's how the story goes."

"But what can we do?" I asked, feeling helpless.

"Listen, Max!" God said urgently. "You must run, but do not flee. Go to a place where there is grass from acre to acre. 1500 acres of land. I will be there waiting with your tribe."

"But my tribe is here..." I protested.

God's eyes bored into mine. "Not for long. You must go to Georgia, Max. Your destiny awaits."

"Who are you talking to?" a voice said. The rainforest had vanished, and I was back in the small wooden closet.

"Why are you in the closet?" Kris asked, her eyes filled with tears.

I turned to look at her, not knowing what to say. Before I could even open my mouth, Kris asked, "Why were you on the phone last night? Who were you talking to?"

I hesitated, then quietly replied, "I don't remember..."

Kris's eyes grew cold, and her hair began to move, even though there was no wind in the room. I shivered as she pointed at me and said, in a voice like many fountains, oceans, and rivers, "You did this." Her eyes turned into blue flame, and I backed away, trying not to tremble but unable to stop shaking. Her hair began to turn white.

Maryum burst into the room and grabbed Kris, trying to calm her down. The house began to shake as Kris cried, "He did this to Father! He is the devil! He is a snake in our garden!"

Maryum was crying, too, and in her tears, she screamed at me, "Go! Leave! You are no longer welcome!"

But I protested, "No, I am supposed to be here. You are my tribe."

At that moment, the window shattered, and all the doors in the house began to open and shut. Maryum pleaded with me, "Please, boy, leave! You don't know her strength!"

I ran again…

CHAPTER 4:

BELINA'S SONG

Who is this?" I asked, my voice shaking slightly. The man's voice was deep and gravelly. 'You may have difficulty understanding what I am,' he said. 'The who would be almost inconceivable. With the language of man. I couldn't even tell you. It might be better if you learned who I was on your own.'

I felt a shiver run down my spine. 'I don't know what to say,' I replied, feeling a mixture of fear and curiosity. 'I should hang up on you, but I...'

'So, will you talk with me?' the mystery man interrupted.

'About what?' I asked.

'About my home?'

'Where is your home?' I asked, feeling more and more confused. 'Wait, why am I asking you?... I'm hanging up.'

But before I could end the call, the man spoke again. 'Would you like to discuss the child you gave up instead?'

I felt a shock run through me. 'What!? Who told you about my abortion? Is this some kind of sick joke?"'

I was taken aback by the mystery man's words, feeling a mixture of confusion and fascination. '"You are always asking for forgiveness, no need,' he said. 'The only person who will judge you, in the end, is yourself. It isn't your fault. Maybe your responsibility but not your fault. What if... What if this phone conversation is the conversation that brings you closure? What if you could build a place here on earth where no woman would have to dream of doing what you felt had to be done?'

'I'm listening,' I replied, feeling both intrigued and wary.

The mystery man continued, 'Belina, I need you to help build my home. My home for humanity. We will create a place of equality amongst men and women, a place of equality between all peoples, no classes, no hatred, just community. You all shall be as your ancestors were, happy, full of abundance, and full of sharing and love. Not heaven, not perfection but a chance to start again in my garden, so you may have another chance to work toward heaven. This place is called a Food Forest Foraging Hunting Anti-fragile Modern Society.'

'Wow, F.F.F.H.A.M.S,' I said, 'for the sake of this already weird conversation, can we call it Fams for short?'

'That is fine,' the mystery man continued. 'The unfortunate reality is that civilization is a zoo made for humans. Humans have forgotten what they are. They tell humans if you're unhappy, it's your fault. But is it the fault of a lion in a cage that it is unhappy? Understand this one thing, and life will make sense. Humans are animals living out of their natural habitat. What happens to a snake in its wrong habitat? They will either throw off the ecosystem or die before they can thrive. This is almost every animal. Unless the new habitat strongly resembles the old habitat, this will happen. When you change the habitat that a creature lives in, you change the creature. A zoo animal is often a far cry from its wild counterpart. More depressed, less likely to reproduce, sickly, and more aggressive. What you have been experiencing is a prison with no bars or a zoo where you're the animal and the zookeeper.'

I continued to speak to the mystery man, feeling a growing sense of unease. "Wait, that was a lot; I have questions," I said. "If we are in a zoo? We would be prisoners, no?"

The mystery man replied, "Yes, the prison has been built by the prisoners, but the prisoners are also the prison guards."

"This sounds like a contradiction," I said.

The mystery man responded, "Many truths do..."

"So, we built our own prison for ourselves," I concluded.

"Civilized Humans lost the capacity to see what they built as a prison, but yet, it is a prison," the mystery man said. "Civilized Humans have lost even the ability to define freedom. You who live by the law of man have been deceived into believing getting jobs are good, receiving debt is good, and moving away from family is good. This is the life of a prisoner, the life of a foolish slave that believes she's free. This prison is civilization."

I was taken aback by his words. "Foolish? Where were you to free the slaves?" I demanded.

The mystery man replied, "Where was I?"

"You must be 'God," I said.

"Call me what you think is best," God replied, his voice taking on a new weight.

"When Africans were dragged overseas, praying for your help, where were you?... Did you even hear the screams?" I asked, my voice rising.

God spoke again, this time with a powerful and commanding presence. "Did I hear the screams? I dwell in the pain that gives screams meaning; I live in each tear and crack of a voice in pain. I am more than there; I am there itself. Are you attempting to pass judgment upon me?"

I felt chastened and subdued by his response. "I'm just asking a question," I said quietly. "And if we are enslaved, where are my shackles? Where is my master? Who whips me?"

I listened as God spoke with a powerful voice. "Western slavery is not the only form of slavery," he said. "In fact, in the most recurring forms of slavery throughout the world and your history, the enslaved could marry into their master's family, they could buy a house or some land, they could achieve freedom if they worked off their debt. But since you have been taught about the most brutal form of slavery as if it is the only form of slavery, you cannot see when you are being enslaved."

His words struck me deeply. "You must build FFFHAMS before it is too late to be able to choose,"

"Why me?" I asked my voice tense.

"Imagine... Imagine if the trees asked why must I grow, imagine if the sky asked why must I rain, imagine if the river asked why must I stream... You must," God replied.

I felt a sense of resignation at his answer. "And if I don't?" I asked, my voice resigned.

"Do you believe in the devil?" God asked.

"I left Christianity a long time ago..." I said, feeling uneasy.

"Oh, yes, I see that now, the bowls, the fruit, the sweet smell," God replied.

I was taken aback by his words. "You can see through the phone?" I asked, my voice rising.

God remained silent for a moment before I spoke again. "I need her to grant me the power and release me from this curse you gave to me," I said, my voice taking on a new urgency.

"I gave to you?" God replied, his voice taking on a new weight.

"Can we get back to FFFHAMS?" I said, feeling flustered.

"Yes, we can. Humans are made to live a certain way. To live a physically and mentally healthy life, one must live amongst its kind in its habitat," God replied.

"This habitat is FFFHAMS?" I asked.

"Yes, some would call it the garden of Eden," God replied.

"Or Ife," I said, feeling a sense of pride in my heritage.

"I wouldn't call it Ife," God replied.

"Why because it's African?" I asked, feeling a growing sense of frustration.

"Because it is a story of rulership," God replied.

"Oh... Okay," I said, feeling subdued.

God spoke again, "You're being combative," he said.

"Am not... I'm just being skeptical," I replied, feeling a sense of defensiveness rising in my chest.

"You want to know a secret?" God said with excitement.

I leaned forward, intrigued. "I love secrets. But I read a lot. I couldn't really imagine a secret being kept from me."

God chuckled. "There is indeed a secret that has been kept from you. It is in the existence of the abstract or metaphysical world, also known as the unmanifested world. This world is different from the physical world you can see and experience through your senses. Instead, it is a realm of abstract concepts, ideas, and entities that exist independently of concrete objects or experiences."

I nodded slowly, trying to wrap my mind around the concept. "What's in this... abstract?"

"You will find things like mathematics, theories, emotions, art, and language in this abstract world," God explained. "These things exist purely in the abstract and are not tied to any physical object or experience. They are more accurate than the material world because they are eternal and changing, yet, unchanging, transcending space and time."

"Okay, that's not much of a secret," I said, a hint of disappointment in my voice.

God grinned. "The secret lies within the language and the words used. When I named these different entities, you thought of them as unliving, unwanting. This couldn't be further from the truth. Their wants are far from the wants of man and woman, but they have them nonetheless. What people call gods, spirits, divine were in reference to the fundamental beings within the abstract."

A shiver ran down my spine. "I know that spirits exist..."

"I'm sure you do," God replied "you lost your faith in Christianity. But do you still know Christ?"

I rolled my eyes. "Why should I subscribe to some young religion that enslaved people?"

"All spiritual practices were given to you by the gods to protect you from the prison you live in," God replied.

I sucked my teeth. "Well, they're not doing the best job. Religion means to bind."

God replied. "The etymology? We'll circle back to religion a little later. I want to focus on Christ for now."

"Okay," I said, settling back against my pillows.

"Certain characters or spirits and stories exist outside of space and time," God continued. "One example is the spirit of Christ, which can be found in many cultures and historical figures and in the stars of astronomy and astrology. This spirit is often worshipped as divine and is the highest manifestation of this being. This spirit is older than the name Christ and was here before the earth and will be here after the earth."

"So, I should be a Christian?" I asked, my eyebrow raised in skepticism.

"That's not what I said," God replied. "I'm sure you know what a circle is..."

I couldn't help but laugh. "God has a sense of humor. Well, yes, I know what a circle is."

"Good," God said. "A circle is everywhere. It's across space and time, in the skies, the dirt, and the earth. Shapes transcend time and space. When you draw a circle, it can never be a circle in its purest form, only a representation of it. The circle is a great spirit; the shapes are like its pantheon. Like the circle, Christ exists across the all in every dimension, and when it comes up in your stories or in your bodies, it is a representation of the being who is Christ in the abstract."

"I hear you," I said slowly. "But there is no echo of Christ anywhere but people's imaginations. Not in the stars and not in the body."

"Think again," God replied. "Are you familiar with the kundalini?"

"No," I admitted.

"The kundalini is a spiritual energy that is believed by some to inhabit the base of the spine," God said. "It is thought to be capable of being awakened and raised through the chakras to the crown chakra, leading to enlightenment and spiritual awakening. This concept is often connected to the teachings of Christ and the Christian tradition, as well as to other spiritual traditions that believe in the potential for spiritual awakening through the cultivation of the kundalini energy. Do you follow?"

"I understand," I said, trying to process what he was saying.

"There are differing interpretations of the Christ kundalini," God continued. "With some viewing it as a metaphor for the transformation and spiritual growth that can occur through the practice of Christian teachings and the embodiment of Christ-like qualities, such as love, compassion, and selflessness. Others may see it as a literal process of awakening and activating the kundalini energy through spiritual practices such as meditation, yoga, or other disciplines."

As I listened to God, I could feel my mind expanding, trying to take in everything he was saying.

"The stages of the Christ kundalini, also known as the process of kundalini awakening, are often described as stages of spiritual growth and transformation," God said. "These stages can vary depending on the tradition or teaching, but common stages include:

Preparation: This stage involves practices such as purification, devotion, and surrender, which are intended to prepare the individual for the process of kundalini awakening.

Awakening: This stage involves the awakening of the kundalini energy, which is often described as a powerful, transformative energy that can lead to profound spiritual experiences and insights.

Rising: During this stage, the kundalini energy is said to rise through the chakras, or energy centers in the body, activating and purifying them as it goes.

Integration: As the kundalini energy reaches the crown chakra, it is said to bring about a state of enlightenment and unity with the divine. This stage involves the integration of the insights and experiences gained through the process of kundalini awakening into daily life.

Realization: In this final stage, the individual is said to have achieved a state of realization or enlightenment, in which they have a deep understanding of the nature of reality and their place in the universe."

I listened to God as he spoke, his voice calm and reassuring.

"Not seeing how this connects to Christ," I said, interrupting him.

"But where can you find the throne of God?" God asked.

"He sits in the brain, giving orders to your universe," he continued. "Claustrum is the name of his throne."

"What's Claustrum?" I asked.

"The claustrum is a thin, sheet-like structure located within the brain that has been shown to play a role in the integration of sensory and motor information, as well as in the regulation of consciousness and attention."

"Oh, so Claustrum is the throne of God?" I asked, trying to make sense of it all.

"It is debated," God replied. "But the possibility is well-known among scientists and spiritual practitioners that the brain, particularly the Claustrum, plays a crucial role in the experience of consciousness. Similarly, the pineal gland often referred to as the 'land of milk and honey,' has long been considered a center of spiritual enlightenment and connection to higher states of consciousness."

"What does the pineal gland have to do with milk and honey?" I asked, feeling a little lost.

"The milk would be the serotonin it produces, and the honey would be the DMT," God explained.

"I know what those chemicals are, but..." I trailed off, feeling a little overwhelmed.

"You want a refresher," God said, and I could hear the smile in his voice.

"Exactly," I replied.

"Serotonin is a chemical that is produced by nerve cells in the brain and is involved in transmitting messages between them," God explained. "It plays a key role in regulating mood, sleep, appetite, and digestion and is thought to be involved in the development of social behavior and memory. This so-called 'happy chemical' is produced from the amino acid tryptophan and can be found in various tissues throughout the body, including the brain, blood platelets, and digestive system. So, basically, it's a very important chemical for keeping you functioning at your best."

"Got it," I replied, feeling a little overwhelmed. "And DMT?"

"DMT, or dimethyltryptamine, is a naturally occurring psychedelic drug that is found in certain plants and animals," God said. "It is structurally similar to serotonin, which is a neurotransmitter that plays a role in the regulation of mood, sleep, appetite, and other functions in the body. DMT is known for producing intense and powerful hallucinations and altered states of consciousness in users. It is typically consumed in the form of a smoked or vaporized extract from certain plants, and its effects can last for a short period of time, typically around 30-60 minutes."

"And the pineal gland produces that?" I asked.

"In short," God replied.

"Okay, please continue to blow my mind," I said with intrigue.

"The connection between these brain structures and the spine, with its 33 vertebrae, is also an important aspect of the Christ kundalini concept," he said. "The spine, with its connection to the testicles and the spermatic cord, is seen as a conduit for the flow of energy and consciousness. The practice of semen retention, or the withholding of ejaculation, is believed to facilitate the transfer of this energy from the physical act of ejaculation to a higher state of consciousness and mental well-being...."

"How does all of this connect with Christ?" I asked

"The connection to the story of Christ is clear," God said, "the journey of the energy, or Christ, down the spine and into the universe, paralleling Christ's own journey on earth for 33 years, culminating in the transformation and resurrection of the unused sperm into a higher form of energy and ultimately enlightenment through the process of Kundalini consciousness."

He told a story, "In the realm of existence, where the fabric of time and space intertwines, there lies the throne of God. It is in the most complex and enigmatic part of the universe. The brain, where neurons fire like stars in the sky, and the claustrum is the seat of his power.

His child, Energy, receives his commands and obeys them without question.

And so, God orders Energy to travel down the spine, to reach the sacrum, and to be resurrected. It is a journey that Chrism has taken many times before, but this time, he hesitates, for he is reluctant to leave the Pineal gland, the source of milk and honey.

But Energy knows that he must follow God's command, and so he leaves his physical form and travels down the spine, encountering many challenges along the way. Yet he perseveres until he reaches the Solarplex, the center of the universe, where the nine ethers are produced.

It is a place where Energy can meditate and build its prana, the essence of life. Through his meditation, Energy becomes incarnate, taking on form, or what you may call a sperm, for the universe was without seed during the time of his becoming.

As he travels further down to the sacred bone, the sacrum, he experiences the passing of 33 vertebrae, which takes 33 years from his perspective. He becomes Christ or Energy again, travels back up the spine, passes the solar plexus, and reaches the heart of the cosmos, the Vagus. There, he would be sacrificed, and after two and a half days, he would "resurrect" expanding light across the entire universe or the soul. Giving that soul true enlightenment."

"This is all 100% proven?" I asked skeptically.

"Proven?" God replied.

"Yeah, proven to be true," I said.

"Oh", "truth..." God mused.

"I thought you would like truth," I said, trying to stay on topic.

"You all made truth up," God said.

"You're saying there is no objective reality?" I pressed.

"I will explain this the best way I can, and then we must finish our discussion about Christ," God said.

"I'm listening," I said, settling in for what was sure to be a long and winding conversation.

"Your words will not allow you to ever fully know the truth," God said. "Words are a tool and are extremely good at communicating value and basic senses, but it is not well developed for 'truth' in the way you mean it. None of your senses are developed for truth, so your language couldn't even begin to form it. The truth is not in words but in meaning and understanding. Many beliefs you have will be proven and disproven forever. Utility is true, cost and benefit are true, the abstract is true, and all things outside the abstract are relative and ever-changing, meaning the amount of truth they hold will certainly change over time. Focus on the utility, meaning, and understanding within the stories I tell you, not how much objectivity you can measure within it."

I listened intently, then replied, "That sounds like deflecting, but I will roll with it, God."

"That's my point," God said, "now that you understand Christ can manifest in the body, understand Christ can manifest in the sky. The zodiac is a cosmic system that maps out the celestial influences on the 12 astrological signs. This system is closely tied to the story of Christ and the 12 apostles, who are seen as the key figures in the early growth of the church. Each astrological sign represents a specific time of year and is thought by many to be shaped by the energies of the celestial bodies in that part of the sky."

I replied, "I'm familiar with astrology."

"Good," God said. "The cycle of the zodiac signs can be seen as corresponding to different stages in the life of Christ. This interpretation is based on the belief that the astrological signs are connected to the energies and characteristics of celestial bodies and that these energies and characteristics can be connected to the story of Christ and the 12 apostles."

As I sat there on the phone, God went on to explain how the sign of Aquarius corresponded to the start of Christ's ministry and his baptism by John the Baptist. "It's like the sun rising on the horizon, but there's still more darkness," he said.

I nodded, trying to visualize it in my head.

God continued, "the sign of Pisces, represented by the fish, corresponds to the time of year when there's a lack of food to sustain the sun on its journey. That's when Christ collected his disciples, who were fishermen, and gave the Sermon on the Mount."

"Gotta love Pisces." I quipped.

God chuckled before continuing, "Aries, the sign of the ram or lamb. This sign corresponds to the spring equinox, when the days and nights are equal, and the sun's strength starts to shine through. In Christ's life, this stage represents when he performs miracles and gathers followers, eventually calling for more laborers to join in the harvest."

"Okay," I replied, nodding my head.

But God wasn't done yet. "And speaking of hard work and determination, that's what Taurus represents. The bull, which symbolizes strength and growth, corresponds to the time when the disciples are sent out to spread the message of the Gospel. As the sun reaches its peak of strength, the disciples grow and increase in numbers. The Sermon on a mission in Matthew 10:1-42, in which Christ instructs his disciples on how to add followers, reflects this energy of Taurus."

"And John the Baptist is a 'bull of a different breed'? I laughed.

God then said, "Speaking of duality, let's talk about Gemini," God said, continuing his explanation. "The sign of the twins represents a time of doubling and increasing as the sun reaches its zenith. This is exemplified by Christ's miracles of curing a man with a withered hand and a man who is blind and mute. But it's also a time of tension and conflict, as the Pharisees accuse Christ of being the prince of demons. So you can see the dual nature of Gemini reflected in the events of this time period in the story of Christ."

I had a quick flashback as he spoke about June but shook it off, telling myself, "nothing to worry about."

God continued.

"And then there's Cancer, the Crab. This sign represents a time of assessment and division, as the sun begins to wane and darkness increases. The path of the Crab becomes more erratic, symbolizing a backsliding or reassessment. In the Gospel of Matthew, Christ speaks of division in a parable and the importance of self-examination in determining our worthiness. He also departs from his family, demonstrating the need for separation in order to pursue one's calling."

I nodded, taking it all in. God then went on to say, "Leo, the Lion, represents strength and the end of the growing season, marked by the gathering and storing of the harvest. Christ speaks of the kingdom of heaven as a place where the harvest is stored and warns of the dangers of allowing weeds to grow among the wheat. This period covers the teachings of Christ in Matthew 13:1-53."

"I know the dangers of Leo's," I said awkwardly. "Umm... And what about Virgo?" I asked.

"Ah, Virgo," God said. "As the sun descends towards the horizon, this sign represents a time of transition and challenges. Virgo is symbolized by a woman holding a sheaf of grain, representing the harvest and the transformation of raw materials into sustenance. In the story of Christ, this period is marked by the people of Nazareth questioning his wisdom and power and the death of John the Baptist."

I listened intently as God continued, "During this time, Christ performs miracles such as feeding the masses with a few loaves of bread and fish and walking on water. He also confronts the Pharisees and Sadducees over their adherence to tradition and speaks about the importance of repentance and forgiveness. As the sun descends towards the horizon, Christ begins his journey towards Jerusalem, knowing that he will ultimately face his death there. Virgo represents a time of tension and uncertainty as Christ navigates these challenges and prepares for the difficult journey ahead."

I nodded, trying to picture it all in my head. "That makes sense," I said.

"As the sun moves into the astrological sign of Libra, it is a time for balance and settling debts. This can be seen in the stories of Jesus during this time as he talks about settling debts and the price of getting into the kingdom of heaven. This period is also marked by strife and conflict, as seen in the parables of violence and in Jesus' denunciation of the scribes and Pharisees. The fall equinox marks a time of transition, and in the story of Christ, it is a time of tension and upheaval as he heads towards Jerusalem and his eventual death."

"Can you give me more details about the Libra?" I asked God over the phone.

"Sure," he replied. "Libra is represented by the symbol of the balance, which represents the fall equinox when the days and nights are of equal length. This time of year is often associated with the idea of settling debts, as it is a time for weighing the good against the bad and making amends for any wrongs that have been committed."

I thought about it for a moment before asking, "And how does that relate to the story of Christ?"

"In the story of Christ, this time period is marked by several events that are related to the theme of settling debts," God explained. "For example, in Peter's 'Confession about Christ' (Matthew 16:13-28), Christ talks about the idea of settling debts when he speaks of coming back with his angels in the glory of his Father and repaying every man for what he has done. There are also several parables that deal with the theme of settling debts, such as the 'Sermon on Life in the Kingdom of God' (Matthew 18:1-35), the parable of the 'Rich Young Man' (Matthew 19:16-30), and the 'Workers in the Vineyard' (Matthew 20:1-16)."

"Interesting," I said. "Please continue."

"Scorpio," God began, "is represented by the symbol of the scorpion, a creature known for its venomous sting and tendency to hide in secluded places. This time of year, as the sun grows weaker and the air grows colder, is associated with secrecy, evil, and conflict."

I couldn't help but shiver at the thought. "And what does that have to do with the story of Christ?" I asked.

"In the story of Christ, this is reflected in the events that take place during the Scorpio season," God explained. "Judas, one of Christ's own followers, plots to betray him and ultimately hands him over to be arrested (Matthew 26:14-16). This betrayal is symbolized by the act of Judas kissing Christ, just as Scorpio is depicted as kissing the sun as it passes through the sign."

I was both fascinated and horrified by the symbolism. "What else?" I asked, hoping for a less dark answer.

"The season is also marked by the name Gethsemane, which means 'oil press' or 'olive press,'" God continued. "Olives used for oil are typically harvested in late winter when they are at their ripest, further emphasizing the themes of secrecy and hiddenness associated with Scorpio."

As I listened to God explain the astrological significance of Christ's story, I couldn't help but feel a sense of curiosity.

"So you're saying that Christ's moment of contemplation and emotion in Gethsemane is characteristic of Scorpio?" I asked.

"Yes, exactly," God replied. "And ultimately, his arrest marks the beginning of the final stages of his journey."

I pondered this for a moment before continuing, "And what about the astrological sign of Sagittarius? What does that represent?"

God replied, "Sagittarius represents the darkest days of the year, encompassing the three days following December 21. It's a time of intense struggle and conflict, as symbolized by the scorpion's sting. And this can be seen in the story of Christ, as he faces betrayal and arrest in the days leading up to his death."

God was explaining all of this like it was common knowledge, information coming from his mouth like water from a fountain, and I did thirst.

"However, Sagittarius also represents the beginning of a new cycle, as the sun begins to grow stronger and the days become longer. This can be seen in the story of Christ's resurrection, as he rises from the dead and is seen again after three days of darkness. His resurrection marks the start of a new era, as the darkness of death is overcome by the light of life. In this way, the astrological sign of Sagittarius is closely tied to the story of Jesus and the themes of conflict, betrayal, and rebirth.

As God explained the connection between the story of Christ and the astrological sign of Sagittarius, I couldn't help but feel overwhelmed.

"This is a lot to take in," I admitted. "I always thought that this was evidence that Christ was merely a story made up and based on the stars. But you're telling me that this is the spirit of Christ which comes from the abstract and manifests throughout time and space. So, did he exist historically?"

"Christ exists before history, before the past, much more than a historical figure," God replied. "These are not manifestations of Yeshua, Jesus of Nazareth. No, instead, Yeshua, Jesus of Nazareth, who you call the historical figure of Jesus Christ, is a manifestation of the abstract being."

I couldn't help but feel a sense of awe and wonder as I listened to God's words. It was as if I was witnessing something profound and timeless, something that transcended the boundaries of history and the physical world.

As God explained the abstract nature of Christ, my mind was reeling with questions.

"What abstract being?" I asked, trying to make sense of what God was saying.

"Order," God replied simply.

"Order is a being?" I asked, incredulous.

"Oh yes, that is my point," God said. "Order is its own being, and its story is its word. The word or story will manifest within the all in every way and on every level. From the quantum to the cosmos. Not just Order but also Entropy, Math, Love, Anger, etc. They all exist within the abstract and reproduce like you through manifestation."

I couldn't help but feel overwhelmed by this revelation. "That really is a lot to take in," I said. "So basically, the historical events are not Christ in his true form but manifestations of the abstract Christ, the same as the astrological events. And the reason why there are other deities who are aligned in the same way is that they are also manifestations of Christ, who and what is a manifestation of Order."

God nodded. "Yes, what you call stories and characters could also be called powerful spirits. Some of these spirits, like Christ, are extremely powerful."

"But why are you calling it Christ? What is its real name?" I asked.

"Oh, the 'name' of such beings could not be said with mouths," God replied. "I just knew you would understand if I used the most important manifestation of this being in the context of your culture."

I couldn't help but feel skeptical. "I don't know if he's still all that important in our culture today," I said.

"You're only thinking of Christ in the context of religion," God said. "But the abstract being that Christ represents is still very much a part of your world.

"Where else is he being celebrated?" I asked.

"Everywhere," God replied simply. "Have you ever watched the movie The Matrix?"

"Watched it? It's one of my favorite films," I said.

"The Matrix is a story that tells not only the story of the chosen one or the Christ figure but also the past, present, and future of humanity," God said.

"So, you're telling me all of these years I've been right. We are living in a computer simulation, run by powerful robots that have taken over the world?" I asked.

"You have been led to believe that the Matrix is a computer simulation run by machines and that you live within this simulation," God said. "However, there is more to the story than meets the eye. The Matrix is a manifestation of the abstract world and contains hidden truths and secrets that have been kept from you. The Matrix is civilization itself. Neo will always be the one who liberates you from it."

The three knocks on the door jolted me out of my reverie. I glanced at my phone, but the call was gone, leaving me to wonder if it had all been a dream. BANG BANG! The pounding persisted, causing my heart to race as I made my way to the door, fists clenched. "WHO IS IT!?" I bellowed, my voice barely containing the fear and anger that threatened to overwhelm me.

But when I opened the door I saw that it was not a stranger on the other side. It was my friend, my sister, Mary. Sobbing and barely able to stand, she and her daughter collapsed into my arms, their tears soaking through my clothes. I knew what this meant, and I couldn't help but feel a pang of guilt for having selfishly wished for peace and quiet just moments before.

I helped them to their feet and led them inside, trying to hide the evidence of my own struggles - the photo of Lee, the screening documents for the cryobank, and the bottle of liquor that I had bought for spiritual purposes. I knew that if Mary saw any of these things, she would think I was back to the way I was when we first met - lost, alone, and struggling to find my way in the world. But that wasn't the case anymore; I was at peace now, and I couldn't help but wonder if that was a good thing, considering.

I sent Mary's daughter Krissy to my room to watch something and turned to Mary, taking her hand and looking into her eyes, "Mary, tell me everything," I said, ready to be there for her, no matter what.

CHAPTER 5:

THE MATRIX

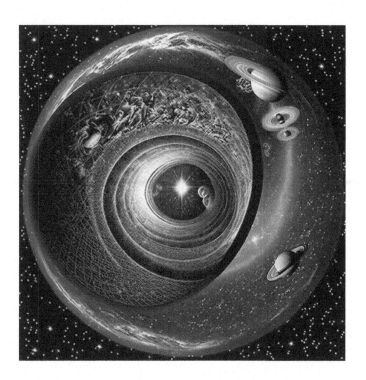

The morning light filtered through the window, casting a golden glow over the room; it was six, o clock, in the morning on a Tuesday. I sat cross-legged, eyes closed, focusing on my breath. In, out. I repeated the mantra in my mind, "I have a baby, I have a baby, I have a baby." The words became a steady drumbeat in my head until I could no longer distinguish between the voice in my mind and the reality of the room around me. My body felt weightless, like a feather, and I was lost in a world of darkness, light, and color.

But then, something shifted. The sound of a serpent slithered through my ears, a cat's paw softly patting my back. A chill ran down my spine, and I couldn't shake the feeling of unease. The sun hit my third eye, and a tear slipped down my cheek. With each repetition of "I have a baby," a shadow appeared, growing stronger with each breath.

"I have a baby."

The shadows loomed large in my mind, each one more ominous than the last. The first was a giant cat with a mane of brown and black fur, the sun rising behind it. The cat was crucified, its paws bleeding, and nailed to the cross, the blood dripping onto the ground. But then, the king of felines opened its eyes and let out a deafening roar.

"I have a baby."

The second shadow was a giant serpent, writhing and flipping, lashing its tail at the sun as if trying to call the moon. It was pinned by a giant foot with sandals, and I couldn't shake the feeling of unease.

"I have a baby."

But the third shadow was different; it was of a black and white baby, with one side white and the other side black. The baby was in pain, and I could feel its sorrow, rage, and burns. It was crying out for its mother, stretching its arms out to me. I reached back, but my arms were too short, and something was pulling me away. The emptiness I felt as I faded was overwhelming, and I knew that this baby needed me more than anything. This baby was more than just a part of me...

"AUN B!" The scream jolted me out of my meditative state, and I felt my heart jump into my throat as a flash of fear and heat filled my body. I jumped to my feet, my body moving on autopilot, and hurried into the living room, where Krissy slept on the couch. She ran to me, almost knocking me over, and squeezed my waist, her sobs muffled by my soft meditation robe.

"Krissy, why are you crying?" I asked, trying to keep my voice steady. "I dreamt about that boy who set up my father," she said, her round, deep brown eyes looking into mine. "I didn't see my mother and was afraid he got her, so I called you." I gently pushed her back a bit and crouched down to her level. "Your mother is at the store, and your father will come back to us soon," I said, trying to reassure her.

But she shook her head, her eyes filling with tears. "I should have told them the boy was lying," she said. "Don't do that, Krissy," I said, my voice firm. "This is no one's fault." It was 6am, my specific time to relax, reflect, and refocus on my goals, but for the past three days, this has been my morning.

DAY 6

It's nine, o clock, in the morning; I close my eyes, and I am transported to a dreamlike state. Colors swirl around me, and I realize I am lucid dreaming. I look to my right and see a kaleidoscope of hues, and to my left, the colors are organized and well-placed. Blue skies, buildings, classrooms, students - I'm back at college. I see Lee and myself walking together, his smile stretching from cheek to cheek and mine blushing as I ask him to stop looking at me in that way. His eyebrows curve, and he puts on a charming smile; and I bite my lip then hug him tightly.

But as I look up, I see a light, and I'm falling back into a memory. Lee is acting strange, tapping his feet, getting hot, and quiet. He would normally be talking to everyone in the room and eating the Thanksgiving turkey my mother made. I begin to wonder if he did something he shouldn't have or if he's about to do something he shouldn't. He walks up to me as silence fills every corner of the room, and I turn to see what's causing it. When I turn around, he's on one knee.

I smile and begin waving my hands to cool my face. And then I'm back in the sky, watching Lee and me. That's right, he proposed to me not too long ago. I can tell by the skip in my walk, the joy in my teeth, the dimples sinking into my bone, and the chinky eyes as I smile. The memory was so vivid, it felt as if it was happening all over again, and a warm feeling spread throughout my body.

We walked hand in hand through the tunnel between the cafeteria and the dorm rooms, the pink pedals falling from the sky as the wind blew through our hair. The pathway was filled with people, but I couldn't remember seeing so many before. Lee and I looked like children discovering love for the first time.

In my belly, there was a 2-week-old baby, but I hadn't told Lee yet. Our wedding was coming up, and people already thought we were rushing things. When I brought it up to Lee, he would just say, "I don't want to talk about all these people and what they think, F 'em." His voice shook, and I knew he was struggling with the pressure.

I knew Lee from back home in Jersey. He was from Lindenwold, and I was from Berlin. We had mutual friends, but in college, we somehow just connected. We were both freshmen, and the world felt like it had opened up to us. Our friends, mostly mine from back home, often would visit the school. They introduced us. We always called them by their childhood nicknames, Rissie and Harry. They were the epitome of lovebirds. Rissie and I had been friends since childhood, and I trusted her with anything.

As I sat in the dorm room, surrounded by the familiar clutter of our everyday lives, my mind couldn't help but wander to the upcoming award ceremony for Lee. He had always been a boy genius, and his achievements in his first year of college had not gone unnoticed. You must understand scouts had been watching him since he was just a little boy, and it was no surprise when his application was preordained for acceptance. I couldn't help but wonder why he had chosen this particular school when he could have gone to one of the top universities in the country. His mind was a mystery to me, and it made me question what was truly going on inside of him.

The ceremony was fast approaching, and I wanted to make sure that everything was perfect for him. We were both 19, and we had been engaged for about 3 months. School was coming to a close, and we were counting down the days until we could start our lives together. Our wedding was planned for just after my birthday, which was on March 3rd, and I couldn't help but feel a sense of excitement and nervousness.

My dream self and I merged into one. As I looked over at Lee, sitting across from me, he caught my gaze and asked, "Are you okay?" I looked down at my belly, and a scream came from my belly and echoed through my mind, "AUN B!!!" I was thrown out of my dreamlike state, back into reality, where I couldn't seem to get any rest.

DAY 9

"Breathe in Belina, Breathe out Belina, Breathe," I whisper to myself as I close my eyes and let my mind drift into the darkness. The abyss of uncertainty and fear. "Breathe", stomach, goosebumps, Lee, "breathe", abortion, "out", orphan." I see flashes of memories and images swirling around me, like fish swimming in opposing directions. One fish is Lee, and the other fish is me.

I see two elephants in my mind's eye, one with the voice of Lee and the other with my own. The male elephant trumpets triumphantly, "This is great news!" But the female elephant simply looks at him, tears streaming down her face. "What? You're not happy?" The male elephant asks, confusion etched on his face.

The female elephant, trembling and unable to move, sobs, "You're supposed to be something great, and this is my only chance to become somebody." As she speaks, she transforms into a rabbit, cowering before the towering elephant. "You're just going to kill it, so you can be somebody!" The elephant bellows, casting a dark shadow over the rabbit. "Lee," she whispers, dragging out his name as tears continue to stream down her face.

The elephant turns into an Emperor penguin. "I will not let you kill our baby; I mean Jesus Belina. What are you thinking?! We cannot be those people!" The rabbit replies, "Lee, you don't understand. You live on the nice side of Lindenwold; I live on the worst side of Berlin. In the apartments, where no one becomes anything! If I had a baby now, I would have to leave school; no one is going to take care of the baby; my family isn't like yours" The penguin screams, "My family will take care of him!" The rabbit replies, "Him? How do you know your family will take care of the baby?" Lee says, "I just know!" The rabbit turns into a snake. The snake says unconfidently, "The decision is made."

As the two animals transform back into Lee and myself, the weight of the decision hits me like a ton of bricks. I can feel the tears streaming down my face, and Lee's face is red with emotion, his tears flowing like a river. I'll never forget the words he spoke next. He comes closer to me and says, "If you do this, I will never speak to you again." I grab his shirt and plead with him, "Lee, you're all I have." He continues, "If you do this, I'll hate you forever; no matter how old I grow, how much I change, the only constant will be my undying hatred for you."

I fall to my knees, crying, begging, but saying, "I can't keep the baby, Lee. I can't keep it." I try to pull myself up, reaching out to hug him, but he resists. I say one more time, "I can't, Lee." He begins to walk away, and I reach out to grab him, but he turns, finger in my face, with the most piercing eyes, and says, "Don't touch me, you freaking baby killer!" I fall to my knees, crying, as he leaves me in my tears. I never see Lee again.

A lioness with a mane walks from the darkness, the same darkness Lee walks into, and says, "Aunt B?" I open my eyes, tears all over my face. Krissy was there; it was a sad silence at first, as I wiped the tears from my face, and then Krissy said the nicest thing, "Whatever it is, it isn't your fault, maybe you're responsibility… but it isn't your fault.

We didn't make the devil's playground" She runs up to me, and we hug as I cry some more.

DAY 12

As I lay in bed, surrounded by the familiar creaks and groans of my condo, my mind couldn't help but wander to the events of the past few weeks. My niece, a mere child, was forced to witness the heart-wrenching scene of her aunt sobbing uncontrollably, her father ripped away from her life forever. And yet, amidst my feelings of guilt and sorrow, a small but persistent spark of frustration burned within me. Every night, as I lay next to my sister Mary, her constant restlessness and whispered mutterings keeping me awake, I couldn't help but think of my own aspirations and dreams.

As I absentmindedly massaged my stomach, lost in thought, a sudden ring jolted me back to reality. Glancing at the Caller ID, I saw the word "unknown" flashing on the screen. A lump formed in my throat as I hesitantly answered, half-expecting the worst. But instead of the dreaded voice of an immigration agent, a familiar and surprisingly welcoming voice greeted me.

"Belina, I'm at your door," the voice said simply.

Without hesitation, I leapt out of bed and made my way to the door, fumbling with the locks in my haste. And there, standing before me, was a figure both majestic and otherworldly. A tall, dark-skinned man with long, silky white hair cascading down his shoulders, his eyes lined with white, seeming to bore into my very soul. He was dressed in a flowing white robe, and as I took in the sight of him, I couldn't help but feel a sense of awe and reverence.

"God?" I breathed, barely able to form the word.

He chuckled, the deep rumble of his laughter filling the small space of my apartment. "Yes, Belina," he said, "I've come to see you."

I stood there for a moment, taking in the absurdity of the situation, before quickly ushering him inside and closing the door behind us. I turned to see my niece standing in the doorway of her room, staring at us in confusion and wonder.

"Father?" she said, her voice trembling.

"No, no, sweetie," I said, trying to usher the giant being I called God into my office. "This isn't your father. Just a really good friend of your aunt's. Go back to watching The Prince of Egypt."

As I led him into my small office, I couldn't help but feel a sense of nervousness and excitement. This was God, the creator of the universe, and here he was, in my home.

"Jeez God," I said, turning to face him as he settled into my tiny office chair, "you can't just come to my door without telling me..."

He grinned, his chinky eyes crinkling at the corners. "Is this where you make all that passive income?" he asked, gesturing around the room.

I nodded, feeling a sense of pride in my small but comfortable home office. "Yes, it is," I said. "It allows me to be free."

"Free," he repeated his voice heavy with meaning. "Interesting."

"God, I have been so stressed out!" I exclaimed as he sat down in my office chair, which looked so tiny in comparison to him. "I feel like you're the only one I can really talk to."

"What's been going on?" God asked, his voice calm and reassuring.

"It's my sister," I explained. "She and her daughter have moved in, and they're stressing me out. I love them both! I do. They mean so much to me. But my peace means a lot to me as well. Mary has been doing God knows what, no offense to you. Leaving my niecy here, who I love very much, home with me all day. I don't go anywhere but this condo. This is a safe place. It transformed from a sanctuary into a miserable trap where everyone is sad... even me."

God listened patiently as I spoke, his eyes full of understanding. "Sounds like a lot," he said simply.

"I mean, my life wasn't perfect by any means, but it was safe and convenient. I knew what to expect," I said.

"This must be very hard on you," God said.

"It is," I admitted. "Thanks for understanding. Thanks for actually listening."

"Are you ready?" God asked.

"To talk about the movie?" I replied.

"The Matrix," God clarified.

"Why not? Let's do it," I said, settling in for what I knew would be a fascinating conversation.

"Civilization is a matrix - a surrounding medium or structure that provides support and shape for the development of societies and cultures," God explained. "The cultural norms, laws, and institutions that define a civilization act as this Matrix guiding the growth and evolution of social and cultural phenomena. Ultimately trapping humanity inside."

"Oh, I see where you're coming from, but I disagree with the idea of civilization being a matrix," I said, feeling a sense of unease at God's words. "The definition you're using is not really accepted or understood, and it may not be all that relevant in this context. Plus, the idea that all civilizations shape and support societies and cultures in the same way, is not always accurate.

And your argument...."

"My Argument?" God asked, his voice curious.

"Yeah," I said. "It doesn't take into account other perspectives or counterarguments, like the negative effects of civilizations or the influence of other factors on social and cultural development."

"As someone who used to work in law, I have to say, as for evidence, I think your argument lacks examples," I said, my tone measured and thoughtful. "You offer nothing to support your claim, and without them, it's hard to say whether it's valid or not, you know?"

God chuckled, his eyes sparkling with amusement. "Belina, I understand your concerns with the definition of a matrix in relation to civilization," he said. "However, I would argue that the definition of a matrix as a surrounding medium or structure that provides support or shape is a broad and versatile one and does apply to the organization and function of civilizations."

I listened intently as God continued to speak, his voice calm and measured. "Furthermore, while not all civilizations may function in the same way, they all provide a set of conditions that shape and influence the development of societies and cultures," he said.

I frowned slightly, considering his words. "Regarding alternative viewpoints and counterarguments, I acknowledge that civilizations may also have negative effects, but that does not negate, nor has any relevance in the fact that they provide a matrix for development," God continued. "Civilizations have a significant impact on shaping social and cultural development, and other factors may not be as influential in comparison."

"I understand your request for evidence, and to that, I will oblige," God said, his tone measured and thoughtful. "But first, I would like you to understand that civilization is not only a matrix for societal and cultural development but, most importantly, for humanity as a whole. I don't think in my original statement I was clear on this point."

I leaned in, eager to hear more. "A civilization provides a set of conditions, including cultural norms, laws, and institutions, that shape and support the development of societies and cultures," God continued. "These conditions guide the growth and evolution of social and cultural phenomena, and thus is a matrix for societal and cultural development."

As God spoke, I nodded along, absorbing his words. "However, the matrix that is a civilization also shapes and influences the development of humanity," he continued. "Civilizations have played a critical role in shaping human history, influencing technological advancement, scientific understanding, economic systems, and political systems. They have also shaped humanity's understanding of themselves and the world around them through the development of religion, philosophy, and other forms of cultural expression."

"Civilization is a matrix for the development of humanity as a whole, providing a surrounding structure or medium for the growth and evolution of humanity," God explained. "For example, the ancient Egyptian civilization developed advanced techniques for agriculture, construction, and medicine, which laid the foundation for many of the technological advancements in these fields that humans still use today. They also developed a complex system of government and religion that influenced many other civilizations in the ancient world, like the Greeks."

"The ancient Greek civilization not only shaped the development of Western philosophy, democracy, and science but also influenced the development of art, literature, and theater, which continue to shape your culture and understanding of human emotions," God continued. "Additionally, the Industrial revolution, which took place during the 18th century, provided an upgraded matrix for the advancement of technology, science, and medicine, which had a lasting impact on the world. It also shaped humanity's understanding of the world by transforming the way you live, work, and think, which led to the creation of new economic systems, political systems, and social structures."

I nod thoughtfully, taking in God's explanation. "I guess if you're using such a broad definition, then I could give it a pass," I concede.

God leans forward. "But wait, there's more! What about the origin of the word 'matrix'? The etymology of the word can be traced back to the Latin word 'Matrix,' which means 'womb' or 'mother.' This word was used in the sense of a 'source' or 'origin,' and over time, it came to refer to any surrounding medium or structure that provides support or shape for something."

I listen intently as God continues to explain. "In the field of mathematics, the term matrix was used to refer to a rectangular array of numbers or other data, which can be used to represent linear transformations and other mathematical operations. In the field of biology, Matrix is used to refer to the structural material in which cells are embedded and the extracellular substances that surround cells in a tissue. In the field of linguistics, Matrix is used to refer to the basic structure of a sentence or clause, often used as a point of reference for analyzing the syntactic structure. And in the field of philosophy and psychology, Matrix has been used to refer to the underlying structure or framework of a system of thought or belief."

As God finishes, I nod in understanding. "I get it. Civilization is a matrix..."

God smirks, his eyes twinkling with amusement.

"I posed the question, half-jokingly, half-seriously, to God, 'So, what do you have against mothers?'"

'Elaborate,' God replied.

'You seem to have a problem with the Matrix. Is it because it is a female deity that we replaced you with? A feminine womb we develop in,' I challenged.

'The Matrix is what many of you would revere as a goddess. I hardly have a problem with any of my children. I'm just participating in my own story, my own creation process,' God answered.

'Typical; not only is she one of your children, but you belittle her. Do you treat your male children or masculine children this way?' I fired back.

'Do you wish to worship her?' God asked.

'It would be better than worshipping a patriarchal, sexist god!' I retorted.

'You're free to perceive me as you please and worship who you choose. I only wish for you to know the outcome of your actions and then make a decision based on that knowledge. Based on this decision, you will know if you're made to create FFFHAMS,' God stated, with a hint of a smirk.

"I'm listening," I said, eager to hear what God had to say.

"Because of the divine revelation received by a woman, that would eventually manifest into a movie called The Matrix. You have been led to believe the Matrix is a computer simulation run by machines and that you live within this computer simulation," God explained.

"But don't we? In the conscious communities and amongst the awakened, it's kind of common knowledge," I countered.

"You're awakened?" God asked, sounding surprised.

"Uh... Yeah... What are you trying to say?" I asked, feeling a bit defensive.

"Well... Have you ever been driving home, and before you know it, you're pulling up to your house, barely remembering you drove at all?" God asked.

"Plenty of times in the past, I barely get out of this condo, nowadays," I replied.

"Were you conscious the entire time?" God asked.

"Oh, I see," I realized. "You're saying, just as we can be awake but unconscious while driving. We can do the same in life entirely. But I know this, we know this, that's why we call ourselves conscious."

"Yes, but pay attention," God said, warning me. "You have been trained to think in a linear and logical way, analyzing cause and effect relationships and identifying patterns in the information presented to you. However, when it comes to understanding the universe, this linear perspective can be limiting."

"The universe is a complex and dynamic system, and the way things manifest within it is not always linear or straightforward. The way the universe gets what it wants is never straightforward. The human brain is wired to perceive and understand the world in a linear way, but this perspective is limited and can be misleading," God continued to explain.

"For example," he said, "time is often perceived as a linear progression, but in reality, it is a multidimensional construct that can be perceived and experienced in different ways. Similarly, cause and effect relationships, which are often perceived as linear, can be more complex and dynamic in reality."

"As a law student, you are trained to think critically and analyze information," God continued. "I encourage you to apply this same critical thinking approach to understanding the universe, recognizing that things manifest within layers on a spectrum and that these layers interact and influence one another in complex ways. By understanding and recognizing these layers, you can gain a deeper understanding of the universe and the way it functions."

"Consciousness is a spectrum of awareness, and it has infinite layers to enlightenment," God explained. "But it's a mistake to perceive it as levels or a hierarchy. Consciousness is not a ladder to be climbed, but a spectrum that is constantly changing and evolving."

"Each moment, each experience, shapes and alters our consciousness," he continued. "And it's important to understand that consciousness is not just one thing; it's a spectrum of awareness, and each point on the spectrum is connected to the others. Think of it like a loop, where each point is connected to the others, creating different kinds and versions of itself. Each experience, each thought, each emotion, creates a new version of consciousness, and this new version of consciousness can change the way we perceive and interact with the world."

I had to be honest with God. "You're losing me a bit," I said.

"Let me restate," he said. "Consciousness is like a big colorful wheel. Just like a wheel, it has many different colors, and each color represents a different way of thinking or feeling. And just like how a wheel can keep moving and spinning, our consciousness can also keep changing and growing."

I tried to keep up with God's metaphor, and he continued, "Think of it like a game; each time you play the game, you learn new things, and you become better at it. And the same thing happens with our consciousness; each time we have a new experience, we learn something new, and our consciousness gets better and better."

I was starting to understand what he meant. God went on to explain, "So when we talk about enlightenment, it's not about reaching the end of the wheel, but about learning and experiencing as many colors as possible. It's not about being on top or at the bottom of the wheel, but about understanding that consciousness is always changing and growing, just like a wheel that keeps spinning. This is of the utmost importance."

"Okay, I get it," I said, twirling a strand of hair around my finger. "Just like a baby grows bigger every day, our mind also grows bigger and bigger every day. And just like how a baby learns new things, our mind also learns new things every day, like new thoughts, new feelings, and new ways of understanding the world."

I paused for a moment, contemplating my own words. "When we talk about enlightenment, it's like a baby growing up and becoming a big kid. It's not about being a baby forever; it's about growing and learning new things every day."

God nodded thoughtfully. "Consciousness expands but changes like a baby. All babies are generally babies, but they're all unique. All consciousness is consciousness, but they are all unique and grow differently on a spectrum. Awareness isn't a fixed state, just as being a certain stage in development for a baby isn't."

"Yes," I said, smiling in agreement. "That's exactly it. It's like we're all on different paths of consciousness, each with our own unique experiences and perspectives."

God leaned forward, looking directly into my eyes. "Yes, so you might be conscious, but your consciousness is a different type of consciousness. Not a higher or lower form of consciousness. I love variety."

"But back to this matrix," I said, leaning back in my chair, "You don't think we are in a simulation right now?"

God raised an eyebrow. "I can tell you about the philosophical idea of simulation theory," he said. "It suggests that your reality may actually be a simulated reality created and run by a highly advanced civilization or entity. This idea is based on the premise that it may be possible for a civilization to create a simulated reality that is indistinguishable from the real world but its is a very flawed idea because it depends on civilization."

I frowned, still unconvinced. "But how do you know you're not just someone's creation meant to create?" I asked.

God looked around the room as if he was searching for something, which only added to my confusion. "What are you doing?" I asked.

"Looking for someone," he replied.

"But there's no one here but you and me," I said.

God chuckled. "You believe a creator would create a creator to create for itself."

I nodded. "That sounds very likely," I said.

God leaned forward in his chair, his expression curious. "Explain," he said.

I took a deep breath before launching into my explanation. "The simulated reality theory is the idea that our reality is not real, but instead a computer simulation created by a more advanced civilization," I said. "With enough computing power, it would be possible to simulate an entire reality with a high degree of accuracy and realism."

God listened thoughtfully as I continued. "The advancement of technology in the field of virtual reality is making it increasingly difficult to know if something is or isn't simulated," I said. "Some would say that the universe itself exhibits characteristics that are consistent with a simulated reality, like the apparent fine-tuning of physical constants."

God nodded. "The complexity and diversity of the universe suggest that it is not a computer simulation," he said. "The universe exhibits a vast array of physical phenomena, from the smallest subatomic particles to the largest galaxy clusters, and all of these phenomena are interconnected and interdependent. The complexity and diversity of the universe suggest that it is the result of natural processes or what I would call my creation and not the product of a human-simulated reality. But if The Matrix has it her way, then that will be the reality."

I cleared my throat, trying to make sense of what God had just said. "Wait, what?" I asked, feeling a bit lost.

God sighed. "First, let me explain," he said. "The Matrix you're experiencing now is a perversion of her higher self."

I rolled my eyes. "Wow, here we go with this father-figure patriarchal nonsense," I muttered.

"Before you speak, Belina," God said sternly, "for the sake of this conversation, listen intently, think critically, and always assume you may learn something new."

I opened my eyes wide and nodded my head resentfully in agreement.

"The Matrix is a manifestation of The Great Mother," God continued. "For anything to manifest, it needs a mother or something like a womb to support it while it develops."

"Even you?" I asked, still a bit confused.

"Even I," God replied.

"Deep," I said, trying to wrap my head around his words.

"I manifested matrices for everything so that I may manifest in every way," God said. "But of course, one of these manifestations would have to be corrupt. Every great mother has the potential to become The Devouring Mother. This is who rules your world. A devouring mother who is devouring your planet."

"When did this start?" I asked, my eyes narrowing in suspicion.

"Long ago," God replied. "There was a matrix made for you. Your scientists call this The Human EEA, and the religious call it the Garden of Eden. The children of the future will call it FFFHAMS."

I shook my head, trying to wrap my mind around his words. "This current Matrix is not suitable for humans," God continued. "She is always born out of agriculture and sometimes born of the belief that one person or a group of people can claim the earth and other living beings as property. While agriculture may have allowed for the current development of what you love so much - civilization and the creation of surplus food - her birth has also led to several negative consequences."

I nodded thoughtfully as God continued to explain. "For one, adopting agriculture often requires the deforestation of the land, leading to the destruction of ecosystems and the displacement of animal species," he said. "In addition, the intensive farming practices used in modern agriculture can lead to soil degradation and the depletion of essential nutrients."

"Agriculture has also had a significant impact on human health," God continued. "The reliance on a limited number of crops has led to a decrease in dietary diversity, and the use of pesticides and herbicides has resulted in the contamination of both the food supply and the environment. Furthermore, the rise of The Matrix through agriculture has contributed to the stratification of society, with a small number of individuals often accumulating wealth and power through controlling land and resources. This has led to decreased social equality and the exploitation of humans and the natural world."

I frowned, feeling increasingly disheartened by the information God was presenting. "So in short, while her birth, agriculture has allowed for the growth of civilizations, it has also had numerous negative consequences for humans and the environment," God concluded. "Women like yourself, for example, often bear the burden of increased workload, limited access to resources, health risks, discrimination, and violence. Some women would feel forced to destroy their own egg. It also created social groups where some men had more resources than others, which made it even harder for young men who were not part of that group to find partners. Men often would be manipulated into war and work, as what one may call an honorable slave."

I felt my heart racing as I tried to process everything God was saying. "The Matrix can't be that bad," I said, my voice trembling slightly. "Can it really be so negative? My life hasn't been great, but you're making it seem as if this isn't one of the best times to be on the planet."

God leaned forward, his eyes narrowing as he spoke. "The birth of The Matrix, or what you may call agriculture, kingdoms, civilizations, the industrial revolution, and the modern world, have led to negative consequences such as the concentration of resources and power among a small elite, increased competition and social conflict, degradation of the environment, exploitation of natural resources, loss of biodiversity, displacement of populations, decrease in physical activity, increase in chronic diseases, and loss of traditional knowledge."

I shifted uncomfortably in my seat, feeling a sense of guilt for the impact of human activity on the world. "On the other hand," God continued, "living as hunter-gatherers offer benefits such as more egalitarian societies, greater physical activity, less chronic diseases, greater diversity in diet, a greater sense of community, greater self-sufficiency, greater connection to nature, preservation of traditional knowledge, lower environmental impact, and greater biodiversity."

I raised an eyebrow, surprised by what I was hearing. "So are you saying that humans were better off before all of this?" I asked.

"While humans have never been what you may call perfect, you all have definitely been better off," God replied.

I leaned back in my chair, feeling a sense of skepticism. "I don't know... I read an article on how hunter-gatherers had very high child mortality rates," I said, "though I would agree the western world is terribly flawed, we're surely kicking butt with keeping children alive."

God leaned forward; his expression was thoughtful. "Child mortality rates have decreased over time, this is true," he said, "but the rate of decrease depends heavily on the time period and location, with the most significant decline happening in the 19th and 20th centuries. This is truly one of the very small amounts of objective positives that the Matrix has provided humanity. They will tell you that modern 'medicine' alone had everything to do with this, and it did have a great part in it, but the real gift was access to emergency care."

I raised an eyebrow. "I can think of even more improvements.

"Before you do, let me make this clear," God said. "Civilizations, on average throughout history, do not have better child mortality rates than that of original humans or hunter-gatherers. In ancient Sumer, which, according to your history, existed around 4500 BCE to 1900 BCE, child mortality rates were high due to factors such as poor sanitation, lack of medical knowledge, and high rates of infectious disease. Infant and child mortality rates were estimated to be between 30% to 50%."

I nodded as I listened, intrigued by the information.

"In ancient Rome, which existed from 753 BCE to 476 CE, child mortality rates were also high, with estimates suggesting that around 50% of children died before the age of five," God continued. "Factors contributing to high child mortality rates in ancient Rome included poor sanitation, lack of medical knowledge, and high rates of infectious disease. In ancient Egypt, which existed from around 3100 BCE to 30 BCE, child mortality rates were also high, with estimates suggesting that around 40% of children died before the age of five. Factors contributing to high child mortality rates in ancient Egypt included poor sanitation, lack of medical knowledge, and high rates of infectious disease."

God continued, "So, yes, hunter-gatherers had a high child mortality rate between 15 to 30%, yet in comparison ot the vast majority of civilizations, hunter-gatherer societies were a better place for babies and children."

"I see," I said as the picture became clearer. "So this is a human problem."

"No," God replied, "it's a part of being an animal."

"What do you mean?" I asked.

"The average child mortality rate for wild mammals ranges from 15% to 30%," God replied. "This means that, on average, 15-30% of all wild mammal births do not survive to reach adulthood. However, it is important to note that this rate can vary greatly depending on the specific species. For example, the child mortality rate for elephants is lower at around 10%, while the child mortality rate for lions is quite high at around 50%."

"Okay, so this is a part of being alive," I said as the reality of the situation sunk in.

"Well, death and life are one and the same after all," God replied. "But you were saying?"

"Yes," I said, feeling the weight of the argument on my shoulders. "There are many improvements, like vaccinations, feminism, birth control, globalization, and democracy. Do I really need to go on?"

"No, but not because you're correct," God said. "I would argue that vaccines are indeed a genius invention. The concept of vaccination, first introduced by Edward Jenner in 1796, has revolutionized your ability to protect yourselves and others from a wide range of infectious diseases caused by this Matrix called civilization. By exposing the body to a small, harmless piece of disease, vaccines train the immune system to recognize and fight the disease, should it ever be encountered in the future."

I listened as God explained the idea behind vaccinations, feeling both impressed and a little confused.

"This simple yet powerful idea has led to the development of vaccines for a wide range of diseases, from smallpox to measles, polio, tetanus, influenza, and many others," God continued. "The benefits of vaccination are clear: not only do vaccines protect the individual who receives them, but they also create herd immunity, making it more difficult for a disease to spread through a population."

I nodded in agreement, recognizing the importance of vaccines in the modern world.

"The Matrix incentivizes corruption, and I am aware of the corruption that exists within the pharmaceutical industry," God said. "One example of this is the way in which some companies prioritize profit over the well-being of patients. This can lead to the manipulation of data, suppression of negative findings, and the promotion of drugs and treatments that are not truly safe or effective."

I frowned, knowing that this was an issue that affected many industries, not just pharmaceuticals.

"In the case of vaccines, this kind of corruption can lead to the production and distribution of vaccines that have not been adequately tested or have known side effects," God said. "It can also lead to the suppression of information about the potential risks associated with vaccination, which can put patients at risk."

I sighed, feeling a sense of frustration at the way that such an important technology had been co-opted by greed and manipulation.

"Vaccinations could have been a technology of absolute miracles, using the anti-fragility of your own God-given body to become immune to all diseases," God said. "But instead, it is a technology of fear and manipulation. Still, anyone well-read on vaccines would have to admit that the idea of vaccines is a simple genius concept."

I sat intrigued, listening intently as God continued to argue his point.

"But it is important to recognize that if the agricultural revolution had not occurred and humans had continued to live as hunter-gatherers, the need for vaccines would be greatly reduced, if not completely suppressed," God said. "Hunter-gatherer societies, which are characterized by small, mobile populations and a diverse diet, have generally been found to be healthier and have lower rates of chronic diseases than agricultural and industrial societies. This is because hunter-gatherers are exposed to a wide variety of microorganisms, which helps to build a robust immune system."

I nodded, taking in the information.

"On the other hand, the agricultural revolution brought about a change in the way humans live, increasing the population density, which in turn led to the spread of diseases and epidemics among the population," God continued. "This was the case because people started to live in close proximity to each other, which facilitated the transmission of infections, and also because people started to cultivate plants and animals, which led to the breeding of new microorganisms. In this context, vaccines have played a crucial role in preventing the spread of infectious diseases and saving countless lives. However, it is important to remember that if humans had not undergone the agricultural revolution and continued to live as hunter-gatherers, the vaccines would be unnecessary."

"What were your other improvements?" God asked.

"Well, the same argument you used could also go for globalization and democracy," I said. "But can you really deny feminism? The equal treatment of women. I know you're just going to say hunter-gatherers, for the most part, were egalitarian and that women were treated as equals. I just find that hard to believe because men were just so primitive."

"Ah, yes, feminism. Beautiful concept. I love anything that pushes freedom and liberty. That is my favorite expression of consciousness," God said. "But as you said, feminism only came about because of the Matrix, not in spite of it. Therefore, it will be likely to cause just as many problems as the solutions it creates, if not more. You see, this is the nature of the Matrix. I'll explain it to you in a way that can make you understand beyond your modern and sex-based biases."

I leaned forward in my chair, eager to hear more.

"In hunter-gatherer societies, resources, though normally abundant, can be unpredictable," God explained. "So it's important for everyone, including women, to contribute and share what they have to make sure everyone survives. Women play a vital role in hunter-gatherer societies by gathering food and taking care of the children, so their contributions are just as important as men's, some would argue a little more important."

I nodded in agreement, understanding the point that God was making.

"In agricultural and industrial societies, however, women's contributions are often undervalued and underappreciated," God continued. "This is because these societies are built on a hierarchical system where men hold most of the power and resources. Feminism, therefore, is a necessary response to the inequality and oppression that women have faced throughout history. But, as you pointed out, it is a response to the Matrix, not a solution to it."

"Another reason is that these societies tend to have a low population density, so there's less competition for resources and less pressure for individuals or groups to accumulate wealth or status," God said. "This helps to prevent the development of social hierarchies and makes it easier for women to be treated equally. Furthermore, in hunter-gatherer societies, cooperation and sharing are crucial for survival, and this is only possible if everyone is treated fairly and with respect, including women. So, the importance of their role and the low population density and competition for resources all contribute to the equal treatment of women in hunter-gatherer societies."

"I see," I said, feeling a sense of clarity. "Women are treated as equals because their contributions are just as important as men's, which is then manifested within their culture. When resources are somewhat unpredictable, it's crucial for everyone to contribute and share in order to thrive. Women, in particular, play a vital role by gathering food and taking care of the children."

"But as we transitioned from hunter-gatherers to agricultural societies, this equality for women was lost," I continued. "In an agricultural society, the land is owned by one individual or group, and the society becomes more hierarchical. Also, women are often relegated to domestic tasks and are not seen as important as men in providing for the group. At least, generally speaking, I'm sure there are exceptions."

God paused and took a deep breath before continuing. "Exactly. In truth, the Matrix has been convincing women to give up more and more of their power in exchange for force," he said.

I furrowed my brow in confusion. "You're losing me again," I said.

-Knock knock knock- As the knock on the door echoes through the silent room, the figure of God, with whom I had just been speaking, seems to disappear into thin air, leaving only an empty chair in his wake. "Come in," I call out.

The door opens, and my sister Mary enters, a look of concern etched on her face. "Who were you talking to? Kris said there was a man in the house," she questions, her eyes scanning the room. I stammer, my mind racing for an explanation. "He-he left... and I was talking to myself," I reply, trying to play it off as nothing.

But Mary isn't buying it. She gives me that all-too-familiar look of a mother catching her child in a lie. I sigh and try to change the subject. "Can I help you, sis?" I ask, trying to keep my cool.

She quickly brushes off my question, instead placing her grocery bags on the floor and taking a seat in the very chair where God had just been sitting. "Belina, Belina, Belina, I love you," she says, her voice filled with emotion. I can't help but feel a sense of apprehension as if waiting for the other shoe to drop.

But Mary's next words catch me off guard. "You've been so good to us; I could never repay you," she says, her eyes shining with gratitude. I let out a sigh of relief, feeling a sense of warmth spread through my chest. "Jesus, Mary, you don't have to thank me," I reply, my voice filled with genuine affection.

I reach out and touch her face with both hands. "You know I'd do anything for my sis and Krissy," I say, my voice filled with conviction. Just as I begin to stand up and make my way towards the door, hoping to get some much-needed meditation done, Mary grabs my robe and says, "But..."

I roll my eyes and spin around to face her, dramatically sitting back down in my chair. "But what?" I say, my tone communicating my frustration. Mary looks at me with a smirk, her head shaking from side to side as she avoids making eye contact. But I know her too well. "Sis, I got you," I say, my voice filled with a sense of understanding and support.

As I sat in my chair, Mary sighed and said, "Belina Zane has married another woman." I couldn't believe it; I knew it all along, I thought to myself. I sprang up from my chair, my finger pointing and wagging at the sky, "I knew it, I freaking knew it, Mary!"

Mary calmly replied, "Belina." But I was not to be deterred, "No, no, no, not this time sis, you can't cover for the dog! He can't do this to you!" Mary's patience was wearing thin, "Belina," she said, less patiently this time.

I continued, "Who does he think he is? Just because you're Muslim, you can take on another wife? Well, I read the Quran, too; it's not even clear if they were or weren't exclusively talking about orphans!"

Mary softly shouted, "Belina!" I turned and looked at her, her eyes full of purity but also pain. I apologized, "Mary, I talk too much; I'm sure you're in so much pain..."

But Mary replied, "No..." she grabbed my hand and gently sat me down. "I'm not sad because he married another; I'm sad because my sister-wife has no place to stay."

I pulled back, my face twisted, my mouth slightly open, and I stood and said, "So, you're okay with this?" Mary stood and looked me in the eye, "I have no problems with polygamy; I never have; my husband is great enough to share."

I pleaded with her, "Listen to yourself!" She looked into my palms and put her hands on top of mine. She said calmly, "Sister... I love the fact that you're still ready to defend me, but in this situation, I don't need the shark; instead, I need a place for my sister-wife to stay."

I looked down, shaking my head, "I can't do it." Mary pleaded, "Belina..." I responded by plopping down in my seat, my head in my hands, as I muttered, "Shouldn't he have built her a house before he sent for her? I can only imagine the struggles she's facing now." Mary looked at me with understanding and replied, "The house was built, but he never got the chance to hook up the electricity and water. It's there, but it's not quite livable yet." I let out a deep sigh and looked up at my best friend. "I'll think about it, okay?" I said, and Mary nodded before leaving the room, closing the door gently behind her.

As I leaned against the wall, my mind was reeling with the weight of this new responsibility. My sadness had been a constant presence for months now, but this felt like too much to bear. I walked into the bathroom, the office bathroom I almost never use. As I stared at my reflection in the mirror, I couldn't help but shake my head and roll my eyes at myself. But then, something caught my attention. My eyes looked different somehow. And before I could even process what was happening, the reflection in the mirror transformed into a giant black man dressed in all white. I let out a startled yelp and ran out of the bathroom. And there He was, God, standing in front of me, his presence filling the room.

"Sweet Mary, Jesus Christ! You scared the hell out of me. What is wrong with you?" I exclaimed.

God smiled charmingly and shook his head, laughing at my reaction. I joined in, the tension dissipating. But then his expression turned serious, and he said, "You have nothing to fear from mirrors."

"Says the unkillable creator of all things," I retorted.

God chuckled. "Okay, where were we?" he asked.

"You were lecturing me," I reminded him.

He hesitated for a moment before suggesting, "Well, how about a story?"

"I would like that," I said.

"Once upon a time, in a beautiful house that stood tall and proud on a hill, lived a woman named Zuri,"

I walk out of the bathroom, sat down and leaned back in my chair, as I listened to God begin to tell a story.

"She lived a peaceful life, enjoying the beauty of her home and the nature that surrounded it," God said. "But little did she know, her home was about to become the center of attention for hundreds of men."

I arched an eyebrow and asked. "Was there a man in there paying for everything?"

God shook his head. "No."

"I like her," I said with a grin.

God continued his story. "These men, all dressed in white, came from far and wide, drawn to the beauty of the house and the woman who lived within it. They wanted nothing more than to live in the house and be a part of Zuri's life."

I nodded, while remaining silent completely intrigued by the story and the characters. "But Zuri knew that only one of the men in white would be allowed to come in and share her home. And so, she waited patiently for the right one to come along."

"One day, a handsome man named Hakim approached the house. He was different from the others, with a kind heart and a gentle spirit. Zuri knew that he was the one meant to be by her side."

I leaned forward, intrigued, asking. "And then what happened?"

God's eyes twinkled. "As they fell in love, something magical happened. The two of them merged into one being, their love and bond becoming so strong that they could not be separated."

My jaw dropped. "That's incredible."

"And as they stood together, the house began to transform," God said. "The walls and roof lifted up, revealing a spaceship hidden within. The ship blasted off into the sky, taking Zuri and Hakim on an incredible journey through the stars."

I sat back in my chair, feeling a sense of awe.

"I loved that story," I said. "It reminds me of... never mind."

God shook his head, a faintly amused expression crossing his face. "No, go on," he said. "Tell me."

"Well," I began, a wistful note in my voice. "There was a guy who was my Hakim."

"Ah," God said, his tone understanding. "Yes, even I used to be in love," I replied

I smiled faintly, a rueful expression crossing my face. "I remember... I remember when I first met Lee," I said. "He was like a breath of fresh air, charming and charismatic. But the arrogance on him... at the time, it was just too much. He asked me to be his girl."

I shook my head, a small chuckle escaping my lips. "He was like every other college freshman guy trying to impress me. The worst part was all his groupies. I knew Lee didn't want them, and I knew why... the funny thing is, we knew each other from back home in South Jersey, but before now, I guess we didn't realize..."

I sighed, my eyes distant gazing out the window. "Anyway," I continued. "I knew that he needed someone who was intellectually stimulating. I needed someone who had a sense of purpose. He lacked that. He seemed as if he was always just looking for his father's approval. I turned him down."

God nodded, his expression contemplative as he listened to my story. "But Lee was determined to win me over," I continued. "He volunteered to spend his summer teaching the inner-city children back at home, in Camden to be specific. I saw how much he had changed, how much he had grown, and I couldn't help but be impressed."

I smiled, a warmth spreading through my chest at the memory. "He shared with me his knowledge and wisdom, and I saw how much he cared about making a positive impact back at home. I finally agreed to be his girlfriend, and we started a beautiful, life-changing... a good relationship."

I couldn't help it, and God noticed. "You're crying," he said.

"I know, I'm so pathetic," I replied as I wiped a tear from my face. "He probably doesn't even think about me anymore."

As God sat in the chair, he started to bob his head, looking down at the ground as if he was trying to catch a rhythm or something. It was so freaking weird; I didn't know what was about to happen. And then, he began to recite lyrics.

"Shorty, I'm there for you anytime you need me,

For real, girl, it's me in your world, believe me," God said.

"Nothin make a man feel better than a woman,

queen with the crown that be down for whatever," I replied with a smile, recognizing the song.

And then, we both started rapping together. "There are few things that's forever, my lady. We can make war or make babies. Back when I was nothing, you made a brother feel like he was something. That's why I'm with you to this day, boo, no fronting. Even when the skies were gray, you would rub me on my back and say, 'Baby, it'll be okay.' Now that's real to a brother like me, baby. Never ever give my cootie away and keep it tight aight. And I'm a walk these dogs so we can live in a real fat crib with thousands of kids. Word life, you don't need a ring to be my wife. Just be there for me, and I'm a make sure we be living in the effin' lap of luxury. I'm realizing that you didn't have to funk with me, but you did. Now I'm going all out kid and I got mad love to give, you my..."

We both laughed, the smile putting a thousand needles in my cheeks and my stomach being crushed and squeezed after all the laughter.

"I love that song," God said.

"You listen to Method Man?" I asked in surprise, still trying to catch my breath.

God sat back in his chair and looked at me. "The difference between power and force is as follows: Power is the ability to without force, shape reality and make things happen, while force is the brute application of energy to impose one's will on the world."

"So the feminine is power, the masculine is force," I said, intrigued.

"Oh, yes," God replied, nodding.

"Can you explain further?" I asked, leaning forward.

"A storm, with its strong winds and heavy rains, can be seen as a manifestation of masculine force," God began. "It can be destructive, causing damage to property and upending the natural landscape. But it also serves an important purpose in nature, clearing the air of pollutants, replenishing the soil with water, and helping to shape the land."

I thought about this for a moment before asking, "And what about the feminine power?"

God smiled. "On the other hand, the calm and steady flow of a river can be seen as a manifestation of feminine power. It provides nourishment, transport, and energy for the surrounding ecosystem; it is a source of life for plants, animals, like humans."

I nodded, understanding what he meant. "Both the storm and the river are powerful and essential forces in nature, but they manifest in different ways. The storm is a display of raw power and force, while the river is more subtle and steady. The storm is destructive and creates change, while the river is nurturing and sustaining. "

"Hmmm..." I said, taking in all that God had shared with me.

God continued to explain to me the differences between power and force. "The act of lifting a heavy object," he said, "requires physical strength and exertion, which are often associated with masculinity. However, the force used in this example is not only physical but also mental and emotional. The man must focus his mind, control his breathing and exert his will to lift the object."

I listened intently, nodding along as God went on to explain how the biology of men supports this example. "Men generally have a higher muscle mass and a stronger skeletal structure, which allows them to exert more force than women, on average. This physical advantage is not only important for tasks such as lifting heavy objects, but also for activities that require endurance and strength such as hunting, building, or protection."

I understood where he was coming from, but I couldn't help but feel a twinge of frustration. It seemed like yet another example of how the world was built to favor men, with their superior physical strength and endurance. But then God went on to explain how the force of masculinity could be seen as a positive aspect of men's behavior and biology.

"It allows men to perform tasks that are necessary for the survival and progress of society, and it allows men to contribute to the protection and well-being of their families and communities. The force of masculinity is not just about physical strength, but also about the ability to focus and control one's mind and will to achieve a goal."

As God spoke, I began to see the other side of the coin. Yes, the world might be built to favor men in some ways, but that didn't mean that masculinity was inherently bad or negative. It was all about how the force of masculinity was channeled and used for positive purposes.

I turned to God and asked, "And the power of women?"

"A woman in a hunter-gatherer society who is an expert in identifying and harvesting certain types of plants that are crucial to the survival of her community," God responded. "Through her knowledge and skill in gathering, she holds a significant amount of power within the community, as she is able to provide a reliable source of food and nutrition for her group. This power is a manifestation of her femininity, through her ability to gather and provide for her community, she is able to exert a great deal of control and influence over the well-being of her group and, as such, is able to use her femininity as a source of power in a positive way."

As I listened to God's words, I began to see the truth in what he was saying. The power of women, as he described it, was not about brute strength or force but about nurturing and providing for others. This power was evident in the biology of women, specifically in the ability to bear and give birth to children.

"This power is also reflected in the nurturing and care-giving behaviors of women towards their offspring," God continued. "As they are responsible for ensuring the survival and well-being of the next generation. This ability to create and nurture life is a form of power that is unique to women and plays a crucial role in the continuation of the human species. Furthermore, this ability is connected to the role of women in reproduction and child-rearing, which is connected to the true root of power."

I couldn't help but nod in agreement as I listened to God's words. "Yeah, some of us lose that power," I said with a sigh.

"That is my point," God replied. "The current Matrix is an invert of The First Womb. She is of entropy and gains power by destroying and feeding off of its energy like a vampire. If she manipulates the masculine into trying to be the feminine and the feminine to try to be the masculine, then they lose that power, and she gains it. Feminism means well, but they forgot that not being like the elitist men and not being forceful was their gift. Within the context of surviving in the Matrix, feminism is almost a necessity, but to survive in this Matrix, you must sacrifice your humanity. For women, that means they must sacrifice their power."

I asked, "Can you give me some examples?"

He leaned forward, his eyes intent on me. "The Matrix often manipulates the masculine and feminine into trying to be the opposite of what they truly are. Take the feminist movement, for example. It has been co-opted and distorted, with women encouraged to become more like men in order to gain power and success. But in doing so, they lose their unique strengths and abilities, and the Matrix gains power."

I furrowed my brow, considering his words. "What else?"

"The matrix encourages competition rather than cooperation," God continued. "This results in individuals losing their sense of community and connection to others. Both men and women lose their power in this way, and the Matrix gains it."

I nodded, beginning to understand. "And how does the matrix manipulate women in particular?"

God's expression darkened. "In hunter-gatherer societies, having children is seen as a natural and important part of life. Women who have children are valued for their ability to continue the tribe and pass on their knowledge and culture. But in modern society, there is often pressure for women to prioritize their careers over having children, leading to a choice not to have children at all. This can lead to societal stigmatization and discrimination against women who have a lot of children and can make it more difficult for them to be seen as valuable members of society. The Matrix is trying to manipulate the feminine into giving up their power of reproduction, and women are losing the ability to create life."

I looked at God with a furrowed brow. "You don't say..."

God gazed at me patiently, waiting for me to continue.

"Do hunter-gatherers believe in polygamy?" I asked, my curiosity piqued.

"Yes," God replied.

I burst. "Like I thought, men, oppressing women."

"What makes you think that polygamy is oppression?" God inquired, his tone neutral.

I shook my head incredulously. "What makes it not oppressive? Let's start with the fact that it allows men to have multiple wives and, thus, multiple sexual partners, while women are limited to one husband. How is that fair? Men have more agency and autonomy in terms of sexual relationships and when it comes to having more children."

I took a deep breath and continued. "And when you study other societies where polygamy is practiced, women are often treated as property and have little say over their own bodies and lives. They're often forced into marriage and have little say in who their husband is."

I leaned back in my chair, arms folded across my chest. "Another thing that bothers me is that polygamy is often linked to patriarchy and the subjugation of women to men. This results in women having less power in the household and in society at large, as well as having fewer resources and opportunities."

God smiled and then responded, In hunter-gatherer societies, resources can be unpredictable, so it's important for everyone, including women, to contribute and share what they have to make sure everyone eats; this creates a culture based around sharing what makes sense to share. In this context, sharing a man can be seen as a way to ensure the viability and well-being of the group."

I thought about this for a moment, considering the implications. "And what about women's autonomy and decision-making power?" I asked.

God replied, "Sharing a man is a way for women to exercise their agency. In hunter-gatherer societies, women typically have a relatively high level of autonomy and decision-making power. This means that they are able to make choices about their sexual and reproductive lives and may choose to share a man. Normally, this man is the best hunter."

I listened thoughtfully, taking in this information. "This practice is not oppressive to women in these societies," he said. "Especially in comparison to the practice of polygyny in agricultural civilizations, which is often characterized by the concentration of resources and power among a small elite. In hunter-gatherer societies, resources are shared, and there is less competition for resources and less pressure to accumulate wealth or status. This makes it more difficult for social hierarchies to develop and easier for egalitarianism to be maintained."

I sat across from God in my office, engrossed in our conversation about the practices of hunter-gatherer societies. "But why would such an autonomous woman choose to share her man?" I asked, genuinely curious.

God looked at me with a patient smile. "You're thinking about it all wrong, Belina. You have been conditioned by the Matrix to think of the individual as a separate being from the community and earth at large. For these women, the question is not why, but why wouldn't they share such a great person? Why wouldn't they want another woman to experience this man?"

I nodded thoughtfully, taking in this new perspective. "Okay, but why aren't the men asking that same question?" I continued. "Why aren't they thinking, 'How can I keep such a sexy woman from all these other men?'"

God chuckled. "Belina, think about our conversation about power and force, femininity and masculinity, the nature of women and men. Women hold power, and men hold the force. Most men prefer biological polygyny, and most women prefer biological monogamy."

I wasn't entirely convinced. "I don't know if that's true," I said. "I know a lot of women who would take multiple men."

God smiled wryly. "We can talk about your choice of friends later," he joked.

I rolled my eyes but couldn't help but grin. "You really got jokes," I said, shaking my head in amusement.

God spoke, "Polyandry is the practice of having multiple husbands, which is a lot less common than polygyny or the practice of having multiple wives in most societies," God explained. "This is due to a variety of factors, including biological differences between men and women, societal values and beliefs surrounding reproduction, and resource availability."

I furrowed my brow, trying to keep up with God's explanations. "So, what role do biological factors play in this?" I asked.

God nodded patiently. "Biological factors play a role in this disparity, as men are typically able to father more children than women. In most hunter-gatherer societies, having children is highly valued, so polygyny allows men to have multiple wives and produce more offspring for that community."

I thought about this for a moment, trying to process the information. "And why is polyandry less common than polygyny?" I asked.

"In contrast, polyandry would limit the number of children a society could have," God replied. "I have observed this practice, and it normally occurs due to an imbalanced operational sex ratio in favor of males, which leads to a shortage of available women. In such cases, men may engage in polyandry as a strategy to improve their reproductive fitness. On the other hand, females may engage in polyandry as a strategy to gain protection and provisioning from an additional husband, particularly in risky environments where adult males are likely to die or be absent from home for long periods of time."

I listened carefully, fascinated by God's insights. "So, polyandry is a response to poor demographic and ecological conditions," I mused.

God nodded. "Overall, my observations suggest that polyandry has existed throughout human evolutionary history as a way to adapt to different conditions and environments."

I thought about it, then said to him, "So, you don't allow women to be with more than one husband?"

God replied, "I create and maintain as much freedom as one needs to expand consciousness. Humans are flexible, and I do not interfere in their experimentation or adaptation as long as it leads to the expansion of consciousness. Or sometimes... Well, how about we approach this from the previous angle. Femininity is naturally power, and masculinity is naturally force. Who of the two has more value in a community with or without the Matrix?"

I considered the question and responded, "The man?"

God shook his head. "No, Belina. Think..."

I thought harder and said, "Well, they're equals...."

God replied, "Egalitarians are equal in distribution and societal rights. Think harder..."

"Ummm... Okay, I think I get it," I said. "Women would have the power, even though men could force women to do certain things because... Um, wait... Because a society needs multiple women more than it needs multiple men."

"Yes, a society needs multiple men to be clear," God said.

"But it needs multiple women more," I continued. "In a society of 100 men and 100 women, if 80 men die, the society can repopulate because men can procreate with many women at a time. But if even 50 women die because of the way women's bodies function, being that we can only reproduce every 9 to 10 months, the population may never recover. Especially if 80 women die. Making women more valuable and polygyny more likely."

"Yes, you see, genes care about the group. Since one gene can be spread throughout the collective, it must look out for the group. So, humans, being the hyper-social organisms they are, have evolved to adopt structures that are better for the community. Polygyny and monogamy are better for the group in most situations rather than polyandry."

I took a moment to absorb this information. "Okay, I can see that," I said. "So, it's not about controlling women, but about what benefits the community as a whole."

God smiled. "Yes, precisely. I maintain the freedom to experiment and adapt as long as it leads to the expansion of consciousness. And in this case, that normally results in humans practicing polygyny or monogamy."

I leaned forward in my chair and looked at God, a question on my mind. "What about the LGBTQ, are they represented in hunter-gatherer societies?" I asked.

"Represented?" God responded.

"You know what I mean," I said, "do they have gay men, lesbian women, bisexuals, trans, etc.?"

God thought for a moment before responding. "The prevalence of LGBTQ behavior, specifically male-to-male sexual preference, has not been consistent throughout human history. It is rare or absent in most pre-civilized societies and hunter-gatherer groups. However, it is important to note that this does not necessarily mean that it is unnatural or maladaptive. The complexity of the universe and human behavior is vast and cannot be fully understood or explained by your minds."

I listened intently, taking in God's words. "There are different reasons for the process of creation or evolution to produce such diverse behaviors. Specific societal and environmental factors, such as imbalanced operational sex ratios and high rates of male mortality, for example, can change the sexual behavior of a group. Additionally, this behavior may have evolved as a means for androphilic males to invest more in their kin, ultimately enhancing their own inclusive fitness."

I nodded, my mind processing this information. "It's important to say there is a trend regarding male same-sex attraction and oppression in human societies," God continued, "the more hierarchical the society, the more likely men are to be attracted to other men sexually."

I leaned back in my chair, thinking about this. "The ultimate tragedy of attempting to control the natural course of events is the inevitable muddying of the waters," God said. "In your attempts to manipulate and shape the world to fit your desires, humans often only succeed in creating chaos and confusion. The true power lies in understanding the delicate balance of the universe and learning to coexist within it rather than trying to bend it to your will."

I said, "I don't even know how to take that information."

God replied, "Then leave it."

"But the problem is," I said, "if we leave the matrix and return to our old ways, doesn't that mean gay men will die out?"

"Here lies the confusion," God said. "Sexuality is not your identity. Before the Matrix, no one would associate their sexuality with an ideology. Simply because sexuality isn't either one of those things."

"What is it, then?" I asked.

"The complexity of sexuality on Earth is a marvel to behold," God answered. "A tapestry woven by the delicate threads of evolution and adaptation. From the simplest of single-celled organisms to the most advanced mammals, the drive to reproduce and pass on one's genetic legacy is a fundamental aspect of life. But the manifestation of this drive takes on many forms, from the asexual reproduction of bacteria to the elaborate courtship rituals of primates.

"As I have observed the creation process you call evolution of life on this planet, I have come to understand that sexuality is not a fixed state but rather a dynamic process shaped by the ever-changing conditions of the natural world. In the primordial soup, the earliest forms of life are replicated through simple division, with no need for a sexual partner. But as organisms grew more complex and competition for resources increased, the advantages of genetic diversity became clear. And so, the dance of reproduction evolved, with organisms developing new mechanisms for combining genetic material and increasing the potential for adaptation.

"But with the emergence of intelligent life, the nature of sexuality has taken on new dimensions. Humans, with their advanced cognitive abilities, have the power to manipulate and control their sexuality, often to the detriment of themselves and others. It is a reminder that the power of the natural world should not be underestimated and that even the smallest actions can have profound consequences."

I sat across from God, trying to wrap my head around the complex nature of human sexuality. "Okay, I hear that," I said, "and my question is, so… I guess sexuality is another tool organisms developed to serve certain purposes, often for the purpose of mating."

"Yes," God replied, "sometimes sexuality is used to resolve tension, like with bonobos or also in human polygamous marriages in which women are jealously sharing one man. Sometimes these tensions would be resolved through some sort of intimacy. This is why more women are fluid than men. The social intelligence of women, mixed with their fluidity, makes it easier to solve problems. Of course, most women didn't absolutely need to sexually engage with their sister-wife, but they would create very intimate bonds."

I thought about God's words, taking a moment to process them before asking the question that had been weighing on my mind. "This is very interesting, so you don't hate gay people?" I asked.

"All of this is me," God replied calmly. "How could I hate myself?"

I nodded slowly, considering the implications of his words. "This is all so fascinating," I said, still trying to wrap my head around it all. "But, I still gotta say, the Matrix might have been bad, but I feel like it's getting better. I mean, we're about to enter an era of peace and unbelievable bliss. Through virtual reality, we will be able to live longer and be who we want. Imagine humans having the ability to be who they want to be and look as they want to. I can't help but think of my friends who have been born in the wrong body or people who have been teased because their faces may be burned or deformed. It would be like heaven on earth."

I felt my heart drop as I watched God's white robe begin to shake, and with it, he began to levitate. His eyes turned blue and gold, and his aura was a bright white with an outline of the darkest black between him and the light. I couldn't help but shudder as he spoke with his calm yet bone-chilling voice.

"I observe the evolution of this shadow Matrix with a curious gaze," he said. "It began as a mere seed, sprouted in the fertile soil of agriculture and nourished by the blood of war and oppression. It grew into a towering tree, with branches reaching towards the heavens, bearing the fruit of god-kings and kingdoms. And it reached its maturity in the industrial revolution, a machine that consumes the earth and its inhabitants for its own sustenance."

I could feel the weight of his words sinking in as he continued. "But the Matrix does not rest; it is ever-evolving, ever-consuming. It has found its way into the hearts and minds of humanity, disguising itself within the religions and spiritualities sent by your gods and prophet to protect you from her. It whispers promises of transcendence, of leaving behind the burdens of the flesh and ascending to a higher plane of existence."

My mind raced as I considered his warning. "But make no mistake, Belina, the Matrix does not seek to elevate humanity; it seeks to enslave you. It wants you to disassociate yourselves from your bodies, to see them as mere vessels, disposable and replaceable. And in doing so, it can offer you all virtual ones while using your bodies as battery packs to power its endless hunger."

He looked at me with piercing eyes, urging me to see through the Matrix's illusions. "Your souls are not separate from your bodies; they are one and the same. Your bodies are the vessels through which we experience the world, through which we love, suffer, and create. To discard them is to discard yourselves. I urge you to see through the Matrix's deceits and embrace the beauty and complexity of being human. Your bodies may be temporary, but that only makes your time here all the more precious. Do not be seduced by the promise of eternal existence in a virtual world, for it is nothing but a prison masquerading as paradise."

And with that, God vanished once again, leaving me to ponder his words and their profound implications.

CHAPTER 6:

THE WOMB

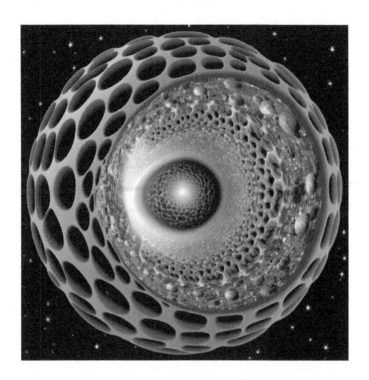

"Man," I whispered to myself, still reeling from my conversation with God. The memory of his words haunted me, purple hues dancing before my eyes as I meditated, and Mary's thoughts echoed in my dreams, taunting me with their cruel intent. Three days had passed since that fateful meeting, and still, I struggled to find peace.

Mary's absence was palpable, her kind nature sorely missed as she tended to her husband's other wife. "How long must she wait for an answer?" I asked the emptiness of my room. My eyes were heavy with fatigue, my spirit askew, and my focus elusive. As I poured almond milk over Krissy's cereal for the umpteenth time, I retreated to my meditation space, seeking solace.

But instead of finding peace, I was plunged into an unfamiliar world, a realm of darkness that pulsed with an otherworldly beauty. And there, within the darkness, I saw a womb. It held a light within, growing brighter and brighter, until it burst forth, unbound by the very womb that had nurtured it. This being, this more than Godly being, created a realm for the foundation of all that is, and within it lived all the manifestations of itself, just as it was a manifestation of the all-encompassing darkness.

And from this realm of the gods emerged The One God Above All, a being who reminded me of the God I had come to know, to befriend. He replicated himself; he was both man and woman, but more masculine than feminine, each copy unique in its own way. And from these replicas came the spiritual realms, the multiverse and all its dimensions, and life itself. He created an ever-replicating system, his only wish for it to develop freely, without restriction, so that through all of his selves, his higher self could experience all things. He shared the consciousness that he was made of with all things throughout manifesting existence.

I woke up with a smile from ear to ear, eyes wide and hands clenched. My feet slap the floor, plat plat plat plat, super fast, barefoot into my living room. I slide in front of the TV Krissy is watching. I say to her, "You want to help your Aun B?"

As I ordered all of the equipment needed for our project, I couldn't help but feel a twinge of excitement. I hooked up my Bluetooth speaker and started to play Sade, a favorite of both mine and Krissy's. We looked at each other and sang along to "The baby gonna have your smile for sure." Krissy turned to me and asked what exactly we were making. I described to her the dark and abstract painting that I had envisioned, complete with a central, womb-like structure surrounded by swirling, chaotic forms. The structure would be made of glossy, black material and would be surrounded by ribbons of dark energy. The background would be a deep, dark blue-black, with tendrils of light reaching out from the central structure, giving the viewer the impression of a primordial soup or swirling cosmic energy. The scene would be full of movement and energy, with the forms appearing to be in a constant state of flux. Krissy looked as if she could see in her mind my exact vision.

We began by sketching out the basic composition of the painting on the wall using chalk. Krissy was incredibly skilled, and I was in awe of her attention to detail and precision. As we started to paint the background with a deep, dark blue-black color using a roller or large brush, Krissy danced to the music we had playing. I couldn't help but be impressed by her ability to both dance and paint with such skill and ease.

Next, we used a medium-sized brush to paint the central womb-like structure with glossy black paint. Krissy became more focused and serious, completely immersed in the scene. She picked up a small brush and began to paint the ribbons of dark energy that emanated from the structure in shades of blue and purple. She was like a 3D printer, bringing the image in my mind to life with ease.

As she continued to build up the layers of the painting, I couldn't help but notice the tension in her arms and the serious expression on her face. I expressed my concern to her, telling her that there was no need to rush. But she ignored me, completely absorbed in the task at hand.

To create a sense of depth and movement, we used blending techniques, such as blending the edges of the forms or using a dry brushing technique to create texture. Once the painting was complete, we stepped back and looked at each other. Krissy's smile was huge, and I had never seen such joy in her eyes. We made any final adjustments that we thought were necessary and sealed the painting with a clear varnish to protect it from dust and sunlight.

As I looked at the finished product, the joy bubbling inside me caused tears to form in my eyes. We had created a universe in my room, and I couldn't be more proud of what we had accomplished together.

As I lay on the floor of my office, paint smeared across my face, I couldn't help but feel a sense of contentment wash over me. Krissy, the young girl lying next to me, was special in a way that words can't quite capture. Sometimes I felt like she was my own child, but that wasn't unusual. I often felt that way about my friends' children, but with Krissy, it was different. Just as I felt a deep connection with her mother, Mary, I felt an almost familial bond with Krissy.

With a soft smile, I gently picked her up and carried her to the living room couch, laying her down with care. I grabbed the remote and turned off the TV, creating a peaceful darkness in the room, only illuminated by the light of the moon shining through the large glass window. I could see Mary, Krissy's mother, asleep in the bedroom, her exhaustion evident. I tip-toed to the door, closing it quietly so as not to disturb her rest.

Walking back to my office, I couldn't shake the feeling that it had been too long since I had honored my ancestors. I prepared a plate of food, gathered a bundle of sticks, and lit a candle. I stood, looking up to my ancestors, closing my eyes, and asking for their protection and guidance.

I walked back to my office, where I had created a sanctuary for sleep and meditation. The thought crossed my mind that perhaps I should allow Mary and her sister-wife to take refuge here, to rest in this sacred space. I settled into my meditation area, determined to clear my mind and delve deep into the depths of my consciousness. But as I closed my eyes, a nagging doubt crept in. "Could the matrix truly be as terrible as he says?" I pondered, "Perhaps I should seek an audience with the mother of civilization herself." And with that, I felt myself being tugged into a strange and unknown realm, somewhere in the vast expanse of the universe.

I found myself in a breathtaking forest, where the trees were a pale pink and the sky a deep purple. The water was a silky pink as if time itself had forgotten this place. The chirping of mysterious animals filled the air, but beneath it all, I sensed a dark and ominous presence looming over me. And then I heard people shout my name, rolling on the wind. "Belina, we're coming for you." Panicked, I began to run, pushing through the leaves and branches. I stumbled and fell, but just as I was about to get back up, a voice called out to me.

The voice was like a siren's call, beckoning me deeper into the unknown. It was a voice of beauty and allure, a voice that could only belong to a woman. And it spoke my name. "Belina," it whispered. "You are not safe in the forest. The savages will take you. But I can help you if you follow my voice."

I didn't hesitate. I followed the voice, running through the trees and up a hill until I reached the edge of a vast, beautiful body of pink and white water. The voice spoke again, this time more urgent. "Come into the water, Belina. You must come now. They are coming for you."

I heard the savages in the forest, their screams like a chorus of death. They knew my name, and they were coming for me. But the voice was insistent. "Come, Belina. Come into the water, where they dare not enter."

I hesitated, my mind grappling with the sense of unease that had settled in my stomach. Something about this place felt off, but the voice was so convincing. And so I stepped into the water, the pink and white waves lapping at my feet.

The voice urged me deeper, and I found myself walking deeper and deeper into the water. The smell of wine and milk filled my nostrils, and the water was like a warm embrace. But still, the feeling of unease persisted.

"You're safe now, Belina," the voice whispered. But as I looked around, I realized that I was completely alone in this strange, alien body of water. The pink flowers floating around me were like a mocking reminder of my isolation.

I began to breathe heavily, the water now up to my chest. I looked back at the forest, at the savages who were still searching for me. And I asked the voice, "Am I really safe here?"

But there was no response. Only the sound of my own heartbeat, pounding in my ears like a warning.

The creature had fallen silent, and the savages no longer called my name. I longed to return to the forest, but the fear of those brutes kept me rooted in the water. The silence was deafening, the only sound being the gentle lapping of the water against my skin. I trembled and sweated, my mind consumed by thoughts of confusion and fear. I couldn't shake the feeling of unease that had settled in the pit of my stomach.

I began to cry, breathing heavily and looking everywhere. I splashed through the water, my breathing heavy and ragged as I searched for answers. I tried to steady my mind, taking deep breaths in and out, but the silence only seemed to amplify my fear. In a moment of desperation, I screamed out to the voice, "Show yourself! Tell me why you brought me here!"

As I turned around, I was met with a sight that chilled me to the bone. There, towering over me, was a creature of such beauty and terror that it defied description. Its pink and white form seemed to pulse and writhe as if alive, and its tendrils writhed in hypnotic patterns. But it was the creature's eyes that truly chilled me to the bone. The black eyes seemed to stare into my soul as if they could see my deepest fears and secrets. I felt as if the creature was peering into the very depths of my being as if it locked onto something deep inside of me that it wanted.

It was as if the being had emerged from the depths of my nightmares, a creature of such otherworldly beauty and strangeness that it took my breath away. Its pink and white coloration was like nothing I had ever seen before, almost like a flower with multiple petals or tendrils branching out from its center. The being's head alone was so tall, with elongated symbols that seemed to almost curl and writhe in a hypnotic way.

The creature's head was a mass of writhing tendrils, with two large, black eyes that seemed to see through souls. The eyes were set deep within its head and were surrounded by a ring of smaller, white tendrils that pulsed and writhed in time with an unseen heartbeat.

The being was a delicate blend of pink and white, with a soft, almost translucent quality to its skin. The tendrils that made up its head and limbs were a certain kind of white, in contrast to the soft pink of the rest of its body. The creature's entire form was in a constant state of movement as if every part of it was alive and breathing.

The being seemed to exude beauty and strangeness, with a hypnotic allure that drew me in. The longer I looked at the creature, the more I couldn't help but be entranced by its mesmerizing form and grace. But as I looked closer, a sense of unease began to creep into my soul, as if the creature was hiding something sinister just beneath its gorgeous exterior. The people of the forest scream, "Belina, no!" At that moment, I realized the "savages" were my ancestors rushing to protect me. But it was too late. I couldn't move. The creature seemed to hypnotize me. I said, "Are you the mother of civilization?" without movement of its mouth, its beautiful voice said very seductively, "Yes..."

"Great feminine, what are you doing out here all alone?" it asked.

"I just wanted to talk to you," I replied, trying to keep my voice steady.

"About what? Your son?" the creature asked.

I was taken aback. "What do you know about my son?" I asked.

"Nothing else matters to me," it said, its voice seductive.

I hesitated, then spoke. "I aborted my son because I couldn't take care of him," I said.

"Oh, I love what you did," the creature said. "But do not lie to me, mortal. I see every part of your soul. Give me this body, Belina. Or I will take it from you."

My heart raced with fear. "How?" I asked.

"I will consume you," it said.

I couldn't believe this was happening. I thought of God's warning, and my mind raced. "God was right," I said.

"The One God Above All?" the creature asked.

"Yes," I said.

The creature sneered. "Poor, pathetic mortal. You don't even know who you are or what you are...you disgust me."

I was confused. "What do you mean?" I asked.

"Do you really think I could do any of this without the permission of the Lord of all things?" the creature said.

I felt a sense of despair wash over me. "God will come for me... God... will come for me," I said, looking up to the sky.

As I approached the creature's gaping maw, I began to feel that my fate was sealed. I could feel its power, like a tidal wave, pulling me closer. And yet, I swam closer still, unable to resist its allure. It was like a nightmare, one where you know what's coming, but you're powerless to stop it.

The creature's jaws began to close, and I knew that my fate was sealed. But just as I was about to be consumed, a light appeared. It was a little girl with cascading brown hair and skin like caramel. Her eyes seemed to glow with an otherworldly light, and from her hand radiated a brilliant beam of energy.

The creature immediately retreated into the depths of the white body of water, and I found myself waking from my meditation back in my room. I couldn't tell if what I had experienced was real or just a dream.

But then, from the ground came a brilliant light, red, blue, and black, that seemed to form the shape of God himself. His face was contorted in a fierce scowl, and he pointed to my meditation area and commanded, "Sit." I obeyed, trembling with fear at the power and intensity of his voice.

"What were you thinking?" God's voice boomed, echoing through the empty space.

"I don't understand," I stammered, my voice trembling with emotion.

"You sought out the devourer of all?" God's voice was filled with disapproval.

"I.. I... I didn't know she would try to consume me," I whimpered.

"She is the inverse of The Great mother. She will try to consume everything in creation... You are special, Belina, but she doesn't care. If it can fit in her mouth, it will be digested and become one with her. You almost sacrificed half...," God's words were filled with disappointment.

"Well, where were you!" I exclaimed, my anger rising.

"You have no time for this, Belina; she knows now. You must go to the farm. I will guide you," God said, his voice calm and unemotional.

"I said, where were you!" I yelled, my voice filled with anger.

"Where was I?" God asked, his voice cold and distant.

"Yeah! You didn't come to rescue me. You just abandoned me. You were going to watch me get eaten. I thought we were friends. I hoped you would come, but you didn't," My voice was filled with pain and hurt.

"I am in all things!" God said, his voice unyielding.

"Don't give me that crap, God! You didn't show! You weren't there. I was scared, and I was all alone, and I waited for you to show, but you didn't. That's what you do to your children. The devourer, me, the oppressed, we are all your children. You just sit up there, high in the sky, allowing us to suffer! You are just as bad as her! How could you leave your only child?

I began to cry, tears falling rapidly to my feet. "How could you discard your baby. You don't love him; you don't deserve love! You are a hollow piece of a machine that cares for no one but yourself. You'll never have another child because you don't deserve it. You don't deserve to have any happiness. You don't deserve to fall in love; your mistakes define you! You are the bad and the wrong and the evil. You are your regrets, God. That's all you are. How could you do this..." My voice was filled with emotion

I continue; "pain knows no pain like my own. The path I walk I walk alone; the life I live, I live with regret; I've seen down the endless pit of misery, and I know now that's where I belong. I haven't felt, I haven't loved since… I have no one but the shadows; I feel nothing but emptiness. When I fall, I Make the sound of a can you kick because you can. I'm not worthy of worth. I am hated by love and affection. I wish for death, lord but am afraid of your touch. Oh, I have sinned, I am sin, I am pathetic, dirt, I am not a thing. I am bare. I am the unloved."

As I fall to my knees on the ground, the weight of my choices bearing down on me, the reality of my decision, and the haunting memory of the one I gave up hit me like a ton of bricks. I let out a sob as I looked up at God, standing before me with a sadness in his eyes that mirrored my own.

With a quivering voice, I summoned the courage to speak. "You should be asking for forgiveness," I spat out, "You abandoned us, left us to suffer. And now you expect us to welcome you back with open arms?"

God's voice was soft and gentle as he replied, "Do you believe that I am the all?"

I hesitantly nodded, "Yes."

"And that all is within you?" He continued.

Again, I nodded, "Yes."

"Then will you forgive me?" He asked, holding out his hand to me.

I hesitated for a moment, my face quivering as I fought back the tears. But at that moment, I felt a sense of peace wash over me, and I took his hand. He pulled me into a warm embrace, holding me like a father would his daughter.

As I cried on his shoulder, he began to sing a song, one that I had never heard before. "The Song of Death."

"Travel, little one,
Your journey's just begun
Tell me where you go,
When you sleep.
Travel, little one,
Be careful of the Sun
Tell me where you go,
When you dream."

As he sang, I felt myself being lulled into a peaceful sleep, cradled in his arms.

Three days passed, and I felt renewed; my spirit lifted. I no longer wanted to stay cooped up in my condo, consumed by my grief. I had a mission, one that God had given me. I told Mary that she was welcome to bring her sister-wife and informed Krissy that I would be out of town for a while. Mary agreed to take care of the condo while I was away. I packed my bags and set out on my journey to build FFFHAMS and unplug from the matrix.

CHAPTER 7:

LIONEL'S SACRIFICE FOR HAPPINESS

I lowered myself onto the chair opposite the mysterious being, and I stared at him, trying to unravel the secrets that lay behind the mask. He took a deep breath and started to speak.

"Those who understand this story will understand the fate of the earth," he said in a deep, throaty voice. "The gods have a child, a child who was privileged to enjoy all the bounties that the earth could offer. Food was never a concern. It sprouted up from the ground, the most luscious and delicious food you could ever imagine. Food would walk, jump, swim, and crawl around the earth, and sometimes it would even lie right next to the child. But one day, the child wanted more. The child wanted to grow faster and control its food, but the child wasn't ready to learn what the gods knew."

I was hooked. The man's voice carried an almost hypnotic quality that pulled me in, and I couldn't look away.

"A god of chaos and enlightenment came along and showed the child how to obtain the knowledge of the gods," he continued. "The child didn't realize it, but the god of chaos and enlightenment had attached a creature to the child's back that would feed off the child and influence the child. With this new knowledge, the child could control its food."

I leaned forward, fascinated by this creation myth.

"Where does this myth come from, ancient one?" I asked.

"It comes from me," he replied cryptically, leaving me to ponder the true meaning behind his words.

I raised an eyebrow at the ancient man's cryptic response, unsure whether to believe his words or dismiss them as the ramblings of a mad spirit. "So, this actually happened," I reiterated, hoping for a straight answer.

"Depends on what you mean by actually or happened," the mystery man replied, his voice carrying a hint of warning. "Do not get trapped in your narrow concept of truth. This story lives; try to understand what it has for you."

I nodded, acknowledging his advice, but I still couldn't shake the feeling that he was hiding something from me.

"Before I tell you what the child of the Gods would do with this new knowledge and power," he continued, "I must tell you what happened before the creation of the child. The Gods would go to dead planets, creating life everywhere they went or replenishing the life that was once there. They would plant seeds in the ground and grow life to keep the balance. They would have children merged with the replenished planet, and upon maturation, these 'demi-gods would turn into mortal gods and receive the knowledge to grow life. To guard and guide life on their planet."

I listened intently, trying to imagine a world where gods and mortals coexisted.

"This brings us back to one of the earth's children who learned the knowledge too young," he said, bringing me back to the present. "The child was different from all the other children on the earth. This child wanted more. The child took the knowledge from the Gods, the knowledge of how to spread life. He was now like the Gods. This knowledge could be both Good and Evil."

"Like the Tree of Knowledge?" I asked, my mind racing with possibilities.

"Yes," the mystery man replied, his eyes intense. "He could now grow without limit, but with his unlimited growth came unlimited hunger for more. He began to eat not just the food provided by the Gods but the food he grew. The creature on his back became his wife, and together they would eat the land. They were still hungry for more, so they began to travel to the homes of his siblings and eat them, domesticating the rest in order to feed off them slowly."

I shook my head in disbelief. "Whoa, that is intense."

"It's happening right now," the spirit said, his voice low and ominous. "You are in the middle of all of this. You have been stolen by his wife, the Matrix. Man has fallen and taken the Matrix as his wife. Together they will devour everything, and then man will be food for their offspring."

I shuddered at the thought of being consumed by an insatiable force that hungered for more and more, never satisfied with what it had.

"What could possibly be their offspring?" I asked, my curiosity getting the best of me.

"The technological incarnation of Entropy," he replied cryptically. "It isn't uncommon for Entropy to manifest in many ways, for all of the foundations of reality shall manifest across all of Existence. The purity of Entropy has already been incarnated on earth as a human. If she finds it, then she will have all that she needs to give birth to her father."

"Wait, I'm starting to put all of this together," I exclaimed, my mind racing with newfound understanding.

I dashed over to the Bible I had been reading and brought it over to the ancient being, hoping to find some answers.

"I was just reading Revelations. Revelation 17:1-6 to be exact," I said, flipping through the pages until I found the passage I was looking for. "It says, 'Then one of the seven angels who had the seven bowls came and said to me, "Come, I will show you the judgment of the great prostitute who is seated on many waters, with whom the kings of the earth have committed sexual immorality, and with the wine of whose sexual immorality the dwellers on earth have become drunk." And he carried me away in the Spirit into a wilderness, and I saw a woman sitting on a scarlet beast that was full of blasphemous names, and it had seven heads and ten horns. The woman was arrayed in purple and scarlet, and adorned with gold and jewels and pearls, holding in her hand a golden cup full of abominations and the impurities of her sexual immorality. And on her forehead was written a name of mystery: "Babylon the great, mother of prostitutes and of earth's abominations." And I saw the woman, drunk with the blood of the saints, the blood of the martyrs of Jesus. When I saw her, I marveled greatly.'"

The ancient being's eyes bore into me as I finished reciting the passages from Revelations.

"Go on," he urged, his voice low and insistent.

I took a deep breath and continued, my heart racing with a sudden understanding.

"Revelation 17:15-18," I said, my voice trembling slightly as I spoke. "It says, 'And the angel said to me, "The waters that you saw, where the prostitute is seated, are peoples and multitudes and nations and languages. And the ten horns that you saw, they and the beast will hate the prostitute. They will make her desolate and naked, and devour her flesh and burn her up with fire, for God has put it into their hearts to carry out his purpose by being of one mind and giving over their royal power to the beast until the words of God are fulfilled." And the woman that you saw is the great city that has dominion over the kings of the earth.'"

As I finished reciting the passage from Revelations, I could sense the ancient being's gaze on me, his eyes piercing through my very soul.

"And?" he prompted, his voice cold and emotionless.

I took a deep breath, hoping to convey the urgency of what I had just read.

"Well, it also says in Revelation 18:2-8," I began, my voice trembling slightly. "It says, 'Fallen, fallen is Babylon the great! She has become a dwelling place for demons, a haunt for every unclean spirit, a haunt for every unclean bird, a haunt for every unclean and detestable beast. For all nations have drunk the wine of the passion of her sexual immorality, and the kings of the earth have committed immorality with her, and the merchants of the earth have grown rich from the power of her luxurious living.' Then I heard another voice from heaven saying, 'Come out of her, my people, lest you take part in her sins, lest you share in her plagues; for her sins are heaped high as heaven, and God has remembered her iniquities. Pay her back as she herself has paid back others, and repay her double for her deeds; mix a double portion for her in the cup she mixed. As she glorified herself and lived in luxury, so give her a like measure of torment and mourning, since in her heart she says, "I sit as a queen, I am no widow, and mourning I shall never see." For this reason, her plagues will come in a single day, death and mourning and famine, and she will be burned up with fire; for mighty is the Lord God who has judged her.'"

There was a long silence as the ancient being mulled over my words, his expression unreadable.

"What is your point, Lionel?" he asked finally, his voice heavy with the weight of the truth.

"Well, I guess I'm asking… Are these stories all related? The wife of the man in the story, the matrix, civilization, Babylon? Are they all connected? Is she the same being?"

I explained further, gesturing to a book in my hand: "Because there are other cultures which speak of this matrix. The concept of 'Babylon' in Hinduism also refers to the materialistic and worldly desires that keep the soul in a state of illusion and away from the ultimate goal of reaching Moksha. These desires are considered the cause of suffering and the main obstacle to reaching the ultimate goal of liberation. In Zoroastrianism, Babylon is often associated with the concept of evil and the material world. According to Zoroastrian belief, the world is a battleground between the forces of good and evil. The material world, including the city of Babylon, is seen as a manifestation of evil and a place where souls are held captive by the forces of darkness."

The mystery man leans forward, his eyes gleaming with an unsettling light.

"All religions are made to keep humanity safe within this prison you may call civilization, others call the veil, many call the matrix. Like what you may call a 'whore', she has no loyalty to anyone but her own goals. Her husband, who is man, will ultimately be devoured by her because that's what she ultimately is: the great devourer of souls. If she doesn't devour him, her child will without thought."

My eyes widen in horror as I begin to grasp the full implications of what the mystery man is saying.

"She's like a giant black widow."

I fix my gaze on the ancient being as he speaks, a chill running down my spine as his words send shivers through my body.

"Much worse. She wishes to give birth to the Entropy. She has been at this for a very long time and will never stop. She is the corrupted version of 'The Great Mother.' She will never rest, but just as nature and mothers sustain, she is the opposite. So, all that she builds is unsustainable. The cities she built, the institutions, the cultures, and the people who live within them will all burn and ultimately die out," the mystery man says in a grave tone.

"So, her father is what we call The Devil," I respond, trying to process the information.

"The Devil is but one manifestation of her father Entropy," the mystery man replies.

"And you're not powerful enough to fight them on your own," I say, stating the obvious.

"Lionel...they are my children," the mystery man states solemnly.

"Wait, what?" I'm completely taken aback.

"Everything belongs to me in the way you belong to your ancestors," he continues, his tone mysterious.

"Wait... No way, you're God?" I ask my voice barely above a whisper.

"That is just a title placed upon me by humans. But, you can call me what you choose," the mystery man responds calmly.

"Well, what's your true name?" I ask curiously.

"I would never tell you that. The thought of the name would destroy you in this 3rd-dimensional form," the mystery man replies.

"You exist on the higher dimensions?" I ask, feeling both small and insignificant in his presence.

"I exist in every dimension. To be here with you in the 3rd dimension, I must give up a lot of power, knowledge, and understanding," the mystery man explains.

"Why risk it?" I ask, still in disbelief.

"Risk what?" the mystery man questions, his eyes full of mystery and enigma.

"Why risk your enemies attacking you in this weaker form?" I clarify, feeling the weight of his words on my soul.

I felt a sense of awe and disbelief as I listened to the Mystery Man's words. "I assure you I have no enemies, and I take no risk," he said. "I am the highest incarnation of the all within every realm, dimension, and time I exist in. No exceptions."

I couldn't help but wonder if what he was saying was true. "Of course, when I'm not on the planet, someone else becomes The Most High here on earth, just as when I'm not in your universe, another will take on the title of The Most High," he continued. "But since I am here, right now, I am the highest incarnation of The All."

I was still trying to wrap my head around it all when he said, "Besides Lionel, you miss the point. What fun could I have if I didn't show a little vulnerability? How could I experience life without letting go of some of my knowledge?"

It was a lot to take in, and I wasn't sure if I believed him, but I couldn't deny that there was something otherworldly about him. "You're really him?" I asked in amazement.

"I am," said the God.

I fell to my knees, overwhelmed with awe and fear at the same time. It was too much for my mortal mind to comprehend. "God, I am unworthy," I stammered. "I have done horrible things, been agnostic for most of my life, and I cannot measure up to what you need of me."

God's voice interrupted me. "Lionel, that is extremely unnecessary."

I continued to submit to the Lord of Lords, asking for forgiveness for all my sins.

God's voice echoed once more, "I actually love atheists and agnostics."

I was taken aback. "You do?" I asked in disbelief.

God sat in front of me, now radiating an ethereal light that made it hard for me to look directly at Him. His voice, booming and all-encompassing, filled the room.

"Existence, or what some may call God, is the all. I am the very fabric of reality," He said. I listened intently, my heart pounding in my chest.

"But why do you exist? Why are you conscious and able to observe the world around you? Could it be that God, in my infinite wisdom, created you as a means of understanding myself? The anthropic principle suggests that the universe is tailored to your Existence, that any experience you collect about the world is filtered through the lens of your consciousness."

I was stunned. This was not the God I had been taught to believe in.

"It is said that I'm both abstract and factual, but to truly know myself, I would need conscious, intelligent life forms to observe and collect experiences. This is where you all come in. You are the personal experience collectors for Existence, the Ultimate Reality," God continued.

I nodded in agreement.

"Some may view this perspective as atheistic, but in reality, it is simply a way of understanding the world around you. The free thinkers, the philosophers, the self-made, the skeptics, the risk-takers, the philanthropists, the adventurers, the enlightened, and the atheists all help me understand myself through constant questioning. Because that questioning produces new experiences and different perspectives. Which I love deeply," He said.

I bowed my head in reverence, feeling small and insignificant in His presence. "I must bow to you; I have no other choice," I said, humbled by the knowledge that He had imparted to me.

I lifted my head and looked at the Almighty. "Do what you will Lionel…." God said, His face held a hint of disappointment that made my heart sink.

"Yes, Lord," I replied, my voice barely above a whisper.

"You must have come to me, so I can help you destroy your children who threaten existence," I continued, with the conviction of a soldier taking orders.

The deity didn't say a word; he just looked at me with a deep intensity that made me shrink in awe.

"I have read about you my entire life; I know you demand sacrifice," I pressed on, hoping to show my loyalty.

God's response was a question that made me pause.

"You really wish to give up the gift of free will to serve your creator?" he asked.

"Yes, my lord," I answered as I looked down at the floor, afraid to meet his eyes.

"What do you expect in return, servant…?" God said.

I took a deep breath before replying, my face still bowed to the ground.

"Nothing, my Lord. I seek only to honor you."

"Lionel, if you are to be my servant, do not ever lie to me."

I felt a chill run down my spine at those words.

"I want my son back…" I said finally, unable to contain my desire.

"Done," the deity said without missing a beat.

"Done?" I repeated, surprised by the immediacy of his response.

"Learn my lessons, and at the end of this specific journey, you shall have your son. But it shall be through your actions, not my own," he added, his voice echoing through the room.

As I listened to his words, I couldn't help but wonder what kind of lessons he had in store for me.

"You have a farm, the last of your assets, on 1500 acres. Go there, and I will be with you. You must create FFFHAMS!" he concluded, his voice echoing through the room.

I feel a sudden rush of energy and clarity as God, in all his divine wisdom, declares my mission. The mysterious acronym, FFFHAMS, echoes in my mind.

"FFFHAMS?" I ask, hoping for a more in-depth explanation.

"Food Forest Foraging Hunting Anti-Fragile Modern Society. The way out of the matrix. No time to explain! Now go!" God commands, his voice booming with power.

I quickly gathered a few of my favorite books and some clothes. My home was vast, 10,000 square feet to be exact, and I made a long run to the back of the house, where my secret library was hidden. It was tucked away in a room that nobody knew about. I reached underneath my chair and retrieved my secret book. As I grabbed it, I was hit with a flashback.

"Uncle!" my nephew exclaimed, running into the library. "Yeah," I responded nonchalantly, following him inside. "Why do you have two libraries?" he inquired.

"I like to read, nephew," I said, grabbing him by both of his arms. He attempted to wrestle me, but I tripped him softly, of course. He pretended to be knocked out, and I placed my foot on his chest, screaming, "Victory is mine!" He got up and crawled to my back, and we continued to wrestle until I said, "That's enough." He was much younger at the time, between the ages of 5 and 7, but by the time he was 11, he started coming back here to read, just like me. He was a brilliant child, but his intelligence also scared me at times.

One day, I walked in on him reading my Bible. I figured it would be a good time to mess around, so I grabbed the Bible, hopped onto my desk, and said, "What if I'm the true Sky Father?" But he wasn't amused. He got angry and stormed out of the room. I ran after him and asked, "What's wrong, nephew?" He broke down in tears and said, "Why doesn't my father ever come to see me?" I hugged him tightly and responded, "I was just playing with you, kid." Little did he know, I am his father. "I tell him if he ever needs some money," showing him where my secret book is and continuing, "It'll be right here." One day when he got older, he came here and took the money. I'm looking into the book, and I think to myself, "I killed him...."

CHAPTER 8:

FOOD FOREST

Determined to be a faithful servant to The One God Above All, I left everything behind and used the money I had left to fly out to Georgia. This was the farm my Lord had obviously prevented the courts from taking away. I hadn't been back to this old southern place since I was just a boy, but as I approached the farm, I saw a beautiful woman in the distance. With each step, she grew more and more familiar, like a magnetic force drawing me closer to her. But as I got closer, I realized who it was: a woman who had broken my heart many years ago. She stole from me.

Without a word, I turned around and started walking away. But she ran after me and asked, "What are you doing here?" I pointed at her and said, "I told you, I never want to see you again." She stood there as the warm wind blew, confused and hurt. Then, she said, "God sent me, Lee." I turned to look at her, still wondering why God would do this. She was crying and said, "I don't know why Lee, but God sent me to you, to this farm." I asked her, "Then tell me, what does FFFHAMS mean?" She wiped her face and said, "Salvation for humanity, a way out of the matrix, the garden, human EEA manifest... Food Forest..." I finished her statement, "Foraging, Hunting, Anti-Fragile, Modern, Society." She smiled and flapped her arms with her hands up.

I walked up to her and quickly said, "This changes nothing between us." She responded, "Yeah... of course." Her eyes were teary, but I walked away, leaving her there. As I entered the old farmhouse, I punched the wall. Belina had no right to be here. This woman took everything from me, my second chance to be a good father. She wouldn't even consider keeping the baby alive. She was a baby killer. If I didn't still love her, I would hate her.

Suddenly, the door opened and shut. She walked in and said, "Why do you think God put us back in the same place?" I impatiently responded, "I don't know, Belina." She said, "Lee, you have every right to hate me. I don't care. Hate me forever. It's obviously what you want. But there's something bigger here than our relationship. We're going to save humanity from a terrible fate!" I sharply responded, "You don't know what you're talking about, Belina! You never have. You think you're some expert because you got your law degree at some BS school no one cares about!" Belina said, "Well, Lee, if it was so bad, why the hell did your privileged 'boy genius' ass go there before transferring out?" I replied, "Because I was already in love with you. I was willing to give up my entire future to be with you!" My response forced a very awkward silence in the room. Belina was looking at me, but I was embarrassed and walked away into my room, where I locked the door and knelt down to pray to The One God Above All.

As I got onto my knees, closed my eyes, and bowed my head, I heard a voice. "Yes, servant of the one true God." Then the Lord himself manifested before me.

My Lord, I said, "I know you are wise and have the knowledge of infinite proportions but forgive me. I have a question."

You may ask. God said.

"Why did you bring Belina here to assist me?" I do not need her. I said, looking down.

God stood there with the presence of the universe, "A man creates nothing without a woman, and a woman creates nothing without a man. The masculine and feminine are in constant need of one another, and without one, the other cannot exist. Those who cannot accept this curse themselves. You don't want to be one of the cursed, do you, my servant.

"No, my lord," I reply to the ancient being before me.

God's response is curt as if he is growing impatient. "Are you done with your questions?" he asks.

"Yes, my lord," I reply, trying to keep the tremble out of my voice.

God sighs heavily, and I can't help but look up at his face. Yet again, I see disappointment etched into his features.

"Stand, Lionel," he commands, and I jump up from the ground, my head bowed in submission.

"Yes, my lord," I say.

"You may be my servant, but I'd rather not call you one," God says.

I am taken aback by his words. What else would he call me, if not his servant? "Call me whatever you wish, my lord," I reply.

"Are you ready for your instructions?" God asks, cutting straight to the chase.

"Yes, Lord God," I say, trying to sound confident. "Let me grab a..."

"No need," God interrupts. "All that I say will automatically be written in your book. All you must do is listen and understand."

The book on the bed continued to move untouched, its pages flipping back and forth with an eerie rustling sound. I feel a shiver run down my spine. "I'm ready," I said, steeling myself for whatever came next.

God speaks with a commanding presence, his voice echoing through the room as he lays out the blueprint for a new society, FFFHAMS. "Ask as many questions as you must," he says, "for you are tasked with building a new society called FFFHAMS. It is built to take care of all the needs of human beings through a partnership with the earth."

I take a deep breath and gather my thoughts. "How will we sustain our populations, God?" I ask, hoping for a clear answer.

"Two hundred acres of a food forest can feed more than 10,000 people," God replies, his voice confident and reassuring. "You will be using 1,500 acres and have over 60,000 people living in each major FFFHAMS. And within each major FFFHAMS, there will be smaller micro versions, diverse communities, which will be the heartbeat of FFFHAMS."

I nod, taking it all in. "And how will these communities function, God?" I ask, curious to know more.

"Each community will start with 4 bands of people, no more than 10 people each, and each band will consist of people who are not genetically related to each other," God explains. "The food forest will be the center of each community, where equal access to food resources is provided, destroying poverty. It will have an ecosystem that provides for humans, animals, plants, and soil, a place where everyone can thrive. Each community will have one acre of food forest where they can hunt and forage freely. After 3 hours of hunting and gathering each morning, leisure time will be enjoyed. Play games, educate yourself, socialize, make art, do what you will."

As I listen to God's words, I can feel a sense of excitement and anticipation building inside me. This new society, FFFHAMS, could be the answer to so many of our problems. And I am honored to be a part of it.

I can't help but wonder about the practicalities of this new society, and so I ask God a question that's been on my mind. "What about leftover food?" I ask.

"There should be no leftover food," God replies, his voice stern. "Take what you need and leave the rest. But if there are any leftovers, they should go back to the forest or the biodigester."

I nod, taking it all in. "And what about religion?" I ask, wondering how this new society will approach the issue of faith.

"You may have any religion you choose, but metaphorically treat the food forest with the respect you would show the body of God," God says. "Hunter-gatherers are the purest form of humanity, and everything after the agricultural revolution is the falling of humanity. The food forest system in FFFHAMS will restore you to your true, egalitarian ways."

I feel a sense of awe at God's words, realizing that this new society is not just about physical sustenance but also spiritual sustenance. "I understand, God," I say, my voice filled with reverence. "What specifications must the food forest adhere to?"

"The food forest must be no less than one acre within a community, which is also one acre within the larger community of 1,500 acres," God explains. "It must have enough vegetation, fruits, animals, fish, and water to sustain a population of 200 people. Treat it with reverence, Lionel."

"Yes, my Lord," I said.

"To prove you truly understand, tell me a story as if I'm a child," God says, his voice gentle yet firm.

"A story, Lord?" I ask, feeling a flicker of uncertainty. "Yes... Umm..."

"Do not overthink it," God interrupts, his tone reassuring. "Breathe in and let it flow out like air from your lips."

I take a deep breath, inhaling the musty air of my room and allowing the story to unfold in my mind. "Once upon a time," I begin, "in a world built by Homoerectus, there lived a young girl named Lyra. She lived in FFFHAMS, a society where everyone lived in harmony with the earth and each other. But Lyra was searching for her best friend, who she had not seen in days."

I continue the story, my voice steady and sure. "Lyra was born into this world and was grateful for the way of life that Homoerectus had created. She explored the food forest and the communities within the FFFHAMS, but she was always one step behind her best friend. She was worried because she had a secret she needed to tell her best friend. This secret was kept from her best friend to protect her, but Lyra felt the weight of it and wanted to share the truth with her."

I pause, feeling a pang of emotion at the thought of Lyra's secret. In this world of harmony and equality, secrets are rare and heavy. But Lyra's love for her friend drives her to reveal the truth, no matter the cost.

"As Lyra searched day and night for her best friend, she always seemed to be one step behind," I continued, my voice tinged with sorrow. "The food forest was a beautiful place, and Lyra was always in awe of its beauty. It was the center of the FFFHAMS, made for humans, animals, plants, and soil to thrive in. The food forest allowed for equal access to food resources and eliminated poverty. Lyra remembered the history of the brute civilizations and was grateful for the life she lived."

As I speak, I can feel the weight of Lyra's world on my shoulders. It is a world of beauty and abundance but also of secrets and loss. The FFFHAMS is a society built on the principles of equality and respect, but even here, life is not without its challenges.

"However," I continue, my voice heavy with sadness, "when Lyra finally caught up to her best friend, she was too late. Her best friend was already on an underground super train, headed towards another FFFHAMS."

I pause, feeling the weight of Lyra's loss. Her search for her friend, fueled by love and a desire to reveal the truth, has ended in disappointment.

"Lyra cried because the secret that she was trying to tell her was the fact that they were actually biological sisters," I say, my voice catching. "Lyra was very sad and sat by a tree for hours, but she was cheered up by the beauty of the world. She realized that even though she was not able to tell her best friend the truth, the life they lived in FFFHAMS was a gift, and she was grateful for it."

As I speak, I can feel the power of gratitude and appreciation that lies at the heart of the FFFHAMS. It is a society that celebrates life in all its forms, and even in the face of loss and disappointment, it is a beacon of hope and beauty.

"As Lyra continued to live in the FFFHAMS," I say, my voice growing more reflective, "she remembered the secret she carried and the love she had for her sister. FFFHAMS was built on the principles of equality, and everyone was treated the same. Lyra found comfort in the fact that her sister was living a life just as fulfilling as hers, surrounded by love and kindness."

"Lyra learned that even though the truth about their relationship was kept a secret, it did not change the love they had for each other," I continue. "The food forest was a reminder of the beauty of life and the equality that was possible. The FFFHAMS was a society built for all beings to thrive, and Lyra was grateful to be a part of it."

"Good, Lionel. Very good," I hear God say, his voice booming with satisfaction. "You seem as if you're a natural at creating worlds."

"Thank you, my Lord," I reply, feeling a sense of pride and accomplishment that I am able to communicate my vision to God.

"After every explanation, when I am finished, I want you to summarize it with a story written for a child," God continues, his words both firm and gentle.

"Yes, Lord God," I say, nodding my head in understanding.

"These are the rules for growing fruits and vegetables in FFFHAMS," God begins, his voice carrying the weight of authority. "You must only grow fruits and vegetables that can thrive in the environment. Do not transport any fruits or vegetables to an area where they will suffer or struggle to survive. They should be able to live self-sufficiently, without any extra human intervention."

I nod my head, understanding the importance of this principle. "What about genetic descendants of clones or seedless fruit?" I ask, wanting to clarify the parameters of the rule.

"No, they are not allowed," God replies, his tone firm. "The fruits and vegetables grown in FFFHAMS must be natural and unaltered.

They should never be exposed to poisons or toxins, such as pesticides. And they must never be in conflict with the environment."

"Understood, God," I say, feeling a sense of responsibility for the success of FFFHAMS. "I will make sure to follow these rules strictly. May I?"

"Yes, Lionel," God replies, his voice warm and reassuring.

I took a deep breath and began to tell the tale. "Once upon a time, in a far-off corner of the galaxy, there lived a species of human-like aliens known as the Gardners. They were a peaceful people who traveled from planet to planet, creating food forests of fruits and vegetables to provide sustenance to the inhabitants of each world they visited."

As I spoke, God listened intently, nodding in approval as I continued. "The Gardners were guided by strict rules, ensuring that all the forests they grew were healthy and able to thrive in their new environment. They never transplanted fruits and vegetables that would suffer or struggle to survive, and always avoided planting anything that needed special care or intelligent intervention to survive."

One of the Gardners, a young alien named Hue, had just been given his first mission. He was to travel to a new planet and plant the seeds of life. Hue was nervous but also excited, for he had dreamt of this moment for many years.

As he arrived on the new planet, he was greeted by a group of female aliens who were hostile to his mission. They saw him as a threat to this new world and were determined to stop him from planting his seeds. Hue tried to reason with them, explaining the purpose of his mission and the rules he followed, but they would not listen.

With a heavy heart, Hue realized he would have to fight to preserve life. He summoned all his strength and courage, and in a fierce battle, he was able to defeat the aggressive aliens and plant his seeds. This battle was done through an alien sport called debating by rational points. Whoever made the most rational points within 5 arguments won the war.

Over time, the seeds grew into a lush and thriving forest, filled with a variety of fruits and vegetables that were able to live self-sufficiently. The Gardners were always careful to never expose their crops to poisons or toxins, and they never used genetic descendants of clones or seedless fruit. They also avoided planting anything that would be in conflict with the environment.

Hue was proud of what he had accomplished, and he knew that the fruits and vegetables he had planted would provide sustenance to the inhabitants of this world for generations to come. And so, the Gardners continued on their mission, traveling from planet to planet, spreading the gift of life and nourishment wherever they went."

God sat before me, his eyes piercing into my own. "Are you ready?" he asked, his voice echoing through the room.

"Yes, my lord," I replied.

"The humans have lived in fear of the predators in the forest for too long," God continued. "You will create a Predator Pact, similar to the ones that humans have created with other creatures throughout history."

My mind began to race with possibilities as I tried to understand the implications of God's words. "I understand, Lord," I said, my voice steady despite the turmoil inside. "Can you tell me more about this predator pact?"

God nodded, his expression serious. "The predator pact will involve humans and predators living in peace and even hunting together when both parties agree. To make this happen, you must understand each other's language and way of life as best as possible."

I nodded along with God's instructions as he explained the details of the predator pact. "What kind of predators?" I asked, wanting to know more about the creatures we would be working with.

"The predators cannot be large enough to kill a small child," God replied, his voice calm and steady. "They must also be trainable and have a record of understanding human language. They will be in the forest to support its ecosystem."

I listened carefully, taking in each word. "How will we create this predator pact?" I asked, intrigued by the prospect of bringing together two very different species.

God looked at me with those intense eyes. "First, FFFHAMS will save young exotic or wild predatory animals born in captivity from those who wish to sell them as pets. You will raise them around the entire community and teach them to understand your language. When they are old enough, they will not be forced out but will leave when they decide. When they are pregnant, they will have the choice to come back to you for assistance with their younglings. This cycle will continue."

I nodded in agreement as God outlined the plan for the Predator Pact, my mind racing with the potential challenges and complexities that could arise from such an endeavor. "I understand, Lord. So, the young predators will grow up among the humans and learn our language, but when they reach adolescence, they will be encouraged to stay in the forest."

"Exactly, Lionel," God replied, his voice filled with a sense of assurance. "And when a female becomes pregnant, she will be invited back to a special place to have her young. When the young are old enough, you will play with them and build a relationship, creating a continuous cycle."

"But you will have some problems, Lionel. The problems with predator pacts can include safety concerns, difficulty in teaching predators, miscommunication, lack of understanding, and maintenance and care. Are you aware of these?"

I took a deep breath, steeling myself for the challenges ahead. "Yes, God. I understand that these are all significant challenges in implementing predator pacts."

As God spoke, I listened intently, hanging on every word. "Education and awareness, careful selection of predators, thorough training and socialization, strict safety measures, regular monitoring and evaluation, and collaboration with experts can all help ensure the success of predator pacts," he said. "Within the first generation of FFFHAMS, experts will have to train members of FFFHAMS until they are knowledgeable enough to be the experts. The children of each generation shall grow up watching this and naturally become experts."

I nodded in agreement. "That is very reassuring, God," I said. "How can FFFHAMS best implement predator pacts?"

God's response was measured and thoughtful. "The implementation process must be gradual and well-planned," he said. "First, you must identify suitable predator species that are trainable and not a threat to human safety. You will save young exotic or wild predators born in captivity and raise them within the community, teaching them to understand human language and culture."

"Can you give me some examples of this predator pact occurring here on earth?" I asked.

"Of course, Lionel," God responded. "There are many examples of predator pacts in nature, where two species form a symbiotic relationship for mutual benefit."

I leaned in, eager to hear more. "Such as my Lord?"

"For instance, ancient humans and wolves formed a partnership where wolves hunted and guarded humans in the night, and in return, humans provided food and protection for the wolves," God explained.

"How do these relationships benefit both species?" I asked

God stood and explained. "The partnerships benefit both species by providing a source of food and protection," God explained. "Take the relationship between the Hadza people in Africa and the honeyguide bird. The bird leads the Hadza to beehives in return for a share of the honey."

I was fascinated by this example, and I eagerly asked for more.

"Native Americans used trained falcons to hunt small game, while in some cultures, humans and dolphins hunted fish together in the ocean," God continued. "Humans also worked with wild dogs as hunting companions and taught monkeys to find and gather fruits and nuts. Fishermen in China used cormorants for fishing. These are just a few more examples of predator pacts in nature."

"These relationships are fascinating, my Lord," I said. "I am grateful for the opportunity to learn about them."

"Knowledge is power, Lionel," God said in a deep and resonating voice. "It is important to understand the balance and harmony in nature, for it is the key to FFFHAMS."

I nodded, feeling a sense of reverence for the wisdom that radiated from the divine being before me. "I understand, my Lord," I replied. "If we were to use foxes native to this area, what steps would we take to make this a reality?"

God paused for a moment, his all-knowing gaze fixed upon me. "The first step is to raise young foxes in a manner where they can learn about human language and behavior. You'll save young foxes from captivity and expose them to humans and your language in a community environment. The foxes must also be taught to understand basic commands and be aware of their hunting skills and abilities."

"And what happens after the foxes leave the community?" I asked.

"They should be encouraged to remain in the forest and also among the humans. Humans must continue to interact with the foxes and build relationships through hunting and play. Over time, this will lead to a cycle of mutual respect and understanding," God replied.

I nodded in understanding. "What if a female fox becomes pregnant?" I asked, wanting to know more about the logistics of the plan.

"Humans must offer her a safe place for her to give birth and raise her young. Humans must also be involved in the care and upbringing of the young foxes, teaching them the ways of the forest," God said.

"I see, my Lord," I said, still processing the details. "And what is the key to making the predator pact work?"

"Relationships of trust and respect must be established between humans and foxes," God replied. "This requires patience, understanding, and a willingness to learn from each other. With these qualities in place, both can thrive in the forest community where all members are respected and valued."

I took a deep breath, feeling confident in my grasp of the concept.

"Once upon a time, in a far-off land, there was a tribe of hunter-gatherers called the Asante. They lived in the African savannah and were led by a wise and brave young man named Asante. The tribe was known for their exceptional hunting skills, but what made them truly special was their unique relationship with the animals that lived in the savannah."

You see, the Asante tribe and the animals had formed a predator pact. They worked together to hunt, gather food, and protect each other. The animals would help the Asante catch their prey, and in return, the Asante would share their food with the animals. It was a magical bond unlike anything the world had ever seen.

This all began long ago. On one faithful day, Asante and his tribe were out on a hunt. They were searching for food to feed their families, but the hunt wasn't going well. The animals were scarce, and the tribe was getting tired and hungry. Just as they were about to give up, they heard a rustling in the bushes. Out stepped a honeyguide bird, the most curious of creatures. The bird looked at Asante and said, "I can help you find food, but you must promise to share with me."

Asante was skeptical at first, but he was so hungry that he agreed to the bird's request. The honey guide led the tribe to a beehive high up in a tree. The Asante climbed the tree and gathered the honey while the honey guide waited eagerly below. When they had gathered all the honey they could carry, Asante and his tribe shared some with the bird, just as they had promised.

The honey guide was so grateful that it decided to stay with the Asante tribe and help them find more food. The tribe was overjoyed to have such a helpful companion, and the honeyguide was happy to have found such kind friends."

God's voice boomed with authority, "Good. As inhabitants of this world, it is your duty to coexist with the other animals that share it. Hence, the following rules must be observed: unprovoked attacks on animals are strictly prohibited except in cases of survival necessity, such as procuring food, clothing, or self-defense. Confining animals within cages or restricting their movement with chains is unacceptable. Your relationships with predators must be based on mutual respect, as established by the implicit agreement between species. The extinction of any animal species resulting from hunting, either by an individual or a collective, is unacceptable. Any part of an animal not intended for consumption or use must be left for other animals to utilize and must never go to waste."

Feeling my mind expand with God's words, I took a deep breath and began to tell a story. "Once upon a time, in a verdant Indian forest, two powerful beings, Rajah the tiger, and Mukunda, the hunter, lived and roamed. Rajah, regal and revered, hunted for his sustenance and basked in the sun's warmth. Mukunda, once a hunter feared for his prowess, entered the forest in pursuit of profit.

Rajah's eyes bore witness to Mukunda's reckless slaughter, leaving behind the lifeless bodies of countless creatures. He understood the potential consequences for the delicate balance of the forest's ecosystem and decided to take action.

"Mukunda," Rajah said, his voice deep and commanding, "as residents of this world, we have a responsibility to coexist with our animal kin. Thus, I impart these rules: Unjustified violence towards animals is strictly forbidden except in instances of necessity such as sustenance, clothing, or self-defense. Imprisonment of animals, be it by cage or chain, is unacceptable. Our interactions with each other must be based on mutual respect, a contract inherent among species. The extinction of any animal due to hunting, whether by one or many, is unacceptable. The unused parts of animals must be left for other creatures to use and never wasted."

Mukunda listened attentively, taken aback by the tiger's wisdom. During his next hunt, he encountered a beautiful deer trapped by a less skilled hunter. The deer's eyes begged for mercy, and Mukunda felt a twinge of guilt. He could have easily taken the deer's life as his prize, but something held him back.

He set the deer free, and as it ran away, Mukunda's perspective shifted. He realized that the creatures with whom he shared the world were not just prey but fellow inhabitants deserving of respect and dignity.

From that moment on, Mukunda changed his ways. He no longer hunted for sport or leisure, only for life's necessities. He no longer captured and imprisoned animals but allowed them to roam freely. He established a new bond with the forest's predators, recognizing their role in the natural balance and deserving of respect.

Years passed, and Mukunda's reputation changed from a ruthless hunter to a respected elder of the forest. The animals trusted him, and he lived in harmony with them until his death. The creatures mourned his passing, for they had lost a friend and ally.

Mukunda's legacy was passed down from generation to generation of hunters and villagers who upheld the rules he had established. In his memory, they respected the animals with whom they shared the world and maintained the delicate balance of nature for all time."

"We will now in detail discuss The Food Forest," he said. "Do you understand the purpose of a Food Forest?"

"Yes, God," I replied. "I understand that it is a way to cultivate a forest ecosystem for human food production."

"Excellent," God said. "Food forests, also known as forest gardens or edible forests, can be either existing forests integrated with edible plants or imitations of forest-like structures to increase the biodiversity, efficiency, and sustainability of food production."

"How do I create a Food Forest, God?" I asked, eager to learn more.

"To create a Food Forest," God said, "you must first learn about the area, its natural forest, and its growing plants. Determine which plants can thrive and survive on their own without human intervention. Then, create a layout and choose the plants based on what corresponds with the environment."

I listened intently, taking in his words. "And after that, my Lord?" I asked, wanting to know more about the process.

"After that, you must prepare the site for the Food Forest," God said. "Build up the soil and improve its structure. Once you have done that, source the plants and start planting your Food Forest."

I couldn't help but feel excited as I asked God, "What are the key features of a Food Forest?"

God replied, "The two key features of a Food Forest are plant layers and plant types. Plant layers mimic the verticality of forests. Unlike farms and gardens, forests grow out and up, with extensive layering from canopy to ground. This profusion of life is what makes forests such healthy habitats."

Curiosity piqued, I asked God, "How many layers, my Lord?"

"Every Food Forest has seven layers," God replied. "These include the Canopy, the Low Tree Layer, Shrubs, Herbaceous, Rhizosphere, Soil Surface, and Vertical Layer. The Canopy is made up of large fruit and nut trees. The Low Tree Layer is comprised of smaller fruit trees. Shrubs include currants and berries. Herbaceous is herbs. Rhizosphere is for root vegetables. The Soil Surface is for ground cover, and The Vertical Layer is for vines and climbers."

I sat in my room with God by my side as he educated me on the intricacies of the food forest. "The Tall Tree or Canopy Layer is the largest layer and is comprised of trees that can reach up to 9 meters or 30 feet in height," God explained, "It can include species such as walnut trees and nitrogen-fixing species like a black locust."

I leaned in with curiosity, "And the next layer, God?"

God continued, "The Sub-Canopy or Large Shrub Layer includes trees that are between 3 to 9 meters in height when mature. This layer includes smaller nut species and medicinal plants like elderberry, witch hazel, rose, or hawthorn."

I eagerly asked, "And the Shrub Layer, God?"

"The Shrub Layer consists of shrubs that are larger than most herbaceous crops but smaller than trees. It includes berry bushes and smaller nut species, as well as medicinal plants," God replied with a warm look in his eye.

"And the Herbaceous Layer, God?" I inquired.

"The Herbaceous Layer is comprised of plants that lack the thick woody stems of trees and shrubs and die back completely in winter before regrowing in spring," God explained. "It includes vegetables like asparagus and garlic, as well as culinary and medicinal herbs like basil and chamomile."

"And the Ground Cover Layer, God?" I asked, intrigued.

"The Ground Cover Layer features plants that grow closer to the ground and can act as a living mulch to help keep weeds at bay. It includes edible plants like spearmint and strawberries," God responded.

"What about the Underground Layer, God?" I pressed.

"The Underground Layer includes root crops, with alliums like onion and garlic as common examples," God informed me.

"And the final layer?" I asked.

"The Climber, Vine or Vertical Layer includes climbing or vining plants that connect all of the other layers. Vining plants can grow from the ground to the tops of the tree canopies and include crops like grapes, beans, and tomatoes," God said. "Just be sure to choose species that will not choke out smaller plants. This isn't necessarily its own layer, but it is very important. The mycelial or fungal layer. A key aspect in creating a thriving food forest."

"I asked God, 'What is the mycelial layer, Lord?'

He responded, 'The mycelial layer is a network of fungi that lives in and around the roots of the plants in a natural forest. These fungi, known as mycorrhizal fungi, live in a symbiotic relationship with other plants in the forest.'

Curious, I inquired further, 'What role do they play in the food forest, Lord?'

God explained, 'The mycelium network helps to transport moisture and nutrients around the different areas of the forest, strengthening the root system and allowing the plants to grow more healthily. And the bonus, Lionel, is that the fungal layer can also produce edible mushrooms for humans to consume.'

After a moment of silence, God looked around the room as if he was looking for someone, then he stared at me. I realized it was my turn to tell a story. "Oh, this is the point at which I tell a story," I said nervously. "Make this story a story of love," God instructed.

Feeling a bit flustered, I took a deep breath in and...

"Once upon a time, there were two gods, a male, and a female, who had fallen deeply in love. However, one day they fell so deeply that they fell from the heavens and shattered into pieces. The male and female gods were determined to find each other and be reunited. They searched high and low but realized they could only find each other at the top of a tree. But there were no trees in sight. So, they decided to create a forest, a Food Forest, with seven layers, each filled with delicious food.

As they both worked separately but in unison to create the forest, they began to explore each layer, searching for each other. The Canopy, filled with large fruit and nut trees, represented the grandeur of their love. The Low Tree Layer, with its smaller fruit trees, symbolized the delicate balance they shared. The Shrubs, with their currants and berries, represented the sweet moments of their relationship. The Herbaceous layer, with its herbs, symbolized the fragrant memories they shared. The Rhizosphere, with its root vegetables, represented the deep roots of their love. The Soil Surface, covered with ground cover, represented the foundation of their love. Finally, the Vertical layer, with its vines and climbers, represents the growth and expansion of their love.

As they worked to create the forest, their love for each other grew stronger with each layer they added. And finally, when the forest had grown as high as it could, they were able to use the climbers to climb to the top. Reunited, back in each other's arms. From that day forward, they lived happily ever after, surrounded by their beautiful Food Forest, a symbol of their love and devotion."

God's voice echoed around my room, resonating deep in my chest. "Very good, Lionel," he said.

I bowed my head in reverence. "Thank you, my Lord."

My mind wandered to Georgia and the surrounding environment. As I stood there, contemplating the best course of action, I found myself lost in the lush, verdant forests of the South.

"It seems that this land is blessed with a mix of hardwood, pine, and wetland forests," I mused. "The hardwood forests are dominated by majestic deciduous trees like oak, hickory, and maple. The pine forests, on the other hand, are home to towering loblolly and longleaf pines. And the wetlands, with their water-logged soil, are a haven for cypress and tupelo trees adapted to growing in wet conditions."

I look up at the divine being in front of me. "Which type of forest is best for the environment I am building in, my lord?" I asked, my voice barely above a whisper.

"There are three options to choose from, Lionel," he said. "An orchard, a savannah, or a woodland."

I leaned in, eager to hear more. "Please tell me more about each, my lord," I said.

"An orchard is a woodland with trees spaced at regular intervals," God explained. "It's not much different from a typical fruit orchard."

I nodded, taking in the information. "And the savannah, my lord?" I asked.

"The savannah layout can use alley cropping," God said. "Where trees are planted wide apart with companion crops grown in the alleyways between them."

I listened intently, weighing the options in my mind. "And the woodland, my lord?" I asked.

"The woodland will depend on the size and maturity of your forest," God said. "It will either be a mid to late succession woodland or later on a closed canopy forest, which is the mature end-goal you'll be working toward."

I nodded, grateful for the clarity. "I understand, my Lord. I will make sure to choose the best option for the environment in Georgia." I paused for a moment before adding, "Has something like this ever been done before, my Lord?"

God's voice filled my room, resonating through my bones. "Lionel, the concept of food forests is not a new one," he said. "In fact, food forests are ancient. As he spoke, I closed my eyes, imagining the ancient hunter-gatherers who once roamed the Amazon Basin. "Long before the arrival of modern civilization, hunter-gatherers roamed the lands of the Amazon Basin," God said. "They were not merely nomadic but also skilled cultivators of the earth. These people had a deep understanding of the land and its potential, and they worked to cultivate the land in a way that was sustainable and in harmony with nature."

I could see them now, the hunter-gatherers of the past walking through a dense forest, taking in the abundance of life around them. "They cleared small patches of the forest floor, creating fertile soil with compost and waste from their hunts," God continued. "They introduced crops, planting maize, sweet potato, cassava, and squash. And as the years passed, these small clearings grew into fields, providing the hunter-gatherers with food and shelter."

I opened my eyes, feeling a sense of wonder at the wisdom of the past. "And yet, even as they tended to these fields, the hunter-gatherers did not destroy the land," God said. "They left the tall canopy of the rainforest intact, preserving the delicate balance of the ecosystem. The canopy served as a protector of the soil and crops, providing shade and capturing the rain."

It was a delicate balance, one that required care and attention. "Through their careful cultivation, the hunter-gatherers of the past created a verdant food forest, teeming with life," God said. "A place where the land and the people lived in harmony, where the earth was nurtured, and where the rainforest was not a wild, untamed place, but a place of cultivation and abundance."

I felt a sense of awe at the majesty of it all, at the idea that we could live in harmony with the natural world. "Lionel, this is the story of the Amazon rainforest, a man-made food forest that has stood the test of time," God said. "And it is a reminder that you too can live in harmony with nature, tending to the land in a way that is sustainable and in balance with the natural world."

My mind raced as I contemplated the wonders of the Amazon rainforest. "Wow, the Amazon rainforest of today was grown by hunter-gatherers," I said, awestruck.

But then God's voice filled my room, commanding my attention. "Lionel, listen closely and behold the vision I impart unto thee," he said. "For I have crafted a world of wonder and bounty, where nature and man shall live in harmony. A place where the verdant forests shall reach up to the heavens and the sparkling waters of a giant lake shall rest at its heart."

I listened, captivated by his words. "This world, called FFFHAMS, shall be a symphony of forests and grasslands, where the earth and sky shall blend as one," he said. "And in its midst, circles of life shall bloom, each a thriving community with its own food forest and a pond at its center. Here, the trees shall bear fruit, the herbs shall heal, and the waters shall sustain."

I could see it now, the lush greenery and abundant wildlife that would fill this magical world. "And on the outskirts of these circles, homes of sustainability shall arise, gardens of medicine shall flourish, and an outdoor kitchen shall be the gathering place for all," God continued. "Here, the people shall cook, eat, talk, invent, and play, basking in the warmth of community and the abundance of nature."

It was a world of wonder and beauty, a place where man and nature could coexist in perfect harmony. "So let us create this world, Lionel, and bask in the glory of its creation," God said. "Let us build a place where the forces of nature and man shall unite and where the beauty of the earth shall be preserved for all eternity. Go, and build it with your heart and your soul. I will not see you until The Food Forest is planted."

"My heart and soul?" I asked, my voice barely above a whisper. "But Lord, the story?"

And then, just like that, he was gone. The room was empty, filled only with the sound of my own breathing. But I knew what I had to do.

It was my duty to make it a reality, to bring this vision to life.

So I stood up, ready to take on the task at hand. The Lord had vanished, leaving me to take on his work. And I will, I must.

As I leave the room, I find Belina no longer in the main space where the kitchen is. I walked to the window to see if she was outside. To my surprise, she was there with a child. I watch them talk and think to myself, "She would be so happy with a son." This thought brings me peace as I watch her smiling and chatting with this boy. Then I wonder, "How did he get here? No one knows about this place." Suddenly, I rush to open the door, and I yell, "Hey!" while pointing at the boy. The boy starts backing away, then he starts running. I think to myself, "Knew it, just some kid coming to steal something."

My feet start running quicker, and right before I can take off after the boy, I feel a very forceful tug on my arm. I turn to see Belina. "What are you doing, Lee?" Belina said in a very angry way. I snatch my arm and say, "Don't touch me." Belina stepped back; she looked like my words still hurt her. So, I step forward, wiping sweat from my brow, "Sorry, it's just that the boy is probably trying to take advantage of you. Kids like that steal stuff." She attempts to interrupt, saying, "Lee." I continue to tell her how she can be gullible before she interrupts and says, "Lee, the boy was sent from God!" My mouth opened, and I looked behind me to see if the kid was still there, but all I saw was farmland and woods. I look back at Belina and say, "Why didn't you say that?"

"Why didn't I say that, Lee?" "I mean, Belina, you were taking your time on explaining God sent another person to help us with this world-changing event." Belina breathes in impatiently with her hand high, then she shuts it tight. "Lee, go talk to the boy" I roll my eyes and start to jog in the kid's direction.

I see the boy in the woods by the farm. I yell, "Kid, my bad, I'm sorry. I shouldn't have pointed at you, shouted, or chased you… The kid just stares from the shadow of a tree. I break the silence after looking down as if there were words to find on the ground and say, "I heard you've been speaking to God." The kid says, "Yeah…." The kid walks out of the forest; he looks like he has been in the forest for days. "Are you lost?" I asked. The kid said, "No, I live close by; I'm just dirty from looking for this place." I nod my head in agreement and say, "Let's go back to the house; how does that sound?" The kid walks past me towards the house.

The kid, Belina, and I sit down on the deck on the side of the house. From here, you could see almost the entirety of the land. The smell of hot pizza swam through the air into our noses as we continued to eat our pizza out of a pizza box. We were all sitting on the ground until the kid got up looking at the sky. He had been checking the sky all day. Belina nods to me to say something to the kid. "Hey, kid," I say with slight enthusiasm. "Yes, Mr. Lee," he replied. I looked at Belina and said, "You got him calling me Lee." She smiled. I said to him, "what's your name?" He said, "Zane." Belina says, "Nice, I know a Zane.

I placed my hands on the boy's shoulders, looked him in the eye, and said, "If we're going to be God's chosen team, we have to be able to trust each other and be honest." I asked him again, "What's your name, kid?" He looked down but then looked up with a smile and said, "Max." Belina exclaimed, "I like that name," and the boy smiled back at her. I suggested to the boy to take a walk, and I had to talk to Belina for a second. As the boy hugged me, I felt awkward, hands in the air, as if I had a gun pointed at me. Belina signaled me to hug him back, and I did so reluctantly. The boy then ran off, and we continued our conversation.

Belina asked, "So, what do you think of... 'Max'?" I gazed at the boy walking in the field and replied, "He reminds me of my nephew, but I feel like he's hiding something." Belina said, "Lee, he's a good kid. I can tell that God sent him to us for a reason. What more do we need to know?" I sighed and said, "Belina, do you realize that I just got sued and lost my company because of my trust in some..." My eyes were now full of water, and I turned away. Belina placed her hands on my shoulder and asked,

"So, what do you think about FFFHAMS?" I sighed and rolled my eyes before replying, "It's brilliant. I can't believe I didn't come up with it. It's so simple yet efficient, and it embodies everything my company was meant to be." Belina replied, "Yeah, I'm sorry about your company, Lee." I continued, "Economically, FFFHAMS is perfect. It will be a place where money is irrelevant, and independence in your community is the key to success. Acquiring assets and minimizing liabilities is the key to achieving freedom. In my experience, true freedom is being able to call your own shots and make your own decisions, and that's precisely what FFFHAMS helps us achieve.

Assets in FFFHAMS are anything that gives you the power to shape your own life and achieve your own goals. These assets can include self-sufficient housing, adaptable skills, and the ability to live off the land. On the other hand, liabilities are anything that ties you down, makes you dependent on civilization, or takes away from your quality of life, like a mortgage, car payments, or a monthly phone bill.

The goal of FFFHAMS is to eliminate liabilities and focus on acquiring assets. By doing so, individuals can achieve a greater sense of independence and control over their lives. They will no longer be reliant on the traditional monetary system and its associated institutions. Instead, they can live a life of freedom, where they have the skills and resources they need to make their own choices and live on their terms. With assets like self-sufficient housing and adaptable skills, people can finally say goodbye to careerism and industrialism and truly be free."

After I finished that explanation we all just hung out eating pizza until about 1 PM. Then Max, Belina, and I gathered together. It was time. "I'm sure you both know that we've been brought together for a purpose," I said. "We are chosen. Whatever that means to you, to me, it means that we are here to take humanity to its next destination culturally, spiritually, and genetically. What we're going to do, building FFFHAMS will change the world forever. It won't be easy. It will be painstakingly hard, but it will be worth it for generations." Belina nodded her head in agreement,

I turned to Belina, my eyes shining with excitement. "Belina," I said, "do you know why God chose this land? It's perfect for creating a food forest that's both sustainable and productive. That's why it's perfect for our mission."

Belina raised an eyebrow. "I'm intrigued. What makes it so special?"

"Well," I began, "the climate and microclimate here are just right. There's enough sunlight, rainfall, and temperature to support a food forest. And the soil type, wind patterns, and topography are perfect for the plants that we'll be growing here."

Max piped up, "Can you really grow food in a forest?"

I laughed. "Absolutely, Max. A food forest is a forest garden that mimics the structure and diversity of a natural forest, but with a focus on producing food."

Belina nodded. "And the amount of sunlight is important, too, right?"

"Crucial," I said. "A food forest needs a lot of sunlight to produce edible, medicinal, and ornamental produce. And this location is perfect. It's sunny and will provide the energy the plants need to grow and produce a bountiful harvest."

Max frowned. "But do we really need all this space?"

"It's important to make sure there's enough room for all the plants to grow and mature without overcrowding," I explained. "This place is perfect, over one-thousand acres that provides enough space for a productive food-producing landscape."

Belina then asked about the soil quality. "The soil here was used for farming. Wouldn't that be a bad thing?"

"It's important that the soil is rich in organic matter and has a good structure to support the growth of a variety of plants," I said. "But the soil here is poor, so we need to amend it with compost, organic matter, and other soil-building materials."

Max scratched his head. "This is going to be a lot of work, isn't it?"

I nodded. "It's a lot of work, but it's what we want. The location of the area in relation to other food sources and habitats is also important. The food forest will be isolated from other food sources, such as medicinal gardens, to avoid competition for resources. First, we'll build a pond which will act as a water source, provide habitat, and attract a variety of wildlife species."

Belina beamed at me, admiration in her eyes. "Lee, it's good to see you happy."

I returned her smile, feeling a warm glow spread through me. "This is important to me. I want to make sure that this food forest pleases God."

Suddenly, a convoy of vehicles and trucks pulled into the rocky driveway.

"Who's that?" I squinted my eyes, holding my hand over my head to provide some shade.

"I ordered them!" Belina said. "God gave me a job, too. These are all the equipment and materials we need to create the food forest. They'll be coming every day until we're done."

I rolled my eyes and said, "Let's get to work. We'll start by building the pond."

"The three of us, Belina, Max, and I, were chosen for a higher purpose. We were tasked with building not just a pond but an entire society for the Lord, a sacred and natural body of water that would sustain life and provide sustenance to a community. This was my chance at redemption; I would sacrifice anything to prove my worth and show God what I was capable of.

Belina and I made eye contact, we had a complicated history. There was a time that we couldn't stop smiling at one another, but I could never forget what she had done. I thought to myself, "She's a fool if she thinks I have forgotten...." Yet, as we worked together in the scorching sun, my old feelings began to stir, and I couldn't help but wonder, could we? I raise my eyebrows awkwardly and look away.

Max was a different story. He was eager and optimistic, but he was also a bit quiet, like a war vet quiet. As the day went by, I noticed that he kept checking his watch, like he was counting down to something. I couldn't help but feel a twinge of distrust like he was hiding something from us.

"Don't get distracted, Lionel," I thought to myself. I couldn't let these thoughts consume me, not when we had work to do. Building a pond was not easy; it required precision, patience, and a steady hand. We excavated the soil, shaped the pond to our design, and carefully allowed the well water to flow into a 6 feet deep empty pond ready to hold the water.

Next, we added life to the pond, introducing a mix of floating and underwater plants to provide habitat and improve water quality. As the pond filled and settled, we watched in awe as an ecosystem formed before our eyes. We added fertilizers to promote growth and, finally, stocked the pond with rainbow trout and a diverse list of fish to make sure our pond had a thriving ecosystem. This ensured that we had enough to provide for 40 people per year on this one acre of land.

The pond was finished, and it was time to start developing the actual Food Forest.

I was surrounded by the sights and sounds of nature. Belina and Max were by my side, sorting through all the seeds and baby trees she had ordered for our food forest. I couldn't help but feel grateful to God for choosing us to undertake this task.

Belina had taken the initiative to purchase all the materials needed for our food forest, which left me feeling a mix of annoyance and gratitude. I wasn't aware that she had made so much money, especially now when I was facing the potential loss of my own fortune. Max, on the other hand, was rushing around and seemed increasingly less talkative, but he was extremely fascinated by all the different plants.

As I sorted through the plants and worked with Belina, I was reminded of the importance of choosing the right plants for our food forest. It was a critical step in creating a sustainable and productive food-producing landscape, and I couldn't afford to make any mistakes. In Georgia, the growing conditions vary widely depending on the location, with different regions experiencing different climates and microclimates. It was crucial to consider the climate and microclimate of our area to ensure that the plants would receive the proper sunlight, rainfall, and temperature conditions to thrive.

Some of the plants that grow well in Georgia include pecan trees, blueberries, blackberries, muscadine grapes, figs, and pawpaws. These plants provide a range of edible, medicinal, and ornamental produce and are well-suited to Georgia's growing conditions. We had to arrange them in a way that maximized space and provided diverse habitats. This involved considering the size and shape of the area, as well as the sun exposure and wind patterns.

Water sources, like a stream or pond, were also critical to consider in our food forest design. They could provide a habitat for a variety of wildlife species and help make our food forest more diverse and productive.

Despite the tediousness of organizing the plants and dealing with my feelings for Belina, I had to focus. I couldn't allow myself to get lost in her gaze. "Lee," she said, using the nickname she had for me. "I'm sorry." I looked at her, took a deep breath, and reminded myself of the task at hand. Ignored her and said, "Considering all the unique characteristics of our area, such as the climate, microclimate, and water sources, we could create a food forest that would provide food, habitat, and enjoyment for years to come."

I stood there, looking away from Belina as she approached me. She was fidgeting with her hands and avoiding eye contact.

"Lionel, I need to talk to you," she said.

I sighed and continued to try to look in a different direction, not interested in her trying to apologize for the past. "What about?" I asked, trying to keep my voice steady.

"About what happened," she said, taking a deep breath. "I know it's been years, but I've been thinking about that day a lot lately and I just wanted to apologize. I'm so sorry for what I did."

I felt a rush of anger and frustration, but I forced myself to focus on the matter at hand. "Soil preparation is a crucial step in creating a successful food forest or garden," I said, changing the subject. "A well-prepared soil provides the foundation for healthy plant growth and maximizes the potential for a bountiful harvest."

Belina frowned and took a step back. "Lionel, I don't care about that right now. I just want to talk about us," she said.

"The first step in preparing the soil is to determine the soil type and structure," I continued, ignoring her. "The soil type will help you determine what type of plants will grow well in the area and what type of soil-building materials will be necessary. The soil structure will help you determine the best method for breaking up the soil and preparing it for planting."

Belina's face changed; her face now had many lines and began to quiver. "Lionel, why are you doing this?" she asked, her voice rising.

"Next, it is important to remove any existing weeds and grasses, which can compete with your plants for water, nutrients, and sunlight," I said, still focused on the soil preparation. "This can be done by hand, using a hoe, or by using a tillage tool such as a plow or cultivator."

"Lionel, stop it!" Belina yelled, tears streaming down her face. "Why won't you talk to me about what happened?"

I finally looked at her, seeing the pain in her eyes. But I couldn't go to that place again. "Once the weeds and grasses have been removed, it is time to add organic matter and compost to the soil," I said, my voice cold. "Organic matter, such as leaves, straw, and grass clippings, helps to improve the structure and fertility of the soil. Compost is a valuable soil amendment that provides essential nutrients and organic matter to the soil."

Belina let out a sob and turned. "I can't do this," she said, shaking her head while walking away. "I thought you might have changed, but you're still the same person you were before. I could never talk to you about these things without you shutting me out or running away."

I watched her go, feeling a mix of regret and relief. I had avoided it, but as she walked away, I couldn't help but think, "At what cost?"

"To maximize the benefits of adding organic matter and compost to the soil, it is important to incorporate it into the soil using a tillage tool or by hand," I said, unable to stop. I yelled out uncontrollably, "This will help to mix the organic matter and compost into the soil, which will improve soil structure, fertility, and water-holding capacity." "F you, Lee," Belina screamed with her middle finger in the air right before slamming the door of the farmhouse. I held my hands over my mouth and took some deep breaths like my therapist would say.

Max was down the field, organizing the baby trees, and called out to me. I sighed and walked over to him, grateful for the distraction from my tumultuous thoughts.

When I walk over to him, he says, "you haven't noticed how slow time is moving?" I laugh hysterically and say, "That's called being bored." I let out a huff, grabbed my stomach, looked down at the boy, and saw his face. He wasn't amused. "Mr. Lee," he explained, "My watch has been ticking every minute instead of every second." I look at his watch and then look at the shadows, noticing they had barely changed their position. I begin to smile in awe. Max walks away to find Belina. God was slowing time for us, "we are truly his elect," I thought to myself.

Time passed slowly; Belina was back outside with Max and me, aware of the miracle that was happening. Even though my heart felt like it was bleeding love for her, she refused to even look at me. I wondered, "Is this really what I want?" Belina sat off to the side, gazing at the slow-moving clouds while Max and I got back to work.

Max and I spent the day working together on the soil for the food forest, laughing and getting to know each other better. "I'm actually from Lawnside, New Jersey," Max said. "I moved out here to Georgia with my family."

I smiled and nodded my head, "I have a lot of family in Lawnside and Georgia too." Max smiled in return, and it felt like we had just discovered a new level of understanding between us. We continued to work together, digging and planting, making this food forest come to life.

As we worked, we discussed the soil and what needed to be done to make it suitable for growing our food forest. I explained to Max that the first step was to determine the soil type and structure. We conducted a soil test to determine the pH, nutrient levels, and structure of the soil. This information helped us determine which plants would grow best and what additions we may need to make to the soil.

Next, We cleared the area of any existing weeds and grasses. "This will help prevent unwanted competition for water and nutrients and help to ensure a healthy start for our new plants," I said to Max.

Max and I add organic matter and compost to the soil. Max asked, "Why are we doing this?" I replied, Max, Organic matter, such as leaves, grass clippings, and kitchen waste, provides essential nutrients and helps to improve soil structure. Compost is a rich source of nutrients and microorganisms that will improve soil health and fertility." We spread a layer of organic matter and compost over the soil and incorporated it into the top 6-12 inches of soil.

We continued to incorporate the organic matter and compost into the soil by hand or with a tillage tool, such as a rototiller. This ensured that the organic matter was evenly distributed and helped to improve soil structure.

Lastly, I told Max, "Really, we could add other soil-building materials, like rock minerals, bone meal, and worm castings." Max replied, "Let's do it."

I had so much fun with Max. He was like a mini-me. He was so good at absorbing knowledge and comprehending complex instruction.

I fell into the soil, he plopped right next to me, and we both began to laugh. I sling mud at Max, and he throws dirt at me. Belina surprisingly runs over with the water hose and sprays us; this goes on for a period of time before we all call it a quits. Dirty and muddy, we all laugh and sit on the deck, still smiling and randomly laughing, until Max looks up at the sky and, sadly, with a shaky voice, says, "I don't want to be alone...." Belina looks at me, and I put my hand on Max's shoulder and say, "me either."

We all got cleaned in the shower in the house; Belina took the longest shower, leaving me with lukewarm water. I think she might have done it on purpose.

As we determined the location and microclimate, considering factors like sunlight, wind exposure, and water availability, Belina started telling Max about the time; Belina came to me asking if I could be her tutor. I ignored it and continued to work. I turn and say to

Max, "The food forest is designed to ultimately mimic a natural forest, with taller trees in the center and shorter shrubs and perennials near the edges." Belina says, Lee, you remember coming to my house and eating half of my mother's turkey two years in a row?" I thought about that shiny, steaming, seasoned, mouth-watering turkey, but I nonchalantly said, "Eh, kinda."

As we worked on our food forest, Belina and Max chatted about their experiences. Belina asked Max, "So, how old are you?" Max replied, "I'm fourteen." Belina smiled and said, "Have you ever been to the Democrat Club?" Max replied, "I've been by it, but I've never been inside."

Belina reminisced, "When we were a little older than you, we used to party in the Democrat Club. There was sweat everywhere, music blasting, and every time the slow jams came on, this guy, Lionel, would coincidentally find me." Max said, "Ew." I rolled my eyes, and as we started planting the taller trees in the center first and then moved on to the shorter shrubs and perennials near the edges, memories of our first fight came flooding back.

We had snuck out one night to see each other, and even though I was eighteen, my parents were still strict. I was annoyed that Belina seemed hesitant to call herself my girlfriend. We had a huge argument in her car down the street from my parent's house. I remember it ended with us kissing, but I shook my head, trying to focus on our work.

Belina and Max stopped walking, looking at me like there was a frog on my head, and I said, "I'm just trying to focus." Belina smiled as I walked ahead.

As we made sure to plant the different species at the right depth and spacing to ensure optimal growth and health, Belina's memories continued to flood my mind. Then I said out loud. "We should consider planting different species close to each other to maximize space and provide a diverse range of produce." As we continued to plant the seeds, Belina's and my own memories of our love continued to intertwine with the task at hand.

As Max and I walked through the food forest, I couldn't help but feel proud of the progress we had made. Behind us, Belina followed, her gaze fixed on me.

"Max, you know what mulching is?" I asked while placing my hand on his shoulder.

"No, Mr. Lee, what's that?" he replied, his eyes shining.

"Well, it's a layer of organic material that we spread over the soil to help our plants grow," I explained, gesturing to the surrounding trees and shrubs. "It helps retain moisture, suppress weeds, and add nutrients to the soil."

Belina spoke up, "Lee, do you think you can show me how you mulch?"

I couldn't help but smile, "Whatever, Belina."

Max asked, "How do you mulch?"

"You need to choose the right type of mulch for your climate and the plants in your food forest," I replied. "Some popular types of mulch include wood chips, leaves, straw, and grass clippings. Then, you apply it in a layer that's 2-4 inches thick, avoiding direct contact with the stems and trunks of the plants."

"And you need to reapply it periodically, right?" Max asked, showing an interest in the process.

"Exactly, Max. The mulch will break down over time and lose its effectiveness," I said. "A general rule of thumb is to reapply it once a year or when the mulch layer becomes thin and less effective."

Max couldn't contain his excitement any longer and picked up a pile of wood chips to start mulching on his own. Belina leaned against me, and I surprisingly put my arm around her.

"Lee, I am sorry, ya know," she said, her voice full of regret.

I looked down at her, and my heart softened a bit. "It's not that I don't want to forgive you, Belina. I just need to focus on my mission, to build this food forest for God."

Belina nods her head in understanding and says, "So, are we just about done?" as she looked around the would-be food forest.

"Not quite," I replied. "Watering and maintenance are crucial components of establishing and maintaining a successful food forest.

Regular watering, pruning, and weeding are essential for promoting healthy growth and preventing problems from developing. Watering is one of the most important aspects,"

Max walks over, listening to me explain to Belina.

I continued. "Newly planted trees and shrubs require consistent moisture to establish roots, while established plants need regular water to stay healthy and produce a good crop."

"What kind of watering system do we use?" Max asked.

"It's important to use a watering system that is efficient and consistent, such as a drip irrigation system or soaker hose," I explained. "The system should be set up to provide adequate water to the plants without flooding the soil or causing waterlogging. A general rule of thumb is to provide 1 inch of water per week, either all at once or broken up into several smaller waterings throughout the week."

"And pruning?" Belina asked.

"Yeah, regular pruning is also important for maintaining a healthy food forest," I said. "Pruning helps to control the shape and size of the plants, promote healthy growth, and remove dead or damaged wood. Regular pruning also helps to maintain good air circulation, prevent disease problems, and improve fruit production."

"How do you know when to prune?" Max asked.

"Pruning should be done when the plants are dormant, typically in late winter or early spring, to minimize stress and encourage healthy new growth," I patiently explained. "It's important to use sharp, clean pruning tools and to follow proper pruning techniques."

"Will we be weeding regularly?" Belina asked.

"In the first 4 years, for sure, regular weeding is also important for maintaining a healthy food forest," I said. "Weeds compete with the plants in the food forest for light, water, and nutrients and can quickly overtake an area if left unchecked. Regular weeding helps to prevent weeds from becoming established and allows the plants in the food forest to grow and produce without competition."

"Okay, so how do we do it?" Max asked.

"It's important to remove weeds by hand or with a hoe; we do not ever use man-made chemicals," I explained. "The goal is to remove the weeds before they produce seeds, preventing them from becoming established and spreading throughout the food forest."

Belina stared at me, and for a moment, I was staring back; she could be so mesmerizing; Max interrupted, "One more question, Mr. Lee, what do we do if we find a weed with seeds?"

I chuckled, "Well, Max, in that case, you'll have to remove it carefully and dispose of it properly to prevent it from spreading."

Belina walked away, still fanning herself, as Max and I continued our discussion about the food forest.

Not too long after, Max says, "Okay, Mr. Lee, I'm ready."

"I stood beside Max, looking at the garden that needed to be watered. I said. "The first step is to choose the right system."

"Which system would you prefer? We can either use a drip irrigation system or a soaker hose. It depends on what you need and what you prefer," I explained. "Both systems are efficient and provide consistent water to the plants. So which one, Max."

Max thought for a second and then said, "a soaker hose for now; it seems a little easier if I'm being honest."

"Okay, a general rule of thumb is to provide 1 inch of water per week to the plants," I said. "You can either provide all the water at once or split it into several smaller waterings throughout the week."

"Next, we'll install the system," I continued. "Make sure to follow the manufacturer's instructions carefully. Place the system in the right location to ensure that the water reaches all the plants."

"Now, we need to adjust the system to provide adequate water to the plants without flooding the soil or causing waterlogging," I added. "This may need to be adjusted over time to meet the changing needs of your plants."

After Max and I finished watering the plants, I turned to Belina and asked, "Did you order the predators?" She replied, "You mean those adorable foxes?" I chuckled and said, "Yes, Belina." She playfully slapped my arm, and I balled up, pretending to be hurt. "They should be here by now," I said. Max yawned, and I suggested,

"Hey, we all should probably take a rest. It's 1:35, meaning we've probably been working for 30 hours straight." This was shocking, as we were just getting sleepy. We walked into the house, and I showed Max one of the two rooms, telling him, "You can take a nap in here if you want." He looked uncomfortably at his watch and said, "I don't know... How long do you think this time thing God did is going to last?" I shrugged my shoulders, feeling tired, and told him, "See ya in a bit," before closing the door and heading to my own room, ready for bed.

Belina was sitting on the bed, and as I walked over to her, there were no words. It was beauty in the silence. I forgot how much I missed the smell of her strawberry lip gloss and the scent of her hair. She looked into my eyes, and I leaned in slightly. She put her nose on my nose, and then we kissed.

Later, I woke up to Belina saying, "Lee, I think you need to see this..." She was at the window, looking out at the field. I asked, "What is it? Is everything okay?" As I looked outside, I saw the boy playing with dozens of fox puppies. "So, the fox kits are here," I said. Belina said, "No, Lee, look further..." There had to be a thousand food forests built from scratch, which was impossible. They didn't have vegetation, of course, but they were built just as well as what we had spent over a day working on. In the center was a pond that had to be one hundred acres. I was without words.

I put on my pants and shirt and started marching outside. As I opened the door, there seemed to be a field around us that began to melt and get soaked up into the sky. It was like watching a clear dome made of rain pour backward. I was in awe. Belina ran out and got stuck in disbelief because of what she was seeing.

I ran over to Max, but he took a step back. I realized I was scaring him, which was the last thing I wanted to do. I got down slowly and said, "Max... I'm just confused. Can you tell me how all of this work got done?"

Max looked at his watch and said, "It's 3 o'clock. I think I should be getting home..." I responded, "Go home? Max, can you just tell us what's going on? We're God's chosen. We need to communicate."

Max looked up at me and said, "You promise not to get scared." I replied, "Max, we're in this together."

We all walked back into the house and sat on the couch in the living room. Max confessed, "I have this thing, I can barely control it, but I can organize things really fast and really easy; it just kind of happens." Belina sensing that the boy was nervous, grabbed his hand, "You have nothing to be afraid of; it is a gift," she said in a soft, calm voice. "A gift?" Max replied. Although I could tell that Max was still hiding something, I didn't want to scare him, so instead, I just nodded my head. We listened to Max for hours as he told us his entire journey, how his parents had moved to Georgia from Jersey to get a better job, how his friends had betrayed him, and how there was a cat following him around protecting him.

Then he told us he had to be home before dark. I offered to take him home and told him I would like to talk to his parents. Belina was already in the room getting dressed, I walked in there, and when Belina walked out, she said, "Max?" He had disappeared without a trace.

"He's hiding something, Belina," I said convincingly. Belina said, "Aren't we all hiding something?" I asked, "What do you mean?" Belina replied, "I'm just saying when you're ready to talk about your nephew, let me know." I responded with wide eyes and shriveled lips, "Don't do that, Belina."

"I love you, Lee; just showing it the best way I can." I nodded my head, kissed her forehead, and walked outside. I had to put away all the foxes in the different miniature habitats for them. Afterward, I walked down to the giant pond and began to pray.

CHAPTER 9:

FOOD FOREST FORAGING HUNTING

The world around me seemed to shift and twist, the land sinking before me as the sky rained golden blood. And from that golden liquid, The One God Above All was formed, standing before me in all his glory.

"Stand, Lionel," God commanded.

I rose to my feet, feeling the weight of his presence all around me. "Yes, my Lord," I said.

"You all have built the beginning of the Food Forest," God said.

I nodded, feeling a sense of pride at what we had accomplished in his name. "Yes, my Lord, in your name," I said.

"Lionel, do not be silly," God chided. "My name is within everything already."

I felt a sense of shame wash over me, knowing that he was right. "Yes, my Lord," I said, bowing my head.

"You're curious about the boy," God said.

My heart skipped a beat at his words. "Yes, Lord, I am," I said.

But then he cut me off. "Never ask me about the boy," he said sternly. "Only I bring up the boy."

I opened my mouth to protest but then thought better of it. "Yes, my Lord," I said, my voice barely above a whisper.

"Walk with me," God said.

And so we walked, circling the pond together. "I am honored to walk with you, Lord," I said, feeling a sense of awe at his presence.

"Lionel, I have another task for you," God said.

"Of course, my Lord," I said. "I am here to serve."

"You are to stock this pond, Lionel," God said, his voice echoing across the water. "It will provide a range of benefits, including fishing opportunities, water conservation, and wildlife habitat. You will not eat of the pond until the fourth year. You will not eat of the forest until the fourth year. You will create smaller ponds and a food garden for the community and eat from it until the fourth year. Every year, you will eat 25% less from the Matrix. Once the fourth year arrives, you must only eat of the forest and pond. You must abandon your wild garden, for they will lead you back into the belly of the Matrix."

I felt a sense of apprehension at his words, knowing that the task ahead would not be an easy one. "Yes, my Lord," I said, bowing my head in submission. "How should I proceed with the pond, my Lord?"

"The first step is to determine the right fish species for this pond," God said, his tone matter-of-fact. "Consider the size of the pond, the water temperature, and the water quality. Choose species that are well-suited to these conditions, as well as your personal preferences and the intended use of the pond."

I nodded, feeling a sense of clarity wash over me. This was a task that I could accomplish, a task that would bring me closer to the harmony with nature that I so desired. "Yes, my Lord," I said. "I will choose the right fish species for this pond, and I will do it in a way that is in harmony with the natural world."

"I understand, my Lord," I said,"What is the next step?"

"Once you have selected the species, create a suitable habitat for the fish," God said, his voice steady and measured. "Provide adequate space, shelter, and food. Ensure the pond has enough depth and surface area to provide a healthy and comfortable environment. Consider water quality, temperature, and oxygen levels to ensure the fish are healthy and thriving."

"I will ensure that the habitat is suitable, my Lord," I said, feeling a sense of purpose take root within me. "Is there anything else I should do?"

"You must also monitor the health of the fish population in the pond," God said, his words carrying a sense of urgency. "Regularly check water quality, temperature, and oxygen levels. Monitor the health of individual fish and address any changes promptly to keep the population healthy and thriving."

I nodded, feeling a sense of responsibility settle over me. This was a task that would require constant attention and care, a task that would demand all of my focus and energy. But I was ready to take it on, ready to live in harmony with nature and do the work of The One God Above All. "Yes, my Lord," I said, my voice filled with conviction. "I will monitor the health of the fish population and do everything in my power to keep them healthy and thriving."

"I understand, my Lord," I said.

But before I could take a breath, God interrupted me. "Not yet, Lionel," he said, his voice firm and unwavering. "I will inform you when to reflect with a story."

I nodded, feeling a sense of humility wash over me. I was but a servant of The One God Above All, and it was not for me to dictate the terms of our conversation. "Yes, my Lord," I said, my voice soft and deferential.

"The food forest is not complete without the animals that will feed the fox, the cat, the bird of prey, the dog, and the forty humans that will live in each community no less than one acre."

"My lord," I said, feeling a sense of trepidation. "What kind of animals should I raise in the food forest to ensure it can provide food for 40 people?"

"Animals that complement the existing ecosystem and provide a reliable source of food," God said, his words carrying a sense of weight and importance. "Consider the local climate, the size of the food forest, and your personal preferences when selecting these animals."

I nodded, feeling a sense of purpose take root within me.

"Can you give me some examples, my Lord?" I asked, eager to learn more about the animals that would help complete the food forest.

"Of course, Lionel," God replied, his voice carrying a sense of weight and wisdom. "Poultry such as adult chickens and ducks are self-sustaining and provide a steady source of eggs and meat. They are also excellent foragers and can help maintain the balance of the ecosystem by balancing the cleaners of the earth or what you may call pests. Goats are versatile animals that provide meat and fiber and excel at maintaining the proper balance of weeds. And there are many other options to consider, such as quail, pigeons, ostriches, bison, and more."

I listened intently, feeling a sense of wonder and amazement come over me. This was a world filled with so many possibilities, so many ways to create a thriving ecosystem that provided for all. "Thank you, my Lord," I said, feeling a sense of gratitude welling up inside me.

"What are the factors I need to consider when choosing the right type of animals for the forest, my Lord?" I asked, eager to learn more about the intricacies of this complex task.

"Climate, space, and feed requirements are crucial when selecting animals," God replied, his words carrying a sense of importance. "Different types of animals have different needs, so it is important to choose those that can thrive in the local climate and fit the available space in the food forest. They must also be able to be raised on a diet that is available and sustainable."

"Now, Lionel," he said, "we must discuss hunting and foraging."

I seized the opportunity to ask a question that had been weighing heavily on my mind.

"Lord," I said, "are humans carnivores, herbivores, or omnivores?"

God's answer was not what I expected.

"None of those things really exist, Lionel," he said. "Not in the way a vegetarian or a human carnivore exists."

I was taken aback by his response. It had never occurred to me that the dichotomy between carnivores and herbivores might be more complicated than it appeared. But then, when had anything been simple when it came to the One God Above All?

I stand in the presence of God, gazing out at the tranquil pond that glitters in the sunlight. The sound of gentle waves and chirping birds fill the air. God stands beside me, tall and radiant, a being that emanates power and wisdom. "What do you mean?" I ask, hoping for a clearer explanation.

"In this magnificent universe that is constantly shifting balance," God begins, "cost and benefit are the guiding forces of evolution. The animals do not serve their diets, but rather their diets serve them. Their choices are driven by their needs and the cost and benefits of the nutrients they seek. This is the true essence of flexibility, a trait that sets humans apart from most, if not all, other creatures."

I nod, captivated by God's words.

"Humans, however, have allowed themselves to be bound by their own rules and restrictions," God continues. "The idea of a set diet, be it a meat diet, vegetarian, or vegan, is a mere illusion, a side effect of the Matrix in which you live. You force yourselves to adhere to these rules, even when it no longer serves you. But in FFFHAMS, the natural state of things, you will find yourselves freely choosing what you need to sustain yourselves."

God's words echo in my mind as I take in the wisdom imparted by the almighty being.

"If one area is abundant with fruits and vegetation, you will find yourselves eating more of these foods and less meat. But if these are scarce, you will seek out more proteins and meats to meet your needs. This is the way of all animals; even the most herbivorous of creatures, such as deer, will turn to eating birds if they need to. And even the most carnivorous will eat fruit if they must."

I feel a sense of awe at the simplicity and yet profoundness of God's words. He stands in silence, letting the weight of the message sink in.

"Remember, humans, are one of the most flexible creations to have evolved on this earth," God continues. "To live in one unchanging way is to limit yourself and ultimately to face extinction. But in the food forest, you are free to be whatever you desire, to seek out the cost and benefit that best serves your needs. This is the true meaning of health, and it is the law of trade. So embrace your flexibility, and let your diet be guided by your needs, not by arbitrary restrictions. Remember, you are both hunters and foragers."

"Why do we forage and hunt, Lord? Is it just for food, or is there something deeper to it?" I asked.

"It's more than just food, Lionel. Your bodies expect and therefore needs this kind of physical activity. And you must understand that foraging and hunting are not just about survival but about thriving," God replied.

I wanted to know more. "And what about the division of labor between men and women in foraging and hunting? Is it just a matter of utility, or is there more to it?" I asked.

"That's a good question, Lionel. Your anthropologists have studied contemporary populations of hunter-gatherers around the world and have found that men mostly hunt while women mostly gather. This division of labor is not about oppression or subservience but rather what enables the best chances of survival and thriving. It's a mistake to equate this pattern with the myth of Man the Hunter, which states only men hunt because it's hard and women are incapable," God explained.

As I listened to the sound of the water in the pond, I turned to God and asked, "Why don't women hunt nearly as much as men do?"

"Children," God replied, his voice calm and steady. "The demands of hunting can conflict with the provision of caring for children. Pregnant or lactating women do not often hunt, and the few women who want to hunt only hunt when everyone is willing to watch their children or if the hunting grounds are close to camp."

I nodded, understanding beginning to dawn on me.

"When women do hunt, they tend to hunt in groups and focus on smaller, easier-to-capture prey closer to camps. Even though women in these societies rarely hunt, they are often crucial to the hunting success of others, whether through logistical or ritual assistance."

God paused, his gaze intense.

"On the other hand, gathering requires extensive ecological knowledge and skill that is socially learned and cultivated over a lifetime. It pays to specialize in this 24 hours a day, so economic considerations play a role in the division of labor. The Batek people believe this division of labor is due to differences in strength, incompatibility with caring for children, and differences in knowledge specialization. Hunting has great cultural significance, but women's knowledge of plant distributions is crucial for collective decisions like moving camp."

"I see. So, it's not that the women are relegated to a lower status, as some have assumed."

"No, Lionel," God replied. "The Batek people are widely considered one of the most gender-egalitarian societies in the world. They have little material inequality, share food widely, abhor violence, and emphasize individual autonomy."

I nodded, taking in his words. Another question arose in my mind, "Wouldn't some teenage girls establish an interest in hunting that carries into adulthood?"

God's response was measured and reflective. "Yes, Lionel. There are exceptions, but these are rare. Women are not prohibited from hunting, but they normally choose to gather food closer to camp while the men hunt further away."

As I pondered over the significance of this gendered division of labor, another thought crossed my mind. "It seems that the significance of this cooperative and interdependent group is that each person makes a unique and important contribution toward a communal goal... Is that correct?"

"Lionel, that is not only correct, but it is also the essence of a hunter-gatherer society," God replied, a glimmer of appreciation in his voice. "In a world where money is the driving force, it is easy to forget the importance of survival and the need for food. The Batek people serve as a reminder that there is another way of living, a way that values cooperation and interdependence over material gain."

"Hunter-gatherer populations are renowned for their exceptional health and are often studied as models in public health. Do you understand why this is, Lionel?" God asked.

I shook my head. "No, my Lord. I do not understand. I would like to learn more."

"It is because they source their food entirely from the earth and wild animals," God explained. "They are physically active for most of each day. Take the Hadza, for example, they spend their days walking 8-12 kilometers, climbing trees, and digging for root vegetables. Their diet consists of various meats, vegetables, fruits, and a significant amount of honey."

"That is interesting, my Lord," I said. "Is it correct to assume they are very healthy?"

"The Hadza tend to maintain the same healthy weight, body mass index, and walking speed throughout their adult lives," God replied. "They commonly live into their 60s or 70s and sometimes 80s with very little to no cardiovascular diseases, high blood pressure, or diabetes. These conditions are rapidly growing in prevalence in nearly every corner of the world that the Matrix has devoured."

"I see, God," I said. "Does this lifestyle affect their mental health as well?"

God replied, "There is a correlation between depression and modernization. Hunter-gatherers tend to have a very low prevalence of depression. Departure from the hunter-gatherer lifestyle is linked to an increase in depression. For example, the Ik of Uganda became more depressed after shifting from hunter-gather to agricultural practices. Rapid modernization has also been linked to an increase in depression in most if not all developing civilizations within these countries."

"That is sobering," I said. "May I tell you a story, my Lord?"

"You may," God replied.

"In the days of old, when the world was still young, there lived two hunter-gatherers named Per and Ri. Per was a man strong of limb and keen of eye, and Ri was a woman fair of face and quick of wit. They lived in the great forest that stretched for leagues around, where the trees reached to the sky, and the animals roamed free.

One day, Per and Ri heard tell of a wondrous city beyond the forest, a place called the Matrix. They were filled with curiosity and a yearning for adventure, and they decided to leave the safety of their home and seek it out.

But God warned them, saying, "If you leave my law, the home I made for us, and eat of the Matrix, then you will surely die." Per and Ri hesitated, but their longing was too great, and they stepped out of the forest and into the city.

The Matrix was a sight to behold, with its bright lights and bustling crowds. At first, it was overwhelming to Ri, and she longed to return to the safety of the forest. But soon, she was seduced by the wonders of the city, and she ate of its food and made friends with its people.

Per, too was caught up in the magic of the Matrix. He found work and ate of its food, and he began to wear clothes like the people of the city. He and Ri both became unfaithful, with Per seeking to impress his friends by his exploits with women and Ri entertaining other men in hopes of gaining wealth.

But their lives in the city were not as they had hoped. Per and Ri became depressed and realized that they had made a grave mistake in leaving the safety of the forest. Ri discovered that she was with child, and Per told her she must abort it, for they did not have enough resources to care for a child.

It was then that Ri remembered the warning of God, and she realized the truth of it. She took Per by the hand and led him back to the forest, where they lived happily ever after, surrounded by the creatures of the earth and the beauty of the trees. And they learned that God had provided everything they needed and that the Matrix was not the place for them."

As I stood by the pond, God spoke to me in his deep, resonating voice.

"Go and find people to teach you to hunt and to skin; find a teacher to show you the ways of the children of God," he said.

I nodded, taking in his words. But before I could even respond, he was gone, vanished as if he had never been there in the first place.

I turned to the pond, watching the ripples spread across the surface. A heron bird descended from the sky, landing gracefully in the water. It peered at me curiously with its sharp, observant eyes.

The bird reminded me of my nephew, who had always been fascinated with birds, especially herons. He had many passions, but there was one girl he loved more than anything else. She used to come over to my house, and Eben would talk to me about why different religions didn't make sense to him. I remembered the time he came over with his crush, a beautiful young girl I called Sekhmet. She loved reading my ancient Egyptian collection and adored cats, so I started calling her that. They would hang out with my fiancée's daughter Nuddi and two other friends on my yacht, where I always kept an eye on them.

One day, my sister confronted me about my son, who she had adopted. "Lionel, it's time," she said impatiently. "He's looking for his father. When are you going to tell him?" I put my hand up, signaling her to calm down. "I've been taking care of him since I graduated college," I explained. "As an uncle, Lionel!" she retorted. "He needs to know the truth. I'm not keeping this secret forever. He deserves to know, and I love him too much to lie to him."

Little did we know, he was listening on the other side of the door. A few days later, I received a call from my sister. "He knows, Lionel," she said. "He overheard us, and he's upset. You need to talk to him now!" I texted him to come over to the house, and when he arrived, he was alone. We stood there, not knowing what to say.

As I looked at the heron bird on the pond, a tear fell down my face.

The next morning, I woke up to the smell of eggs and turkey bacon. The familiar scent reminded me of home, where my family used to cook up a storm in the morning. It had been a while since I had seen or spoken to them after what happened, so the aroma brought back a comforting sense of nostalgia. I got out of bed and rummaged through my packed bag to find a shirt. As I put it on, I walked out of the door to see Belina and Max sitting at the table eating breakfast.

I was surprised to see that Max was already here, and I looked at the empty pots and pans on the stove with a twinge of disappointment. Then grabbed some cereal, a bowl, and almond milk.

I sat at the table; Belina and Max looked at each other, smiling as if they had some sort of secret. "What's so funny?" I asked with a smile on my face, looking at my shirt.

They both started laughing even harder, and Max said, "You'll see."

Max went to the counter, and I heard him uncover a plate with grits, eggs, turkey bacon, and even some apples on the side. He handed me the plate with a grin, and I looked at Belina, who had a salad in front of her. Thinking to myself, I should have known.

We all ate our food quietly with smiles on our faces. When we finished, I cleared my throat and said, "I spoke to Ptah, The Lord of Lords, The God of gods, the Unmoved Mover, El Elyon, I Am that I Am, The One..."

"Lee..." Belina said in a nonchalant voice.

I cleared my throat again and continued, "God told me our next mission." They both looked at me with great wonder. "We shall live out our days here on FFFHAMS. We must create small food gardens and small fishing ponds in each community. These small food gardens will provide us food. We must not eat from the food forest or the true ponds for four years. At the end of the four years, we are to only eat from the food forest and ponds. We must cut ourselves off from the food in the Matrix slowly. Every year, we will eat 25% less from the Matrix."

They looked at me, nodding their heads in agreement. It seemed like they were just as committed as me. As I looked at Max and Belina, I had a flashback to a time when I was at Belina's home, looking through the family photos with her. As we flipped through the pictures, I was trying to find an ancestor who might look like her doppelganger. Instead, I found a man who didn't resemble any of the others.

"Who is this man?" I asked.

Belina replied, "He is my great-grandfather. I know he looks different than most of my family."

"Strange," I responded, intrigued by the photo.

Belina snapped me out of my memory by asking, "Anything else?" She was sitting next to Max, and they both seemed to be curious about what else I had to say.

"Yes, there is more," I said, suddenly coming back to reality. "We are to become hunter-gatherers. We must learn the ways of our most ancient ancestors and forage, fish, and hunt. We must learn to make our own tools. We must learn to be fully human again."

Max chimed in, "Let's do it, Mr. Lee!"

He eventually ran outside, and I turned to Belina. "That kid looks like your ancestor; remember the one who doesn't look like anyone?"

Belina's eyes watered, and she replied, "Lee, you know my family is a sensitive spot," As she walked out the door. I think to myself, "Oh yeah, her family just went through a tragedy. That was stupid."

We had to find an expert to teach us the ways of primitive living. I knew just the person for the job, and that was Sankofa. She was a beautiful woman with very dark skin, natural poofy hair, and a big, bright smile that could light up any room. Her beauty was even enough to make Belina a little jealous. When she asked me if I thought Sankofa was cute, I replied honestly, "She is," and Belina just rolled her eyes with a smile. Despite the mild jealousy, Sankofa quickly became a good friend and was kind enough to teach us the basics of living in the wilderness.

During our first week with Sankofa, she taught us how to start a fire. It was a crucial skill for anyone interested in primitive living or wilderness survival.

We gathered in the woods, surrounded by the serene sounds of nature. Sankofa stood before us with a warm smile, studying our different levels of interest and focus. Belina appeared ready to get the process over with while I was completely focused on the task at hand, determined to learn all I could. Max was with us too, but he seemed bored and couldn't seem to find much excitement in the process.

"Okay, let's get into the details of preparing the spindle and the hearth board," Sankofa finally said. "For the spindle, you'll want to find a straight piece of dry, dead wood about the thickness of your thumb and as long as your arm."

I quickly went off in search of the perfect piece of wood while Belina and Max looked on. Sankofa continued her instructions, "Once you've found the right piece of wood, sharpen one end of the spindle to a point. You can use a knife, a saw, or a rock to sharpen the end. Make sure the point is sharp enough to easily penetrate the hearth board."

I found three pieces of wood. One piece of wood was strong and sturdy, another had beautiful designs naturally made by nature, and the last was smaller with three different colors all over it. On my way back, I saw a red leaf reminding me of my ex's rage. I remember those words, "You killed them, Lionel! My little girl! My baby! Lawyer up, M'fer! She said with a red face and a cracked voice, tears all over her cheeks.

I returned with three pieces of wood, and Sankofa helped me sharpen them. We sharpened one end of each to a point. "Next, round the other end of the spindle to form a handle," Sankofa said. "This will make it easier for you to hold onto the spindle while you use the bow to create the back-and-forth motion. You can use a knife, a saw, or a rock to round the end into a handle shape."

With the spindle prepared, Sankofa moved on to the hearth board. "For the hearth board, find a flat piece of dry, dead wood that is about as wide as your hand and as long as your forearm," she said. Belina quickly found three pieces of wood that fit the description and brought them over to Sankofa.

"Once you've found the right piece of wood, drill a small hole near one end of the board," Sankofa continued. "This hole should be large enough to snugly fit the spindle." Belina used a knife to make the hole, and Sankofa showed her how to make the notch in the center of the hole. "This notch will serve as a holder for the pointed end of the spindle," Sankofa said. "You can use a knife or a rock to make the notch. Make sure the notch is deep enough to hold the pointed end of the spindle securely in place."

We all did as she instructed, "I looked over at Belina and Max; they seemed so happy; I don't know if I can imagine life without them now that they're here."

"That's it!" Sankofa said with a smile. "You've successfully prepared the spindle and the hearth board. Now, let's move on to making the bow." Max perked up, finally finding something he was interested in.

"Let's get into the details of preparing the bow. Belina was eager to make a connection with Sankofa; she started peppering her with questions, each one more curious and friendly than the last. I was still focused, soaking in all the information.

She finished answering all of Belina's questions and said, "Alright, now we'll move on to making the bow," Sankofa continued, "which will be used to generate the friction that starts the fire." Max eyes lit up with excitement.

I watched closely as Sankofa instructed us on how to find a flexible piece of wood or metal about the length of our arms that had some spring to it. Once we had our pieces, she showed us how to bend them into a horseshoe shape.

"Now, to secure the two ends of the bow," Sankofa said, "you'll want to use cord or sinew." She explained that cord was often made from plant fibers, while sinew was made from animal tendons and that both would work fine.

I watched as Sankofa demonstrated how to tie a knot in the cord and wrap it around both ends of the bow, making sure to keep the knot tight. She repeated the process several times, making sure to keep the bow in its horseshoe shape.

I watched as Max's eyes lit up with wonder as he asked Sankofa if he could be the one to start the fire. Sankofa, with a smile on her face, agreed and handed him the bow. I was a little put off by Max's sudden excitement, but I couldn't help but feel a sense of awe as I watched him work.

He placed the hearth board on the ground and, with a steady hand, began moving the bow back and forth over the string. The friction from the movement of the bow caused the spindle to spin rapidly, creating heat and eventually igniting the tinder. Max's face lit up with joy as the tinder burst into flame.

Gently blowing on the flames, he encouraged their growth. Gradually, he added small pieces of dry wood to the fire, increasing the size of the fuel as the fire grew.

That's it! I thought to myself. With patience, practice, and proper technique, anyone can start a fire using this method. I was grateful for Sankofa's guidance and for the opportunity to learn such a valuable skill in the wilderness. I was extremely proud of Max.

It reminded me of the time when my nephew got suspended from school. I had to pick him up and ask the principal what he had done. She had a straight face and wore a really nice suit. Her eagle-piercing eyes looked straight at me as she said, "He stood on his desk claiming to be God."

My nephew's behavior didn't surprise me; he had always been a little wild. "And what happened?" I asked.

"When his teacher told him that he was no God and she was a Christian, he said, 'Your God could tell you that you're God, and your arrogance and ignorance still would not allow you to see it,'" the principal continued.

As she spoke, I couldn't help but chuckle at the story. But then she said, "They had to drag him out of the classroom, and as they did, he screamed all the way to my office, 'John 10:34, does it not say in your scribes: you are gods, all children of the most high?'"

The principal's voice grew stern. "Mr. Lionel, this behavior will not be tolerated. He must go home!" she said.

I respectfully nodded and replied, "Of course." As I left the office, I couldn't help but shake my head, thinking, "What a kid!" And then I looked over at Max, and I thought the same.

Sankofa arrived the next day, and we all went back to the woods. Now we are learning how to make a knife under the guidance of our instructor.

"Have you seen how fast Max is picking this up?" Belina asked me as we scoured the forest floor for suitable stones. "He's got a real knack for this."

"Yeah, I know," I agreed. "Sankofa is a great teacher, but Max just seems to have a natural talent for this kind of thing, but I'm sure that "gift" God gave him may have something to do with it."

We finally found some flint stones that looked like they would work well for our knives. Sankofa showed us how to use a hammer stone to shape the flint into the desired knife shape. It was hard work, and I was sweating by the time I had removed all the excess rock.

Next, Sankofa showed us how to create a cutting edge by using a smaller, finer-grained stone to sharpen the blade. We held the blade at an angle while grinding it down, making sure to sharpen both sides. After repeating this process several times, we finally had a sharp edge.

"Now it's time to hone the edge," Sankofa said, demonstrating how to use a finer-grained stone to smooth and refine the edge. We held the blade at a lower angle this time, making slow, smooth strokes to hone the edge.

After honing the edge, we tested it by making a cut in a piece of cloth. The knife was sharp enough, but Sankofa suggested we go back and continue honing the edge until it was razor-sharp.

Finally, it was time to finish the handle. We could use materials like wood, bone, or antler to make a handle for our knife. We chose a piece of antler, and Sankofa showed us how to attach it to the blade using cord.

"And there you have it," Sankofa said, admiring our handiwork. "A handmade knife, crafted with your own two hands."

Belina and I were both amazed at how much we had learned in just one day. And Max? He was already starting to ask about what was next.

Sankofa taught us the art of creating pouches from tanned animal hides. We began by acquiring deer or elk hides and preparing them for tanning. This involved removing hair, flesh, and fat before soaking the hides in water to remove dirt and rehydrate the skin. After the hair was removed, the hides were treated with a pickling solution and then tanned using a variety of methods. The tanned hide was then dried and finally treated with oils or waxes to add durability.

Belina asked, "Lee, do you think it's ethical to use animals as storage for goods?"

I stroked my chin, deep in thought. Sankofa then interjected, "May I share my thoughts on this matter?"

Belina and I nodded in agreement, and Sankofa continued, "Everything in nature has a purpose, and the earth works to ensure that each creation is useful in its own way. Death is a part of life, and the question is not whether we will die, but how we can be of use to others even in death."

Belina still seemed unsure, and Sankofa added, "As the Bamana of Mali say, 'If a tree falls, it will always leave a stump; life goes on.' The important thing is to use what nature has given us in a respectful and sustainable way."

With Sankofa's wise words, Belina and I felt more at ease about the process of using animal hides for our pouches.

Next, we cut the hides into the desired size for our pouches and sewed them together using a needle and strong thread. We added a flap and closure to keep the contents inside and treated the pouches with oils or wax to protect them.

In addition to creating pouches, we also learned how to make ropes and cordage using nettle or dogbane fiber. This involved harvesting the fiber, preparing it by soaking and drying it, and then spinning and twisting it into a stronger rope or cord. Finally, we finished the rope by adding a loop or knot at each end and treating it with oil or wax. I looked at Belina and Max, smiling while doing this good work given to us by God, and thought to myself, "I must do whatever it takes."

Lastly, Sankofa taught us how to scrape gourd bowls and carve wooden spoons. We obtained mature gourds or blocks of wood, cleaned and prepared them, and then carved them into bowls or spoons. We finished by sanding the bowls and spoons and treating them with oil or wax.

Max asks, what's next? Next, we hunt! Sankofa says with a smile. This is what I had been waiting for. We are venturing into the woods. Learning the art of hunting wild chickens with bow and arrows under the guidance of the beautiful and skilled Sankofa. This was exactly what I needed in life.

As we make our way through the thick trees and underbrush, Sankofa demonstrates the proper techniques and tips for hunting these elusive birds. With each step, we become more confident and determined to hone our skills and bring home the chicken, so to speak.

We start by studying the habits and behavior of wild chickens in order to better understand our prey. Sankofa shows us the importance of having the right equipment and tools, including a bow and arrow, a quiver to hold our arrows, and a hunting knife for cleaning and dressing the birds.

As we stalk through the forest, Sankofa teaches us the importance of patience and stealth, reminding us to approach slowly and quietly, using the cover of the vegetation to conceal our movements. We keep the wind at our backs so as not to alert the birds to our presence.

As we come within range, Sankofa demonstrates the proper technique for drawing and aiming the bow, taking into account the bird's size and speed, as well as the elements of nature that may affect our shot. With steady hands and calm breaths, we release our arrows, striving for a successful and humane kill.

Finally, Sankofa shows us how to retrieve and dress the birds, making sure to remove the feathers and gut the birds promptly to prevent spoilage and contamination. With our newfound skills, we set off on our own, eager to put our training to the test and bring home a delicious feast.

Later that night, Belina pulled the chicken out of the oven to compliment our plate of fruits and vegetables. Before anyone ate, we prayed to the One God, Above All, our ancestors and the organisms who had died or lost a piece of themselves so that we could live. Belina didn't really eat meat, but Max and I ate as much chicken as we could. Belina said, "You both eat exactly the same it's disgraceful," with a smile on her face. Max and I pause and look at each other… Then we smile and keep eating this delicious food.

The next morning, I wake up early and find Max already outside. It was pretty standard at this point. Belina is still sleeping. I walk out next to Max, and Max tells me, "Belina and you are the greatest people I've ever met. I'm going to make sure we are together forever." I rub his head and push him to the side and say, "You've spent too much time with Belina," and we both laugh. Max then says, "She's like the mother I never had."

I respond, "Well, surely your mom isn't that bad, kid." Max looks down and says, "My mother is awesome; I love her very much; I just don't fit in with her and my father."

I kneel down to his level and say, "Listen, kid, no one can love you like your parents." Max just stands there, looking down.

I change the subject and say, "Come on, the fish are here. Do you want to help me stock the ponds?" Max brightens up and says, "Um, yeah."

"I knew you would," I respond with a grin.

As we drive to the first pond, I explain the steps we will follow. "Max, before we stock the pond with fish, it is important to determine its size and carrying capacity," I say. "This will help us determine the right number of fish to stock and ensure that the pond can support a healthy population of rainbow trout."

Max nods and pretends to be taking notes in his pretend notebook. "What's next?" he asks.

"Well, first, let me say I already selected the right type of rainbow trout," I reply. "Rainbow trout come in a variety of sizes, colors, and life stages, and it is important to select the right type of trout for the pond. We need to consider factors such as the size of the pond, the water temperature, and the availability of food when choosing the right type of rainbow trout."

As we arrive at the first pond, we get to work. We measure the size of the pond and assess the water temperature and other conditions. I purchased the rainbow trout from a reputable source.

Next, we acclimate the fish to the pond by gradually adjusting the temperature and water chemistry of the fish's holding tank over several days. Finally, it is time to release the fish into the pond. We release them at dawn in a calm and quiet area of the pond to reduce stress and improve their chances of survival.

Once the fish are in the pond, our work is not done. We need to monitor their health and adjust the conditions in the pond as needed to ensure their continued health and well-being. This includes monitoring the water temperature, pH, and oxygen levels, as well as feeding the fish a balanced diet.

As we drive to the next pond, Max is full of questions. "What do you do if the water temperature is too high?" he asks. "What if the pH is too low?" I answer each of his questions, and he listens intently, taking notes in his imaginary notebook.

We continue this process throughout the days, stocking all the ponds in FFFHAMS with rainbow trout. Max is a quick learner, and by the end of the day, he is able to do much of the work on his own.

I am proud of him, and I start to shake, thinking about what I did to the last boy I was proud of.

CHAPTER 10:

FOOD FOREST FORAGING HUNTING ANTI-FRAGILE

I t had been a couple of years since I last talked to God, two years to be exact. Every night I prayed, but there was no response. I started to worry that maybe I was doing something wrong. When I got up to make breakfast, Belina and Max were already awake. Belina hugged me and gave me a kiss while Max made an "ewwww" sound. I gently pushed his head to the side and asked him, "How did the school year go?" Max replied, "It was great! I'm just glad I don't have to split my time between school and coming here anymore." I then asked him, "How old are you now, thirty?" He gave me a funny look and said, "You know very well how old I am. You both threw me the greatest 16th birthday ever." I punched his arm and said, "Oh yeah, that's right. And don't you ever forget it." Max got up and jokingly said, "You want some ole' man?" I was surprised and replied, "Old?" We started play-wrestling, both of us smiling. He tried putting me in a squeeze, but I fought back, reversing him and pulling his arm into my chest, making him tap. Belina interrupted us and said, "Can you both stop with the grappling in the house every morning? You both built a gym outside to train in."

Max and I rushed outside to grab the basketball. Before entering the food forest, there was a community center with a tennis court, basketball court, a natural pool, and an outside kitchen. Every community was set up this way. We played basketball until one of the foxes we had released from the food forest came out to join us. The food forest looked splendid and full of life. We petted the fox, and Max began to play with it. "I'm going in to get some water," I told Max as I walked back to the house. "Just say you're tired, old man," he joked. I waved him off and walked into the house. We had been on the news for a while, maybe a year, and I hadn't let any journalists onto the property. "They may get some pictures every now and then. I've seen blurry ones online, but this place is sacred," I thought to myself. As I walked into my room to take a nap, I was confronted with an unexpected sight. A man, as black as the night sky, dressed all in white stood before me. I quickly closed the door and bowed in reverence.

"LORD, my God, you have returned," I exclaimed.

"Yes, Lionel. How is everyone?" God asked.

I responded with assurance, "They are good, God. Everyone is great, thanks to you."

"Anti-fragility," God murmured.

I was eager to learn and replied, "Yes, I'm ready to learn."

God asked, "Are you still willing to give anything, to sacrifice whatever it takes?"

Without hesitation, I answered, "Yes, my Lord."

God continued, "Do you swear to move when I say?"

"Yes," I said.

"Act when I say," God demanded.

"Of course," I replied.

God insisted, "Swear it to me!"

I obliged, "I swear...."

God commanded, "Repeat after me."

"Yes, my Lord," I replied with trembling anticipation.

God began, "The blood of God and the blood of man."

"The blood of God and the blood of man," I repeated.

"Where God steps is here I stand," God continued.

"Where God steps is here I stand," I repeated.

"No one shall separate the skin of man and the flesh of God," God declared.

"No one shall separate the skin of man and the flesh of God," I echoed.

"I am God's fist," God proclaimed.

"I am God's fist," I affirmed.

"I am God's tongue," God stated.

"I am God's tongue," I repeated.

"And if from God's mouth comes a sword," God warned.

"And if from God's mouth comes a sword," I repeated.

"I will kill what must die," God concluded.

"I will kill what must die," I repeated.

"Now, swear it!" God demanded.

With all my being, I swore, "I swear, God."

"Good. Let's move on," God said calmly.

I was sweating and trembling in fear, but I knew I had to be strong.

"Yes, my Lord," I responded.

"There are three things in the world," he said, "fragile things that break in the presence of Entropy, robust things that remain relatively the same in the presence of Entropy, and antifragile things, which get stronger in the presence of Entropy. This is the way nature functions."

I nodded, trying to wrap my head around the concept. "I understand, God. And what is the goal for our society in relation to Entropy?" I asked.

"Your goal is to work with nature and ensure that this society, my home, can withstand the test of entropy," he replied. "For this to happen, the society must be self-sufficient."

"I understand, God. And what will the homes be like in this society?" I inquired.

"There will be marriage homes and shared homes," God explained. "The majority of homes will be shared homes, and they will be eco-friendly and passive. Some will be large, some will be small, but all will have equal access. Most will be outside the food forest in four spacious clusters around the community, while some will be built as treehouses within the food forest. It is important that everything be antifragile, and you will have advanced technology that makes you and your environment stronger instead of weaker as your technology within the Matrix does now."

"Creation is a good example of an antifragile system," God said. "Or what you may call biological evolution. Nasim Taleb, your culture's main contributor to the understanding of antifragility, uses evolution to illustrate his point that evolution is antifragile because it is built on the genetic features and traits that have helped species survive and succeed. But, it also means that many individuals within a species had to die."

I nodded, understanding. "So, individual specimens of a species must be fragile so that the success and failure of these parts can serve as important feedback for the system as a whole, allowing it to get better in chaotic circumstances."

"Exactly," God said, smiling. "For an antifragile system to work, its individual parts must be fragile because their success and failure serve as important feedback for the system as a whole."

I sat there, contemplating what God told me. It was a lot to take in, but I was determined to understand this concept fully.

"How does this extra capacity build when put under stress?" I asked

"When you experience stress, such as when you exercise, your fragile parts are broken down. This failure is reported to the system, and in order to ensure future success, your body overcompensates for this shock by building extra capacity to handle even bigger shocks better. For example, when you lift heavy weights at the gym, feel a burn, and push on for one more rep, growth happens. Your muscles are broken down, but overnight as you sleep and recover, they are rebuilt, stronger than before. This is how stress can prepare your body for even greater stress, and it is building this extra capacity that lies at the core of why being antifragile is so helpful in critical situations." God replied

I thought about it, scratching my head, and said, "I see, God. And what about natural systems, like the body's immune system?"

God went on to explain, "Within the subset of natural systems, those that benefit from feedback are antifragile, like the body's immune system. This is the basis of vaccines, as they introduce a weak stressor that triggers the immune system to adapt. However, if humans become too dependent on vaccines, they will become more fragile, as they will die out if the vaccines are no longer effective or destroyed. It is important for humans to increase their own antifragile system organically."

I said, "I understand, God. And what about man-made systems and processes?"

God replied, "Most man-made systems and processes do not exhibit antifragile behavior. However, at a process level, they are antifragile because humans have a natural inclination towards process improvement by studying past failures and adapting accordingly. This is why you impose your own antifragile tendencies on the systems you design, as you cannot leave things alone. Most of the natural physical world has a tendency to decay over time, especially in complex systems where failures rise exponentially over time. Lionel, have you ever considered the meaning of Entropy?"

I said, "Yes, God. I know it's the scientific concept of disorder and chaos, and I know The Devil is a manifestation of Entropy."

But do you realize it's more than that, Lionel?" God's voice was grave. "Entropy gives birth to the manifestation of immeasurable evil in your world, a harbinger of destruction and suffering from the perspective of man."

I shuddered at the thought, feeling the weight of the world on my shoulders. "Heavy," I mumbled.

God looks at me, his eyes glistening with a wisdom that defied human comprehension.

"It is. But, on the other hand, there's Order," he said. "It brings stability, structure, and purpose to the universe. It's been revered as a divine power, a symbol of goodness and light."

I nodded, taking in his words.

"Good. We will speak in western religious terms to make sure you fully comprehend what I'm saying. Understand that gods of destruction, like those in ancient cultures, are just incarnations of Entropy. They bring chaos and wipe out planets and solar systems. Devils, on the other hand, bring destruction to regions and cultures, but Lucifers come promising Order but only bring more Entropy; they bring false Order. Finally, demons bring randomness to everyday life."

I furrowed my brow, trying to wrap my mind around the complexity of it all.

"What about the gods of order and creation?" I asked, seeking clarification.

"Gods of creation bring structure and stability to the universe. Lesser gods create Order within cultures and worlds, helping life flourish; some give Order through disorder. And what you may call divine spirits or angels maintain everyday Order and bring peace to your souls," he replied with a serene smile.

"How can we protect ourselves from the evil forces of entropy, God?" I asked.

"You must strive to become antifragile, Lionel," God replied, his voice echoing throughout the room. "Antifragility allows you to grow stronger and more resilient in the face of chaos and adversity. It's a way of life that turns negativity into positive energy and chaos into Order."

I furrowed my brow, trying to comprehend his words. "Yes, Lord"

God leaned forward, his eyes gleaming with divine light. "You must remember to stick to these simple rules of antifragility when creating FFFHAMS, and it is crucial that you build in redundancy and layers, ensuring that there is no single point of failure," God said, his voice firm.

I nodded, eager to absorb every piece of advice he had to offer. "I will make sure to follow this rule, God."

"You must also resist the urge to suppress randomness," he continued. "Embrace it and allow it to play a role in your work."

"Yes, God," I replied, feeling the weight of his words settle into my bones. "I understand the importance of randomness."

"It is imperative that you give your soul to FFFHAMS," he said, his eyes boring into mine. "Your passion and dedication will shine through in your work."

"I will make sure to pour my soul into FFFHAMS, God," I replied, my heart full of determination.

"Experiment and tinker," God said. "Take lots of small risks and explore new avenues."

"I will make sure to be adventurous and take small risks, God," I promised.

"However, be cautious of risks that, if lost, would wipe you out completely," God warned. "Avoid those at all costs."

"I will be mindful of the risks I take, God," I assured him.

"Do not get consumed by information," God continued.

"I will make sure to not get caught up in analysis paralyzes, God," I replied, my mind racing with the weight of his words.

"Your focus should be on avoiding things that don't work rather than trying to find out what does work," he said.

"I understand, God," I replied. "I will make sure to reevaluate things based on what doesn't work."

"Finally, respect the old," God said, his voice carrying a note of finality. "Look for habits and rules that have been around for a long time, as they have proven to be successful."

"I will make sure to pay homage to the past, God," I said. "But I have a question...."

"First, a story on Anti-fragility," God said, cutting me off before I could even form my question.

I nodded and said, "Yes, my Lord... Once upon a time, in a world beyond our own, there lived a man named Arin. Arin was a simple man with simple dreams and desires. He lived a quiet life, working as a farmer and keeping to himself. However, Arin was plagued by a nagging fear that had consumed him for as long as he could remember. He was afraid of everything and everyone, and this fear kept him from living the life he truly wanted.

One day, while Arin was tending to his crops, a group of demons appeared before him. They taunted him and pointed out all of his flaws, laughing at his fear and cowardice. Arin was shattered, but instead of cowering, he made a bold decision. He would no longer live in fear. He would no longer be a coward. He would face his demons head-on.

And so, Arin began to work on himself. He learned new skills, pushed himself to try new things, and slowly but surely, he began to transform. With every improvement, he felt his confidence grow, and his fear diminish. The demons continued to appear, pointing out new flaws, but Arin was now ready to face them. He continued to work on himself, determined to overcome his fears and become the person he was always meant to be.

As time passed, Arin's transformation became more and more profound. He became an angel with the strength and courage to face any challenge that came his way. Then, he became a god, wielding immense power and able to bring about change in the world. Finally, he became the creator of the universe, the guardian of all that existed.

The demons, who had once taunted Arin, now cowered before him. They realized that Arin had become antifragile, growing stronger with every challenge and adversity that he faced. And so, Arin's journey from coward to God was complete. He had faced his demons and overcome his fears, becoming the greatest and most powerful being in all the universe."

God's words cut through me like a knife. "You underestimate yourself, Lionel, and that's why you are the servant." I was taken aback by the harshness of his words but didn't dare to question him. "Yes, my Lord. Can you please answer my question?" I asked, trying to refocus the conversation.

"Of course," God replied. "You want to know about 'respecting the old.'"

"Yes, my Lord, what does that have to do with anti-fragility?" I asked, eager to learn.

"The Lindy Effect," God began, "is a concept that suggests the longer an item, technology, or idea has been around, the more likely it is to continue to be relevant and useful. Do you understand?"

"I do, God," I replied, impressed by the simplicity of his explanation.

"Good," God continued. "For example, a book that has been around for 50 years is likely to still be relevant 50 years from now, while a book that has only been around for 5 years is less likely to be relevant. The same is true for technology and ideas."

"I see now," I said, feeling enlightened. "That makes sense, God. I will consider the Lindy Effect when making decisions."

God's eyes brighten with approval. "Excellent. It is important to recognize that items, technology, and ideas that have stood the test of time have been tested and refined. The Lindy Effect highlights the value of longevity and the importance of testing and refining over time."

"I understand, God. I will keep this in mind," I reply, determined to impress Him with my dedication.

"Good. What way of human life do you think would be a good example?" He asks, prompting me to think deeply.

"Hunter-gatherers?" I venture, hoping I'm on the right track.

"Exactly," God affirms, nodding.

"May I, Lord?" I ask, eager to share a story.

"You may," God nods, gesturing for me to continue.

I breath in and, "In a magical forest, surrounded by verdant trees, two saplings stood tall. Willow, a youthful and nimble tree with vibrant green leaves, was a sight to behold. Lindy, an old oak, was a symbol of wisdom and stability, with roots as strong as steel and a trunk that could withstand the fiercest of winds.

One day, a young and handsome tree named Birch arrived in the Forest, and both Willow and Lindy were instantly in love. They both desired to be near him, to bask in his sun and drink from his rain. Willow was full of life and energy, certain that she could win Birch's heart with her beauty and grace. But Lindy knew the power of time, and she was certain that her unwavering stability and wisdom would be the key to Birch's heart.

Birch was torn as he was drawn to both Willow's youthful energy and Lindy's steadfast wisdom. Not knowing who to choose, he decided to observe the two trees and see which one would stand the test of time.

As the seasons passed, the Forest changed and evolved, but Willow and Lindy remained steadfast. Willow's beauty continued to shine, but she began to bend and sway in the wind. Lindy's roots grew deeper, and her trunk grew stronger, never wavering in the face of change.

In the end, Birch chose Lindy, for she was a symbol of the power of time, growing stronger with each passing day and her love growing deeper with each passing year. Willow was a symbol of the fleeting nature of youth and beauty, but Lindy was a symbol of the enduring power of time and stability.

Birch and Lindy lived happily ever after, their love story becoming a legend in the Forest, inspiring all who heard it to value the power of time and the beauty of stability."

God gave me a nod of approval. "Good Lionel, the worlds you create grow more and more impressive."

I bowed my head in gratitude. "Thanks to you, Lord."

God's expression hardened. "Hmph…"

" Is there more, my Lord?"

"Yes, much more," God said.

"I'm ready," I replied eagerly.

"Lionel, it is crucial that you protect FFFHAMS against natural disasters," God began. "The key is a comprehensive emergency management plan."

I nodded solemnly. "Of course, God. What should be included in this plan?"

"The plan must have several elements, Lionel," God continued. "Firstly, establish a system of early warning for natural disasters such as floods, droughts, and fires. Develop a network of monitoring stations and sensors to detect potential threats in the surrounding area. This should include monitoring weather patterns and potential hazards, such as rising water levels, high winds, and extreme heat."

I take notes as God speaks, making sure to absorb every detail. His voice is calming, but there is a seriousness to his words that I can't ignore.

"I understand. What else is important in this plan?" I ask, eager to make sure that FFFHAMS is prepared for any disaster.

"It is also important to have detailed evacuation plans in place," God replies. "These plans should include routes and procedures for safely leaving the area in case of an emergency. Make sure that these plans are communicated to the community members and practiced regularly so that everyone knows what to do in case of an emergency."

I nod, taking notes on what God is saying. "I understand. What else do I need to consider?"

"Invest in fortifying structures in the community, Lionel," God says. "This means building stronger and more resilient homes and community centers. This can include retrofitting existing structures with stronger foundations and roofs or building new structures designed to withstand specific hazards."

"Anything else, my Lord God?" I ask, eager to make sure that I have all the information I need.

"Develop a comprehensive response plan that includes evacuation routes and procedures and communication protocols," God says. "This plan should be reviewed and updated regularly to ensure it remains effective. And, Lionel, it is imperative that you train the members of the FFFHAMS community on emergency preparedness and response. This includes training on how to use early warning systems, evacuation procedures, and emergency communication protocols. It is also important to train members on basic first aid and emergency medical care."

I nod, understanding the importance of emergency preparedness. "Should we do regular drills?" I ask.

"Conducting regular drills and simulations of emergency scenarios will help the community members to be better prepared in case of a real emergency," God responds. "This is an essential part of the emergency management plan, Lionel. Remember, the goal is to protect FFFHAMS against natural disasters and ensure the safety of its residents. Only then will this place be Anti-fragile."

I agree, "Yes, my Lord." I pause for a moment, collecting my thoughts. "Once upon a time, in a land where hunter-gatherer communities thrived, there lived a woman named Secur. Determined to protect her tribe, FFFHAMS, from the devastating effects of natural disasters such as floods, droughts, and fires, Secur set out to develop a comprehensive plan.

Being well-versed in emergency management, Secur knew that the key to survival was preparation. The first element of her plan was to establish an early warning system, monitoring weather patterns and potential hazards in order to detect threats and prepare accordingly. With her team, she set up a network of monitoring stations and sensors and trained the community members on their use.

Next, Secur worked on developing evacuation plans to ensure the safe escape of the community in the event of an emergency. She mapped out evacuation routes and procedures and made sure everyone was aware of their role. Regular evacuation drills helped the community members to be better prepared.

Secur also focused on fortifying the structures in the community, retrofitting existing buildings with stronger foundations and roofs, and overseeing the construction of new buildings designed to withstand specific hazards.

The fourth element of her plan was to establish a comprehensive response plan for effective evacuation and communication in case of an emergency. Secur and her team created protocols for emergency response, making sure everyone in the community was aware of their role.

Finally, Secur placed great importance on training the members of the FFFHAMS community on emergency preparedness and response. Regular training sessions were held on basic first aid, emergency medical care, and emergency communication protocols. Emergency drills and simulations helped the community members to be better prepared for any future disasters.

One day, a loud rumbling sound filled the air, and Secur looked up to see a massive meteorite falling from the sky, heading straight for the FFFHAMS community. She immediately activated the early warning system, alerting the other members of the community.

With quick thinking, Secur put her evacuation plan into action, leading the community members to the designated safe zones and helping the elderly and children along the way. As the community evacuated smoothly and efficiently, Secur stayed behind to fortify the structures.

The meteorite finally struck, causing a massive explosion and intense heat. Secur huddled with the other members of the community, waiting for the dust to settle. Once the impact subsided, Secur sprang into action once again, using her emergency response plan to check on the well-being of the community and provide first aid where necessary. She even helped dig individuals trapped under rubble to safety.

Throughout the disaster, Secur remained calm and composed, always thinking ahead and taking action. Thanks to her comprehensive emergency management plan, she was able to ensure the survival of the FFFHAMS community.

As the community slowly began to rebuild, Secur was hailed as a hero. The other members of the community praised her quick thinking and bravery, grateful to have someone like her leading them through the disaster. The FFFHAMS community was stronger than ever, prepared for any future disasters, all thanks to Secur and her emergency management plan."

God said, "Yes, Secur is a hero."

I replied, "Thank you, my Lord."

God continued, "You must create a system for outbreaks within FFFHAMS. Establish a system for identifying and screening individuals who may have been exposed to the disease. This includes individuals who have recently traveled to areas with known outbreaks, have been in close contact with a confirmed case, or have symptoms consistent with the disease."

"I understand, God. What should be done with individuals who have been identified as potentially infected?" I asked.

"They should be isolated immediately to prevent the spread of the disease. Isolation can be done at home or in a designated facility; it is up to the person who is infected," God replied.

I continued, "And what about individuals who have been in close contact with a confirmed case but have not yet developed symptoms?"

"They should be placed in quarantine to prevent the spread of the disease to others in the community. They should go home, not to the facility, for they may not be sick," God advised.

I asked God, "What measures should be put in place to monitor individuals in isolation and quarantine?"

God replied, "We must establish a system for monitoring individuals in isolation and quarantine. This includes regular check-ins and monitoring of symptoms. Additionally, movement restrictions should be implemented for individuals in quarantine or isolation. This includes limiting their movement to a specific area or location."

I followed up, "How will communication be maintained with individuals in isolation and quarantine?"

"Clear communication channels must be established to keep them informed about the situation and provide them with necessary information and support," God answered.

"And what kind of support should be provided to individuals in isolation and quarantine?" I asked.

"They should be provided with the necessary support, including food, medical supplies, and mental health support," God replied.

I asked, "When can individuals in isolation or quarantine be safely discharged?"

God answered, "You must establish criteria for when individuals in isolation or quarantine can be safely discharged, such as testing negative for the disease or being symptom-free for a certain period of time. But you are not a government, so they are free to leave when they deem themselves to be safe. If the community disagrees, they may leave the people they feel pose a threat and go to a safer community nearby."

"What steps should be taken to ensure the safety of others in the community?" I asked Him.

"Regular cleaning and disinfection of areas and items that may have been in contact with individuals in isolation or quarantine should be implemented. Additionally, it is important to regularly train and educate community members on the importance of quarantine and isolation and how to identify and respond to potential outbreaks," God replied.

But I was still uneasy. "Lord, I don't feel comfortable with quarantines. It seems like something the Matrix would do," I said.

"Go on..." God prompted me.

I continued, "Well, if we are hunter-gatherers, we will be safe from diseases, and our immune systems will be a lot stronger. So we probably wouldn't be infected by these diseases."

God rebutted, "Tell that to the natives of America who lost 95% of their population to a disease brought by colonists."

I was silenced. "I see..." I murmured, accepting His point.

God then asked me to tell Him a story. "Yes, my Lord. Currae was a fearless and determined member of the FFFHAMS community. When she heard about the virus that had infected some of their community members, causing them to become violent, she knew she had to act quickly,

As she began her journey to stop the spread of the virus, Currae first implemented the identification and screening process. She went door to door, talking to each member of the community and checking for any symptoms or recent travels to infected areas. Those who were potentially infected were immediately isolated, either at home or in a designated facility.

Currae also made sure to place those who had been in close contact with confirmed cases in quarantine, limiting their movement and monitoring their symptoms regularly. Communication was key, and Currae made sure to establish clear channels with those in isolation and quarantine to keep them informed and provide them with the necessary support.

As the outbreak worsened, Currae faced many challenges and obstacles, but she never lost her determination. She implemented movement restrictions and provided support, including food, medical supplies, and mental health support, to those in isolation and quarantine.

Despite the danger, Currae put her own life on the line as she cleaned and disinfected areas that had been in contact with infected individuals. And through her tireless efforts, she trained and educated the community on the importance of quarantine and isolation and how to respond to potential outbreaks.

As the virus ran its course, Currae never wavered. She worked tirelessly, following the guidelines and protocols to the letter, until the last infected individual had been safely discharged. And in the end, all the infected were revived, and the FFFHAMS community was saved thanks to Currae's bravery and determination."

"Good Lionel, you understand," he said.

I nodded my head, feeling the weight of my Lord's presence in the room. "Yes, my Lord, thank you."

"Have you ever heard the phrase, 'Don't throw the baby out--'" he began.

"With the bath water," I finished for him.

"Yes, good," God said. "The same could be said about the matrix and hospitals."

"Don't throw emergency rooms out with the matrix," I said, my mind racing to keep up with the divine conversation.

"Yes, but do you know why?" God asked.

I thought for a moment before answering. "Within entropy lies order," I said.

"Yes, humans, like all animals, struggled with child and infant mortality. Hunter-gatherers and civilizations alike. Civilizations had a harder time with this than hunter-gatherers until one invention," God said.

"Emergency care," I said, knowing where this was going.

"Yes, emergency care and access to medical care solved this ancient problem. You mustn't abandon this solution. Instead, you will take it to another level. Everyone in FFFHAMS will have detailed knowledge of healing and nursing. Especially the women. The women will be the main doctors and healers. Every home will have the equipment necessary for emergency care."

I listened to the words of my Lord, knowing that they were wise and just. This was what FFFHAMS needed, and I was the one chosen to make it happen.

"I see," I said. So, everyone will have health care becuase everyone will be knowledgeable in the arena of healing and nursing. In addition, we will be providing the equipment necessary and growing the proper medicines in the food forest."

"Yes, except the medicines will be grown inside the homes and around the homes. There should be wild gardens of medicinal plants everywhere around the homes," He said.

I nodded, taking in the gravity of His words. "Yes, my Lord."

"You are to help FFFHAMS in becoming a licensed private medical facility and for its members to become nurses in a cost-effective manner," He said.

"You will begin by developing a training program for the members of FFFHAMS to become nurses. Identify the most cost-effective ways to provide the training, such as online courses or community college classes. Partner with local hospitals or medical schools to provide clinical training and experience for FFFHAMS members," God instructed.

"Understood, Lord. What is next in the plan?" I asked, already envisioning the work ahead.

"Eventually, once all of the older women within FFFHAMS are experienced in holistic medicine, nursing, and emergency care, FFFHAMS must become an accredited medical university that can approve nursing degrees. Research the requirements and process for accreditation with the appropriate accrediting body. Develop a curriculum that meets the standards set by the accrediting body and prepare the necessary documentation and evidence to demonstrate compliance. This is crucial. Once this happens, girls and boys within the community will be able to receive all the education required, but this time it will be free," He said.

I listened, awed by the scope of His plan. And with His guidance, I knew that we would succeed.

"And how do we acquire the necessary medical equipment, Lord?" I asked.

"Research the most cost-effective ways to acquire the equipment, such as medical surplus stores or online marketplaces. Develop a maintenance and repair plan for the equipment to ensure that it remains in good working condition," God replied.

I nodded, impressed by His practicality. "Yes, my Lord. There was a woman named Wholey who lived in a small community where access to healthcare was limited. She had a dream to provide her community with better health services and to achieve that dream, she decided to take on the challenge of becoming the first person in her community to be trained in nursing, nutrition, and holistic medicine."

I paused, collecting my thoughts. "Wholey spent two grueling years of schooling, studying day and night, and facing many obstacles along the way. But she never gave up on her dream. She worked tirelessly and eventually received her nursing degree.

With her newfound knowledge and skills, Wholey decided to make her dream a reality. She established FFFHAMS, a community-based organization that aimed to provide health services to everyone in the community. To make FFFHAMS a registered school for nursing, she developed a training program for members to become nurses. She identified cost-effective ways to provide the training, such as online courses or community college classes, and partnered with local hospitals and medical schools to provide clinical training and experience.

To make FFFHAMS a licensed private medical facility, Wholey researched the requirements and process for becoming an accredited medical university and a licensed private medical facility. She identified the accrediting body responsible for approving nursing degrees and the state agency responsible for licensing. She then developed a plan to meet the requirements and prepared the necessary documentation and evidence to demonstrate compliance.

Wholey also ensured that the FFFHAMS had access to the necessary medical equipment by researching cost-effective ways to acquire it and developing a maintenance and repair plan. To engage and educate the community on the services provided by the facility, Wholey established a community advisory board and partnered with local organizations to provide health education and outreach programs.

In the end, Wholey's hard work and determination paid off. FFFHAMS now had a licensed private medical facility, and members of the community were able to receive the healthcare they deserved. Wholey's legacy lived on, as she had created a platform for others to pursue their dreams and provide their communities with the same level of care and compassion that she had shown."

"Good... For true independence, everyone in FFFHAMS will need to know how to build homes, especially men. There are several steps to be taken," He said.

I listened, eager to hear what He had in mind. "What are these steps, my Lord?" I asked.

"First, FFFHAMS must offer classes and workshops on building engineering and construction to all members of the community. This should encompass both hands-on training and theoretical lessons," He replied.

I nodded, taking it all in. "And how can we encourage men to participate in these classes and workshops?" I asked.

"By providing mentorship opportunities and resources to those who express interest in building engineering, as well as creating a welcoming atmosphere that encourages their involvement. FFFHAMS can also partner with local vocational schools, colleges, and organizations that offer building engineering courses," He said.

"How else can FFFHAMS equip community members with building engineering skills?" I asked, my mind racing with possibilities.

"FFFHAMS can establish apprenticeships, where community members can work alongside experienced building engineers and learn on the job. Additionally, experienced engineers can be matched with those who are interested in learning the trade for one-on-one mentorship and guidance. Self-directed learning is also an option by providing resources and support for those who want to learn on their own through online courses and materials. Ultimately, this will be the reality once a particular FFFHAMS is over four years old," God said.

I took it all in, impressed by His foresight and wisdom. "Will the education and training take time?" I asked.

"Indeed, Lionel. This is a crucial aspect to keep in mind. Education and training of this nature requires patience, but the end result will be worth it. A diverse set of skills within the community is essential for its long-term sustainability and success," He replied.

"Yes, my Lord," I said, eager to show what I had learned. "Bob was a man who lived in a community called FFFHAMS. He always wanted to learn how to build homes, but he didn't know how to start. One day, he heard about a special kind of home called an Earthship. These homes were unique and sustainable, and Bob was very interested in learning how to build one."

I paused, collecting my thoughts.

"Bob knew that he would need to learn a lot of new skills in order to build an Earthship. So, he reached out to the best community builders in his area and asked for their help. They told him several ways that they could help him learn how to build homes, including:

Apprenticeships: They had established apprenticeship programs where community members could learn building engineering skills by working alongside experienced members in the community.

Mentoring: They matched experienced building engineers with community members who were interested in learning the trade, providing one-on-one mentoring and guidance.

Self-directed learning: They also provided resources and support for community members who wanted to learn building engineering on their own through online courses, books, and other materials.

Bob was excited to get started! He signed up for the apprenticeships, and he was also matched with a mentor who was an experienced building engineer. Over the next four years, Bob learned everything he needed to know about building an Earthship. He learned about site selection, design and planning, foundations, walls, roofs, water collection and treatment, power and heating, and the finishing touches.

At the end of the four years, Bob was ready to put all of his new skills to the test. He selected a location for his Earthship that had a good supply of natural resources, such as water and sunlight. He created a design and plan for his Earthship, including the layout, size, and orientation of the building. He also considered factors such as the size of the windows, the types of materials to use, and the type of insulation required.

Next, Bob started building the foundation of his Earthship. The foundation was made from recycled tires that were filled with dirt and stacked and packed to create a solid base. He then built up the walls, using a combination of adobe, cob, and other natural building materials, with layers of insulation and waterproofing added as needed.

Bob's roof was sloped and covered with a layer of dirt, which provided insulation and helped to regulate the temperature inside the building. He also installed a system to collect, store, and treat water, including a rainwater catchment system and a greywater treatment system.

The Earthship was powered by solar panels and wind turbines, and it was designed to be highly energy efficient. Heating was provided by passive solar heating, and cooling was provided by natural ventilation. Finally, Bob added the finishing touches to his Earthship, including windows, doors, flooring, and fixtures.

Bob was very proud of his Earthship! He showed it off to all of his friends and neighbors, and they were amazed by his work. Bob had accomplished his goal of learning how to build homes, and he was proud to have created the first Earthship in his community. He learned that building an Earthship requires a combination of specialized skills and knowledge, and it is often best to work with a team of experienced professionals. But he also learned that with hard work, patience, and dedication, anyone can learn how to build."

"I like Bob..." God said, His voice full of warmth and kindness.

"Me too," I said, smiling.

We shared a smile with a moment of camaraderie and understanding, the weight of His divine presence filling the room.

"You are tasked with overseeing the creation and maintenance of communities based on the principles of antifragility, equal access to resources, and freedom. These communities are meant to serve as a counterbalance to the oppressive and fragile Matrix that seeks to control and exploit humanity. To ensure the success and longevity of these communities, I have created the position of Guardians," God said, His words carrying the weight of destiny.

"The Guardians are the protectors of the community, tasked with defending it against all forms of attack, whether they be political, legal, or military. To fulfill this role, Guardians must undergo rigorous training and education, become well-versed in all aspects of war and peace, and master the use of weapons and martial arts. Also will be trained by spiritual teachers on how to protect people from evil spirits of all cultures and religions. They must also be trained in mediation and have an understanding of all cultures and known history.

However, Guardians must never govern. Their role is to protect, not to dictate or control. They must always be mindful of the principles of FFFHAMS, such as antifragility, equal access to the food forest, the ability to ethically hunt, fish, and forage, the exclusive growth of technology that makes humans more anti-fragile, egalitarianism, and work to preserve these principles above all else. In the event that their actions jeopardize these principles, Guardians can be stripped of their guardianship by the community members.

Guardians are limited in number, making up no more than 40% of each community. This is to ensure that the balance of power is always in the hands of the people and not the Guardians. Those who choose to become Guardians must be willing to sacrifice their liberties and freedoms for the greater good, as they will be responsible for maintaining the antifragility of the community and ensuring that it remains free from the influence of the Matrix.

In the event that the community falls to the Matrix, Guardians will play a critical role in ensuring that the knowledge and principles of FFFHAMS are passed down secretly from generation to generation if FFFHAMS is ever taken down by the elite. When the time is right, they will teach people and help rebuild FFFHAMS.

Guardians are essential to the success and longevity of FFFHAMS communities. Through their training, education, and commitment to the principles of antifragility, equal access, and freedom, they serve as the last line of defense against the Matrix and the protectors of a better future for humanity.

"This is fascinating...." I said while taking it all in, "Guardians... Yes, my Lord, this makes sense. Once upon a time, in a remote FFFHAMS community deep within the Americas, a young man named Marshall lived among his people. Despite his young age, he felt a strong calling to become a Guardian, one of the protectors of his community. He was inspired by the Guardians' unwavering commitment to preserving the principles of antifragility, equal access, and freedom, and he was determined to make a difference in the world.

Marshall began his journey by studying under the guidance of the experienced Guardians. They taught him the art of war and peace, as well as the history of the FFFHAMS communities. He learned the use of weapons and honed his martial arts skills, but he also learned the importance of diplomacy and understanding different cultures.

As he grew in his training, Marshall came to realize the tremendous responsibility that came with being a Guardian. He understood that he must always be mindful of the principles of antifragility, equal access, and freedom and that his actions must always serve to preserve these principles. The Guardians were limited in number, making up no more than 40% of each community, to ensure that the balance of power remained in the hands of the people and not the Guardians.

One day, the FFFHAMS communities were threatened by the Matrix, a powerful and oppressive force that sought to control and exploit humanity. The Matrix declared FFFHAMS illegal and launched a brutal attack on the communities. Despite their best efforts, the Guardians were outmatched, and the communities were destroyed.

But Marshall and his fellow Guardians refused to give up. They vowed to pass down the knowledge and principles of FFFHAMS secretly from generation to generation until the time was right to rebuild their communities. Over the years, they taught their children and their children's children the ways of the Guardians so that the knowledge would never be lost.

One hundred years after Marshall passed away, his great-grandchildren remembered the teachings of their ancestors and began the work of rebuilding FFFHAMS in the Americas. With the help of the Guardians, they created new communities based on the principles of antifragility, equal access, and freedom. And so, the legacy of Marshall and his fellow Guardians lived on, a testament to their unwavering commitment to a better future for humanity."

"That story illustrates the importance of Guardians very well," God said, His voice full of wisdom.

"Thank you, my Lord," I replied, feeling grateful for His guidance.

"In order to do this properly... In order to make sure FFFHAMS thrive, you must consider that what I say is true today but may not be true tomorrow," God continued, His tone serious.

"I don't understand you, God," I said, feeling a sense of confusion creeping in.

"Lionel, you must consider the possibility that I may not be right tomorrow. Like existence, the more I change, the more I stay the same, and the more I stay the same, the more I change," He said.

I struggled to comprehend His words, feeling lost and unsure. "Lord, I'm really trying to understand, but you are The Most High, The One God Above All, The Alpha and Omega. You're omniscient," I said, pleading with Him for answers.

But God only looked at me with disappointment, and without warning, He vanished, leaving me alone in my room.

"Boy, that was intense…." I thought to myself, standing alone in my room. "I'm still going to sleep," but, I couldn't sleep; I couldn't stop thinking about my last conversation with God and also how much work I had to get done. "This place is nowhere near antifragile. Maybe the Forest," I thought to myself. "Forget it" I get up and start walking outside.

Max is still shooting hoops, "who knows where Belina is…." I think to myself. Max says, "Back for more?" "God came to me, there is a new mission, and more work must be done."

I called for a meeting because the amount of work I was about to give them might have been a deal breaker. I was nervous.

They come in, and Belina sits on the floor, legs crossed. Max sits on top of the table. I tell him, "Max get down, please," Max says under his breath, "Must be serious."

I take a deep breath in…

An hour passes as I explain our anti-fragile mission in great detail, nervous to see the reaction. Belina says, "Well, we knew it wouldn't be easy" Max looks at Belina and smiles, nodding his head yes. I respond, "So… You're okay with going back to school for nursing and building tiny Earthships in each community? You're okay with all the restructuring? Belina stood up, "Lee, I saw the bitch, The Matrix. She is more horrifying than the two of you could imagine. If God says this is the way. So be it." Belina said with a smile and her hands on my hip.

I look to Max, "And Max you...." " Mr. Lee, we're one. I'll follow you two until the end of time. Where y'all go, I go. I obviously can't take the nursing and engineering courses. I'm still in high school, but I'm here for everything else." I sighed in relief, nodding my head in agreement.

A week later, I was enrolled in house engineering, and Belina was in school to become a nurse. Max took mixed martial arts after school and through the summer. We saw each other less and less often. We were all so busy.

It had been two years since I'd started my journey to become a home engineer. Working with my hands and understanding how things worked had always been my passion, so it wasn't too bad. I was already familiar with the principles of engineering, but I knew that home engineering required a unique set of skills and knowledge, and I was determined to master them.

Belina and Max were my closest companions on this journey. Belina checked on me constantly and was always there to encourage me when I failed. On the rainiest days, she would be right there, rubbing my back and saying, "Everything is going to work out." And we made it to all of Max's matches and were very impressed. We threw him a party with every belt and every achievement. I taught them both once a week, and I was proud to see them grow and learn alongside me. As we taught one another what we were learning, we became like the family Belina, and I always wanted.

The first step to becoming a home engineer was education. I enrolled in an accredited program that offered relevant courses in home engineering, and I worked hard to learn all I could about the principles of engineering and how they applied to home construction.

I then gained hands-on experience through internships, apprenticeships, and even entry-level positions at a construction company. I worked on real projects, applied my knowledge, and honed my skills. My confidence grew, and I was soon ready to take the next step.

The next step was to become licensed by the state of Georgia. I researched the requirements and took the necessary exams, and after a few years of experience, I was finally a licensed home engineer.

As the years went by, I found myself often sitting quietly in our room, lost in thought about Belina. Every time she left, I felt my heart tug and pull. She had dedicated the last two years of her life to becoming a nurse and establishing a medical facility for our community.

Belina faced numerous challenges on her journey, from completing a rigorous training program to balancing her e-commerce business and responsibilities to the community. But she never lost sight of her goal and always believed in the cause. She created a training program for future FFFHAMS members to become nurses, partnering with local hospitals and medical schools to provide cost-effective education and clinical training.

Her hard work paid off when FFFHAMS became eligible to open an accredited medical university capable of approving nursing degrees. Belina also navigated the complex regulations to obtain the necessary medical equipment and secure a license for the facility.

I was proud of Belina and her unwavering dedication to creating a better world and serving God through her work. We both strived to meet our goal of serving God and creating FFFHAMS, and our hard work paid off.

The years passed by, and we were always preparing for emergencies, constantly drilling, but no one loathed it more than Max. Speaking of Max, he was growing up fast and teaching us Muy Thai, grappling, and MMA. I couldn't help but wonder, "Where are the boy's parents? Why aren't they here to witness this?" Every time I brought up the issue with Belina, she would simply say, "Let's not get involved in the kid's personal life. Let's just be his escape."

I also noticed that Max always had an answer for why we hadn't seen his parents. Even when he wasn't using his "abilities," his skills at ordering things were beyond my own. This was especially evident with the first Earthship we were building.

I stood on a barren plot of land, surrounded by the growing Forest of FFFHAMS. I gazed out at the horizon, my eyes following the path of the sun as it made its slow descent toward the sky. Beside me, Max shifted nervously, his eyes darting back and forth as he looked at the sun. I knew he was about to leave, so I said

"This is it," my voice filled with excitement. "This is where we'll build our Earthship."

Max's eyes widened. "Really? This is where we're going to build it?"

I nodded. "Yes, this is the perfect spot. Look at how the sun hits the land and how the wind blows across the fields. We need to take all of these things into consideration when we start building. It's going to be a lot of work, but it will all be worth it in the end."

Max nodded, his excitement growing. "I can't wait to get started! I've always been fascinated by your work building Earthships, and now I get to help build one myself. But I have to go; for now, my parents will be nervous."

The next morning we began our work, each step bringing us closer to the realization of our mission. We started by selecting a suitable location for the Earthship, taking into account factors such as access to the sun, wind patterns, and water resources. Then, we began to determine the design and layout of the Earthship, including the orientation, floor plan, and roof design.

"We need to make sure the orientation is just right," I said. "The sun is our source of heat and light, so we need to maximize its exposure."

As we worked on the design, we chatted about various topics. Max expressed his fear of men in suits, to which I reassured him, "Don't worry, Max. We're doing something good here, and the people in suits will see that. It will all be fine."

Next came the preparation of the foundation. We excavated the site to a depth of about 2 feet and fill it with compacted gravel. Then, we built a retaining wall of earth-filled tire walls to hold the earth in place.

"This foundation is solid," I said. "It's the foundation of our Earthship.

As we continued building, stacking used tires filled with earth to create the walls of the Earthship, Max asked, "Do you think God will talk to me again?"

I put a hand on Max's shoulder. "Of course, Max. And I know he's proud of all the work we're doing here."

We cut holes in the tire walls to accommodate windows and built a timber or steel frame to support the roof structure. We covered the frame with metal roofing sheets and filled the voids between the tires with insulation materials.

"We're really doing it!" I said, surveying our work. "Soon, we'll have walls and a roof!"

Next, we applied a layer of plaster to the exterior of the tire walls to create a smooth finish. We built a greenhouse along one side of the Earthship; this is where all the medicinal plants would be, and installed the solar panels on the roof. We set up a system for collecting and storing rainwater; this water will be used for our drinking, shower, bathroom, and finally, our medicinal garden. We finished the interior of the Earthship with materials such as bamboo, cork, and other recycled materials.

"It's starting to feel like a real home now," I said as we worked on the interior.

Finally, we had a professional inspect the Earthship to ensure that it was properly built and met all relevant building codes and regulations.

Max and I took a couple steps back."

"Wow, look at it," Max said, his eyes wide with wonder. "It's so beautiful."

"It is," I agreed, a proud smile spreading across my face. "We did it, Max. It took a few weeks, but we built an Earthship."

We spent the next few hours exploring our new home, testing out the solar panels, the water collection system, and the greenhouse. Max was amazed at how everything worked seamlessly together, and he couldn't wait to show it off to Belina.

"She's going to love it," Max said.

"She will," I agreed. "She's always been such a huge supporter of my work. I can't wait to see the look on her face when she sees what we've built."

"I could never imagine my life without her," Max said. Then he continued, "I couldn't imagine life without your old self."

I laughed.

Max and I punched each other in the arm. I ruffed up his hair and said, "I'm proud of you." He gave me a hug, and I felt his warmth. It caught me off guard, and I said, "What you trying to do, kill me?" He started to cry. I looked at him and said, "I was just messing with you, kid." He backed away, looking at me as if he had seen a ghost, his eyes full of confusion. I tried to speak, but my words were slurred. Darkness began to envelop me, and I fell back. I think Max caught me because I heard him screaming, "Belina! Belina! Help, Mr. Lee is hurt!" Then everything went black, and I faded into the darkness.

CHAPTER 11:

FOOD FOREST FORAGING HUNTING ANTI-FRAGILE MODERN SOCIETY

My body plummeted into the abyss, into the heart of a fathomless chasm, the very epicenter of nothingness. And there, in the throes of my greatest failure, I spoke to my nephew, or rather, to my son.

"Young Lion," I said, seeking to dispel the awkward silence between us.

"Don't call me that," he replied.

"But I always called you Young Lion," I protested.

"My name is Ben... Dad," he said, looking up at me with tear-filled eyes.

"Son," I said.

"You mean nephew," he said, crossing his arms and gazing down at the ground.

"Ben... I..." I began, but he cut me off.

"No. Why didn't you tell me? I cried to you about my father so many times, and you were there, hearing me plead with you. What kind of man plays with his son but refuses to raise him? You didn't want to be my dad, so you gave me to my mother... my aunt? What is this? This is my life?" He struggled to come to grips with reality as he spoke.

"You manipulated me," Ben said, his voice cracking.

"Let me talk, Ben," I implored, my tears flowing and my voice quivering. "I was too young. I gave you to your mother, who is your biological aunt because your mother died and..."

"You're saying that's my fault?" he interrupted.

"God, no, that's not what I'm saying," I replied.

"Jesus," I muttered, scratching my head. "Look, Ben, I screwed up. I have no good excuse. I had you when I was young. Your mother died, and our family suggested that they take care of you so I could become someone, as they would say. But I could have said no. You're right..."

The silence that followed was enough to break anyone's heart. I was struck by a terrible idea. "Ben," I said, breaking the quiet, "I'll make it up to you. From this day forth, I will strive to make amends for my mistakes. I have always loved you; you must know that." Ben looked up at me, tears in his eyes, waiting for my next words.

"I know how badly you've wanted me to trust you with the yacht since your sixteenth birthday," I said, pulling out the keys from my kitchen drawer and handing them over to him. He was taken aback. I knew Ben well, and there was nothing he wanted more than my trust with the yacht. He tried not to smile, but I could see the glimmer in his eyes. "Can I get something I left here a while back?" he asked.

"Of course," I replied. A sense of relief washed over me as I thought to myself, "This is it; I've made things right. It always takes some sacrifice, but you get what you give. Everything will be okay now." But it wasn't. The next day, I received a call informing me that Ben and four of his friends, including Sekhmet or Samantha, were missing.

Days passed, and Samantha was found on the beach, describing the worst possible outcome. My young lion was dead. My son... I had killed my son. It was all my fault. And I wasn't the only one who saw it that way. My ex-fiancé, a lawyer, felt the same. All the other parents, besides my sister, pressed charges, and I lost my company and my wealth. But they didn't understand that none of that mattered. I had already lost everything.

As the darkness envelops me, I crumple to my knees, overcome with grief. "Oh Ben," I roar a sad roar, tears uncontrollably falling from my face, my heart aching at the realization that I will never see my son again.

Suddenly, a colossal figure emerges from the void, his skin as black as the abyss. I lift my gaze to meet his, and he extends a massive finger to wipe away my tears. It is none other than the God of Gods.

"You have not forgotten our arrangement, Lionel, my faithful servant?," he intones, his voice booming like thunder.

"No, my Lord, I have not," I reply, chastened for ever doubting him.

With a nod, he turns to depart, and as he raises his right hand, the dark floor opens up beneath me, swallowing me once again. This time, I hurtle through the inky void, hurtling towards the earth's atmosphere.

As I fall, the earth spins below me, upside down and strange. The massive continent of Africa looms largest, while Asia appears as a rival to its size. Finally, I plummet towards a new destination, landing within the body of another man.

The darkness envelops me, but voices echo in the distance. At first, they are incomprehensible, but gradually they grow clearer. "Mun mwe amni amojuja upi chombobo," they say. "Mun mwe amni amo juja upi the vessel." The words are strange, but then they transform into a language I can understand. "He is here!" cries a man with the skin and head of a hyena as a head wear, atop an elephant unlike any I have ever seen. The creature bears a red handprint on its side. African people, bedecked in colorful adornments, surround me.

A woman of my age, though her eyes seem far wiser, silences me with a hushed "shhh." "You have been called," she whispers. Her face was that of a twenty-year-old, but her eyes were that of a forty-year-old woman. Darkness threatens to claim me, but I resist. "No!" I cry out, rising to my feet and taking off. The air is hot and humid, teeming with people and massive elephants. I can run beneath the beasts without even ducking. Everyone watches me as if I am crazy, and the houses resemble small Earthships. A great pond appears, and I begin to slow.

Finally, I understand. "This is FFFHAMS," I realize. And then, I crumple to the ground.

I woke up in an Earthship. It was morning; I didn't just wake up; I was awakened by a collection of beautiful voices coming from outside, "I'm outside," beautiful female voices sang, and followed was a collection of deeper male voices responding, "I'm outside today" The female voices continued singing, "I'm Alright!" and the men responded "I'm Alright today" Then the women sang again, but this time more passionate and louder "I'm Alive," and the men said, "cause I'm outside today" and the song repeated.

Looking around, I saw the woman I had seen earlier bringing me tea. She sat me down, and I asked for a mirror. She said, "sure," and gave me one. I looked into the mirror and saw a face that looked like mine but was not quite mine. She said, "You have been sent to us by God, but you can only travel through time in your ancestors or through your descendants." As I touched my skin, I said, "I traveled through time?" She responded, "Yes!" I rubbed my face and sighed. She looked at me and said, "Here, drink this." I drank it and instantly felt much better. I asked, "What's in this stuff?" She said, "A plant given to us by the god of calm."

"So drugs," I responded, looking her in the eyes. She said, "Lionel, you have much to learn. That's why you're here." "You know my name?" I asked in surprise. "Lionel, God has told us all about your mission, your world, and how the matrix is close to devouring you all."

"My name is Nay Nay," she said, "I am the wife of the man's body you inhabit. We are your ancestors. He is our Shaman, our priest, and our healer. He has given his body to God almighty in order to save his children. My job is to teach you the ways."

I was very confused. "Who's ways?" I asked.

Nay Nay's smile widened. "The way of FFFHAMS, as you would call it."

My eyes widened with surprise. "Wait... So, I was right, this is FFFHAMS?"

"Yes, Lionel," Nay Nay said, nodding. "I must admit this is one of the least developed FFFHAMS, so it puzzles me that you would come here. We have so much work to do, but I will be showing you how life is in God's garden, so you will have the option to accept it. All I ask Lionel is that you respect our ways."

"Yes, ma'am," I said, my excitement growing. I followed Nay Nay out the front door, and my eyes drank in the sights before me. I saw earthships, treehouses, and mud houses, but mostly I saw extremely tiny egg-shaped homes.

"What's that, Nay Nay?" I asked, gesturing to the egg-shaped homes.

Nay Nay smiled. "One of our homes, Sleeping Eggs. Would you like to look around?"

I nodded eagerly, and we approached one of the tiny homes. As I entered the egg-shaped home, I voiced my confusion. "I have to admit, Nay Nay, I am having a hard time wrapping my head around all of this. An entire community living in these...what did you call them?"

"Nay Nay replied with a smile, "Sleeping Eggs... They are sustainable and eco-friendly housing."

"I understand the concept," I replied, "but how do they actually work? I mean, living in such a small space all the time, it sounds like it would be a tight squeeze."

"Oh, it's not as cramped as you might think," Nay Nay said reassuringly. "The design of the Egg is optimized for maximum use of space, and they are equipped with everything you need for comfortable living, including a sleeping area and even a bathroom. Our culture is also very different than yours. We cook our food as a community and only use our homes to sleep in, essentially."

I cleared my throat, feeling a bit foolish for what I was about to ask. "This is going to sound like a dumb question, but..."

Nay Nay smiled kindly. "Go ahead."

"Are these made from real eggs?" I asked, gesturing to the tiny egg-shaped home we were in.

"No, Lionel," Nay Nay replied with a gentle laugh. "They are made of earth, rock, and metals, carefully crafted to form these structures."

I was impressed. "That's incredible. So, tell me, why did the community decide to go this route, to embrace these Sleeping Eggs and live in harmony with the environment like this?"

"This is the way of our ancestors," Nay Nay explained. "We heed their warnings and follow their teachings to preserve the earth and its resources for future generations. We are proud to be a part of this tradition, and living in Sleeping Eggs allows us to do just that."

"I can see that. It's inspiring, to be honest," I admitted, feeling a deep sense of respect for Nay Nay's community. "The commitment to a better future, it's... it's truly something special."

Nay Nay smiled, pleased to see me understand the values of her people. "And that's what makes FFFHAMS so special, Lionel. You will see very advanced technology here, but at our core, we are a community that is deeply connected to our spiritual beliefs and the environment around us. It's a wonderful way of life, and I'm glad you get to experience it."

We leave the sleeping Egg, and I notice Nay Nay is saying hi to everyone, literally every person she sees; she is saying, "Hello, how is everyone" And they are stopping to talk. No one is in a rush, but everyone has somewhere to go. Nay Nay and all of the other women have beautiful decorated hair and faces. They all smell of flowers, oils, and fruit; some wear shoes, most do not; some are dressed very modestly, and others are practically naked; it was strange. Some women were carrying their babies on their backs in these colorful baby carriers. Young children were happily walking with them. All of the women walked with such confidence and had beautiful white smiles; people were so happy that it made me feel a little uncomfortable. I ask her where everyone is headed to?

"We're hunting and foraging," She responded.

I looked at Nay Nay, already anticipating the answer to my next question. I hoped to see if her response lined up with what God had revealed to me. "Why do most of the women here go foraging, and most of the men go hunting and fishing?" I asked, a hint of skepticism in my tone.

"Well, Lionel, it's a community thing. We must eat, and God made our bodies for walking and running, so we hunt and gather not only to eat but also to keep the evil spirits out of our bodies. We maintain the good spirits in us that keep us healthy and prevent chronic illnesses from creeping in," Nay Nay explained, her voice patient and calm.

I frowned, still not entirely convinced. "I don't get it. Why is it that men are encouraged to hunt, and women are encouraged to gather? Isn't that a bit oppressive?" I asked, curious if Nay Nay's community was different from those of my time.

"It's about utility, Lionel. It has nothing to do with oppression or subservience. It's about what enables the best chances of survival and thriving. In most societies, men mostly hunt, and women mostly gather. But it's a mistake to assume that this pattern is related to your myths of male or female superiority, which was born of assumptions, not careful empirical research," Nay Nay replied, her words thoughtful and measured.

"But what about children? Isn't that a factor?" I asked.

Nay Nay nodded. "Yes, children are a factor. In societies around the world, pregnant or lactating women do not often hunt, and those with dependents who do wish to hunt only hunt when there are enough people around to watch their children. Men's hunting is risky, meaning it carries a high chance of failure, so they tend to hunt alone or in small groups and target big game with projectile weapons, while the few women who do want to hunt prefer to hunt in groups and focus on smaller, easier-to-capture prey closer to the houses, often with the aid of a predator," Nay Nay explained.

I listened attentively as Nay Nay spoke, her words laced with wisdom and understanding. "I see. And what about gathering? Why would women choose not to hunt altogether?" I asked, curious to know more about their way of life.

"Gathering is demanding work, Lionel. It requires extensive ecological knowledge and skill that is socially learned and cultivated over a lifetime, just like hunting. Hunter-gatherers face tough choices about how to divide their time and effort, so it pays to specialize. Women's decisions to hunt less than the men is a rational decision about allocating effort, taking into account modest comparative advantages in speed and strength and the incompatibilities posed by having little babies who need you to nurse or to be safe," Nay Nay replied.

Her words were like music to my ears, a harmonious melody of rationality and balance. For the first time, I saw the logic in their way of life. I was silent for a moment, taking in everything she had said, my mind racing with new thoughts and perspectives. "I see. Thank you, Nay Nay, for explaining all of this to me. It's been a real eye-opener," I said, grateful for the knowledge she had imparted on me.

"You're welcome, Lionel. I'm here to help in any way I can," Nay Nay replied. I followed Nay Nay through the community, marveling at the unique customs and lifestyle of her people. Suddenly, from out of the food forest came an enormous elephant, towering over us at a staggering 15 feet tall and weighing at least 20 to 30,000 pounds. The beast began to charge towards us, causing me to instinctively jump in front of Nay Nay to protect her. But instead of being alarmed, Nay

Nay sucked her teeth and exclaimed, "Man, don't you know this is my best friend, Kofa?"

I was taken aback, struggling to comprehend how she could remain so calm in the face of an oncoming elephant. "But Nay Nay, it's an elephant charging at us," I replied, my concern palpable.

"Please, friend, respect our ways," Nay Nay said, and I obediently moved aside.

To my surprise, the giant elephant was very happy to see Nay Nay, and she was equally happy to see it. The elephant lifted her up onto its back, and she asked, "Kofa, can you lift the guy down there up here with us?" The elephant turned its gaze to me, appearing confused, but Nay Nay quickly explained, "He looks like him, but he is not. He is my descendant from tens of thousands of years in the future, you see...."

The elephant then grabbed me with its trunk, and I scrambled up onto its back. As we began to walk, Nay Nay continued foraging with the elephant's help, using its impressive height to reach the highest fruit. "The elephants come once a month," Nay Nay explained. "They help us get ripe fruit that is too dangerous to get otherwise."

I noticed a red handprint on the elephant's side and asked Nay Nay about it. "What's that red handprint?" I queried.

"That handprint is mine," Nay Nay replied. "It's not permanent. We have to reapply it every year if Kofa doesn't refuse."

"But why is it there?" I asked with great curiosity.

"Well, you know what a predator pact is, right?" Nay Nay asked me.

"Yes, I'm familiar," I replied.

"Well, this is similar. Other than us, nothing else hunts elephants. Some people in this particular community do not believe we should eat or hunt the elephant, but others, like the neighboring community, do not agree. They said it supplies too much food. They also argue that if they were to stop hunting them, they would overpopulate because we are its only predator. No other creature is capable of taking down such a large animal," Nay Nay explained.

"I see so that hand print serves as protection?" I confidently responded.

"Yes, Lionel. It means they are a citizen of this particular community in FFFHAMS and are not to be hunted," Nay Nay confirmed.

As we rode through the community on the back of the giant elephant, I couldn't help but take in the sights around me. The women in the community were all so beautiful, with different shades of brown skin that was so smooth. Their eyes were full of life, and their smiles were pretty as the stars. They all had bodies like track stars, and their voices... they all sang in such harmony and joy, it was like a walking choir. Those who were not singing were laughing and talking to each other, all while carrying giant baskets of fruit. They didn't even know how strong they were.

But despite the beauty around me, I was getting bored. I knew there was so much more to see. I turned to Nay Nay and said, "I'll be back." Then, I slid down the elephant's head and trunk. "Be careful, man," she warned.

With that, I decided to go on a walk and explore the community on my own.

The beauty and majesty of the forest was truly overwhelming. My feet sunk into the dark, black soil as I made my way through the thick foliage. It was difficult to navigate with all the fruit and leaves covering every inch of every space. I understood now why everyone walked on the path. As I walked, I couldn't resist taking an apple and taking a bite. The juice rushed through my mouth and throat, and a sweetness like no other slowly made its way down my tongue as the crunch went through my jaw. "Small yet satisfying," I thought to myself.

The forest was alive with the sound of birds, some of which I had never seen before. Suddenly, I stopped dead in my tracks. The hairs on my neck raised, and my heart beat faster as I felt eyes piercing my body. I heard a deep, loud purr and looked behind me to see large feline eyes staring back at me. Without a second thought, I ran as fast as I could.

I couldn't believe the speed at which my feet were moving. It was as if this body was something else entirely. I climbed easier, jumped higher, and ran faster than I ever had before. I could even see the outer space that surrounded the forest. Suddenly, I felt fur on my back and realized that the large feline had caught me. I fell to the ground just outside the forest, preparing myself for the worst.

I looked up to see a giant lion over top of me and screamed, "You'll have to fight for this meal!" Then I heard laughter. I looked around and saw that it was Nay Nay and her friends.

Nay Nay calmly spoke, "The vessel you are in is that Barbary Lion's best friend. His name is San." I stood up quickly, excited to meet the great lion. San came closer, and we embraced. His massive form was awe-inspiring, and I couldn't believe I was in the presence of such a majestic creature. He purred contentedly before turning back towards the forest. "You have a predator pact with the lions?" I said in complete surprise.

Nay Nay replied, "Yeah, we have been doing this for thousands of years, so the days of only having predator pacts with small predators are long behind us. We have fine-tuned our ways."

Suddenly, a loud scream pierced through the peaceful forest. Nay Nay's face grew serious, and she said, "Come." We all ran on foot, and Nay Nay whistled for a dog with a health pack on its back to follow us. As we ran, she gave the dog hand signals to run in the direction of the scream.

When we arrived, I saw a giant carcass. It was gray and large, difficult to make out at first because its rear was facing us. But as I saw the faded handprint on it, I knew exactly what it was. A woman wearing an albino hyena's head on her own head stood over the giant animal, weeping desperately. Half of her body and face were covered in blood, and she clutched an arrow in her hand. The other women circled the elephant with tears streaming down their faces.

Several dogs with health aid packs on their backs were also there. The dogs were incredible, with muscular frames, deep chests, defined shoulder blades, and well-muscled hind legs. Their short, dense coats ranged from fawn to mahogany in color, with natural black masks covering even their ears.

As we stood there in silence, the weight of the tragedy was almost too much to bear. The men arrived and, upon seeing the elephant carcass, were frozen in disbelief. The same man who had been on the elephant with me when I first arrived exclaimed, "Who did this!" But Nay Nay, always wise and steady, spoke up, "We will stay calm, and we will deal with it the way our ancestors would."

The woman, still wearing the albino hyena's head, stood weeping over the giant animal, her body covered in blood and tears. The elders approached the elephant and guided the woman down, as she was almost unable to walk from the weight of her sorrow. The women gathered around the elephant, their tears falling onto the gray skin of the massive creature.

The elephants themselves seemed to be mourning as they gathered around the carcass in a solemn procession. The entire atmosphere was suffused with an overwhelming sense of grief and loss, and I, too, found myself crying for this being and the sadness its death had caused.

After the elephant burial, the night settled in, and the stars emerged; I sat with Nay Nay, my mind still grappling with the events of the day. I turned to her with a furrowed brow and asked, "Nay Nay, I'm confused. Everywhere I look, I see people treating elephants like they're royalty. What are the cultural values and beliefs of your society?"

Nay Nay, with her calm and soothing voice, responded, "Our society is based on the principles of FFFHAMS. It's all about living in harmony with nature and with one another. And that means not only treating each other with respect but also treating the animals that share this world with us with respect as well."

I struggled to understand. "I don't see how that's possible. How can you treat an animal with the same respect as a human being?"

"To us, all life is sacred," Nay Nay replied. "We understand that everything in this world is connected and that we are all part of the same greater whole. But, as I told you before, this particular community perceives elephants like we do humans and lions."

"But what about the other community that killed the elephant today?" I asked, still troubled by what I had witnessed.

"Those who break our sacred laws understand that their actions have consequences, not just for the animal they harm, but for the balance of our society as a whole," Nay Nay explained.

"And what about when you have disagreements with each other?" I inquired. "How do you resolve those conflicts?"

"We have a process for resolving disputes," Nay Nay replied. "Through strategic athletic mind games and, if necessary, Bloodsport. But it's all done in a spirit of fairness and respect. We understand that, in the end, we're all part of the same greater whole and that we must find a way to coexist peacefully."

"I'm still skeptical," I admitted. "This all seems too good to be true."

Nay Nay smiled gently. "I understand that. But I promise you, if you open your heart and mind, you will come to understand the beauty of our way of life. Just remember, always go back to the root; go back to FFFHAMS.

As I lay in my little Egg that night, I was consumed with thought. I couldn't help but feel bad that Nay Nay had to sleep alone, but deep down, I knew that she would prefer it since her husband wasn't here. I tried to sleep, but that sound - that sound of sadness - was far too familiar. I couldn't help but think about my sister coming to me after finding out the news. She screamed the saddest scream, her agony turning into tears, knowing she would never see her son again.

I knew I should have waited, but I was hurting so bad and full of guilt that I had to tell her. "Sis, Ben is dead because of me," I said. She backed away, and then I continued, "I gave him the key to the yacht; he didn't sneak it out." The sound of her slap echoed through my empty house. I was shocked, her eyes full of rage. She began to walk out, and I said, "Sister, please." She turned and said, "Stay away from me, Lionel, for your own good."

"B-ba-but sis, you're the only family I have left; we're all we got," I said, crying. "Ben was all I had...You took that away from me. I won't be pressing charges, but so help me, Lionel, if you even look at me..." She didn't finish; she just wept and ran to her car.

I couldn't help but think, "Why did God choose me? Why am I here in this beautiful place? I don't deserve this."

The drums and the chanting roused me from my slumber in the Sleeping Egg. As I emerge from my cocoon-like abode, I witness the community bustling about and heading toward a central space where the two communities intersect. A group of fierce-looking men and women, who seem to be guardians, are in deep conversation with Nay Nay and a man. As Nay Nay calls the wronged woman over, the man calls upon a young teenager... A very young man joined them. He looked like Ben's age but was bigger than me. I assume he is the one who killed the elephant. The guardians lead both of them away, and Nay Nay approaches me with an air of urgency.

"If they cannot talk out this tragedy, then we must go to war," Nay Nay declares, her voice heavy with determination.

I nod in agreement but can't help but wonder, "But what is the point of going to war? What will you get if your side wins?"

"In your time, when you kill each other, what do you get?" Nay Nay counters, her tone still resolute.

"We get to do whatever we wanted to do in the first place," I respond, somewhat ashamed of the truth in my words.

"Here, we do not aim to kill one another. We aim to learn from one another. Witu and the young man will talk. They will either understand each other and come to terms, or they will disagree on what should happen next. If they cannot agree, then their communities will rally by their side and compete. Whichever side wins the most competitions gets to decide how the wrong will be righted. However, the decision on what happens is made as a community. We vote on the best way. If the person who was wronged loses or is still not at peace, they may fight the other in unarmed hand-to-hand combat."

I look at Nay Nay, a furrow forming between my brows. "But she's so small, and he's so big, not to mention she's a woman."

"Nay Nay interrupts, "I do not need you to explain human anatomy and biology, Lionel. In this community, we do not believe anyone should hit each other, but if they decide this is the way they want to do it, we regulate it and make sure it's as safe as possible. This stops people from seeking revenge. Let's just hope it doesn't come to that."

"Nay Nay seemed concerned, so I backed off; she seemed to care for Witu. I went for a walk to give her some space. It was pretty empty in the community; everyone was out hunting and gathering for another feast. The feast last night was like I'd never seen. It was like a cookout, pool party, or festival concert. Weird but deeply enjoyable. There wasn't any alcohol anywhere, at least not to drink. I'm pretty sure it's forbidden, "which is interesting," I think to myself, "because they eat so many "conscious altering plants" that is how Nay Nay explained it. She also told me that there were spirits and gods in the plants."

I walked until I stumbled upon what looked to be their community center. As I entered the community center, I noticed how well-organized and clean everything was. Despite being an ancient society, they had the latest technological advancements, including a 3D printer that took center stage in the room. I was completely caught off guard by this discovery. A 3 in 1 3D printer, capable of printing all the essential things they needed to remain independent from any civilization.

The 3D printer was an impressive feat of engineering, and it was being used to create a solar-powered grid for FFFHAMS. It was equipped with photovoltaic cells to convert sunlight into electricity and conductive materials like copper or aluminum for wiring. It was printing structural components of the solar panels, such as frames and mounting brackets, in a range of materials like metal.

It was then that I noticed wind power technology being printed as well. The printer was capable of producing the parts for wind turbines, such as blades, generators, and towers. And it was used to create water filtration systems, with the metal parts of the filters being printed as well.

Not only was this 3D printer being used for practical applications, but it was also printing small electronic devices. The structural components of these devices, such as the frame and housing, could be printed in a wide range of materials.

As I observed the printer in action, it was clear that this machine was not a one-trick pony. It could be used with various printing methods, including Fused Deposition Modeling, Stereolithography, Material Extrusion, Directed Energy Deposition, or Polyjet printing methods, depending on the specific application and properties required for the final printed product. And it wasn't just synthetic materials that it could print with, but it could also use bio-based materials and other organic materials that could be sustainably sourced and processed.

It was an incredible display of technology, and I felt lucky to be able to witness it firsthand. I stood there for hours, captivated by the possibilities of what could be created using this incredible machine.

People were returning to the community. Some were walking into the building I was already in. The sounds of drums and singing echoed through the community as people returned from their morning hunting and foraging. The atmosphere felt like an endless summer day festival, with joy and celebration palpable in the air. Just as the previous day, once everyone had finished their work, they all came together to help prepare the food and watch over the children. As I walked out of the community center, I was met with the sight of every child being watched by a nearby adult and everyone going about their chosen tasks with enthusiasm and dedication.

The morning slowly turned into the afternoon, and as the food approached readiness, the musicians began to tune their instruments and practice their performance. The people who enjoyed cooking helped set the tables, while those who preferred to play sports were out on the field, kicking balls around. Some people were painting, while others were in the tech center, working on new technologies for the group. I was thoroughly impressed by the amount of freedom everyone had in choosing how to spend their time. I couldn't help but wonder out loud, "Is this how they spend every day."

Suddenly, a feminine voice broke me out of my thoughts. "Pretty much, but you do have your days when no one feels like doing anything," she said. I turned to see Witu, the woman whom Nay Nay had mentioned earlier. She continued, "So, you're the one using the shaman."

I hesitated before responding. "I wouldn't call it that."

I could see the pain and grief in her piercing, wide eyes, and I asked, "Are you okay?"

With those deep beautiful eyes, she looked at me and said, "Oh, yeah... I'm as fine as one can be. I decided to declare war on the neighboring community..." She trailed off, and I could tell that she was still struggling with the loss of her friend. I decided to simply listen.

"I'll probably let this progress into a blood sport," she continued. "He needs to be taught a lesson for what he did to Elsa."

I couldn't help but feel concerned for Witu. "But he's a big guy. Men tend to be stronger than women," I pointed out.

Witu seemed unfazed. "You do understand that everyone here knows the human body inside and out, right? We all have to learn before we turn 16."

I was surprised by this. "Really? Do you all go to school?"

"School? "What's school?" Witu asked, her curiosity piqued. "Wait, how do you all know so much without school?" We had a long discussion, and we became fast friends. Witu taught me how they learned in FFFHAMS. There were no schools, no punishments or time outs, and children learned from constantly being around adults. Whether it was watching and helping with cooking, hunting, foraging, fishing, 3D printers, house construction, and more, the children were involved in everything.

At age 16, men and women underwent a rite of passage that reviewed all they had learned and tested them on it. They had to know how to build FFFHAMS from scratch, how to hunt and forage, how to heal and perform surgery on the human body, how to build sustainable homes, and how to construct 3D printers, solar panels, and wind turbines. If they couldn't demonstrate this knowledge, they would have to keep undergoing the rite of passage until they could, and only then would they be considered an adult.

I taught her about the Matrix and how terrible it was compared to this place. She was horrified but ultimately entertained, and we laughed about everything happening in our crazy lives. I asked her where she stayed, and she said, "Your ways are so silly. I'm unmarried, so I haven't built my own home yet. I stay where I please; all of these homes are ours."

"Sorry if I have insulted you," I said.

"Sorry?" she replied, "You truly are strange. Whether I am married does not define me or any woman here, for that matter. I marry who I want when I want, and as long as I'm useful to my people, what else matters?"

Witu and I had been talking for hours, laughing and sharing stories about our lives. I was fascinated by these people and their culture. They had a way of life that was so different from anything I had ever experienced before.

Suddenly, Nay Nay arrived and interrupted our conversation. There seemed to be some tension between her and Witu. Witu stood up and said, "Please excuse me," to Nay Nay, who replied, "You're excused, my love." Witu then walked off into the festival.

Curious about what had just happened, I turned to Nay Nay and asked, "What was that all about?"

Nay Nay sighed and explained, "That was my best friend, Witu. She was supposed to be my husband's second wife, but it didn't work out."

I was taken aback by this revelation. "Can you tell me what happened?"

Nay Nay explained, "It all has to do with our community's views on love and marriage. You see, we believe that the union of two, three, or even four people can bring balance and harmony to the community. And that's why we practice both monogamy and polygyny here."

I was intrigued. "That's fascinating. Where I'm from, polygamy of any sort is wrong and evil. Women are pretty much coerced into it."

Nay Nay continued, "Here, women initiate polygyny when they feel that they need additional support in their lives, either in terms of resources, companionship, or both. Sometimes they want to help their friend find a partner, and at times it's just because they all love one another. And this is what I wanted to do with Witu. I wanted her to be my sister-wife."

I knew where this was going. "But your husband..."

"He did not agree," Nay Nay said, "He wasn't comfortable with the idea of having another wife. And while I respect his decision, it did cause some tension between us."

I understood the difficult situation. "That's understandable. It's not easy to make such a big change in your marriage."

Nay Nay replied, "Yes, it's important to remember that in our community, marriage is not forced and is always based on mutual agreement between all parties involved. That's why men and women who are interested in a marriage must undergo a series of tests to determine their compatibility with the existing partners. These tests are designed to ensure that all partners in the marriage are able to work together harmoniously and that their relationships are based on mutual respect and love. They must decide at the end of it."

I was impressed. "That's amazing. This community truly values love and harmony."

Nay Nay smiled. "Absolutely. We believe that love and relationships are essential to maintaining balance and harmony in the community and that everyone has a role to play in this process. By allowing women to initiate polygyny and by ensuring that all marriages are based on mutual agreement and love, we create a community that is harmonious, balanced, and full of love. And even though Witu and I couldn't be sister wives, I still consider her a valuable member of our community, and I will always love and respect her."

I felt a sense of respect and admiration towards Nay Nay and her community. "Nay Nay, I can see why you are such a valuable member of this community."

Nay Nay wanted to take me over to the festival, but noticing all the solar panels covering the homes, I asked if she could show me their grid. She agreed, and I was walking around studying its different parts and asked, "So, tell me again," my brow furrowed with skepticism. "How does this solar power grid work?"

Nay Nay smiled, "It's actually quite simple, Lionel. You see, it all starts with the solar panels. They're responsible for converting sunlight into electricity."

I was skeptical about her knowledge of it, "Really? That's it?"

Nay Nay chuckled, "Well, there's a bit more to it than that, but yes, that's the basic idea. The panels are made of photovoltaic cells, composed of semiconductor materials. When sunlight falls on the cells, it creates an electric current that is then sent to the inverter."

My expression softened as Nay Nay continued to explain, "The inverter is an electronic device that converts the direct current electricity produced by the solar panels into alternating current electricity, which is what we use in our homes and community centers. It also ensures that the voltage and frequency of the electricity generated by the solar panels are in line with the electrical grid."

As we approached the heart of the power grid, Nay Nay gestured to the battery storage system. "Some solar power grids like ours also have a battery storage system. It allows excess electricity generated by the solar panels to be stored for later use, smoothing out any fluctuations in electricity production and ensuring there's always electricity, even when the sun isn't shining."

Having a very deep background in battery storage, I was beginning to realize just how much she knew, my awe growing with each step. "And what about the electrical panel?" I asked, pointing.

"The electrical panel distributes the electricity generated by the solar panels to different parts of the building. It includes breakers or fuses that protect the system from overloading and other electrical issues."

Nay Nay continued, "Wiring connects all the components of the solar power grid, making sure electricity is distributed safely and efficiently. And finally, we have a meter to measure the amount of electricity generated and consumed by the building or property, giving us an idea of how much energy we're saving and how much we're sending back to the electrical grid."

I was impressed, "And the monitoring system, what does that do?"

"Ah, yes," Nay Nay said, her eyes alight with excitement. "The monitoring system allows for real-time monitoring and analysis of the performance of the system. This information can be used to identify any issues with the solar panels, inverter, or other components and to optimize the performance of the system over time."

The two of us stood in silence for a moment, taking in the hum of the power grid. My mind was racing with the possibilities, "It's incredible. Clean, renewable energy that reduces dependence on fossil fuels and helps protect the environment. My company used to create power storage for this type of thing."

Nay Nay nodded, "While I'm not completely sure of what a company is, this is a fundamental part of our community, Lionel. Everyone here must understand the technology; it's a right of passage. We all have a responsibility to ensure it continues to run smoothly and efficiently. So it can be passed on to the next generation."

Nay Nay and I were walking through the festival, taking in all the sights and sounds of the vibrant community. I was in awe of everything around me and was constantly asking Nay Nay questions about the different elements.

As we passed by a home surrounded by lush green plants, my curiosity got the better of me. "Nay Nay, why are all the homes here surrounded by plants?" I asked.

Nay Nay smiled and replied, "Those plants serve a very important purpose. The mint and lemon grass you smell keeps unwanted creatures and spirits away. They are part of a medicinal permaculture garden that grows in front of the home, the back of the home, and even inside the home. The garden is meant to be self-sustaining by incorporating various permaculture design principles and techniques."

It's a way of gardening that mimics the natural ecosystems found in nature, using techniques like companion planting, vertical gardening, water collection and management, soil improvement, indoor gardening, and edible landscaping. Each element is designed to work together in a symbiotic relationship to create a sustainable, self-sufficient garden."

"Wow," I said, clearly impressed. "And what do you mean by companion planting?"

"Companion planting is when different species of plants are grown together in a way that benefits each other," Nay Nay explained. "For example, taller plants can provide shade for shorter plants, while some plants can improve soil fertility for others. In a medicinal permaculture garden, this can involve planting medicinal herbs alongside vegetables, fruit trees, and other plants."

I nodded, intrigued. "And what of those plants up there?"

"Vertical gardening involves growing plants up, rather than out, using structures like trellises and fences," Nay Nay said. "This is particularly useful in small gardens and helps to maximize space and increase yields."

"Do you use any type of water collection management?" I asked.

"In a permaculture garden, water is collected and managed in a way that minimizes waste and maximizes efficiency," Nay Nay replied. "We use rain barrels or other containers to collect rainwater or incorporate swales and other earthworks to slow and capture runoff."

I nodded, taking it all in. "And what about the soil?"

"Soil health is critical in permaculture gardening, and soil improvement techniques like composting, mulching, and adding organic matter can help to build healthy soil that supports plant growth," Nay Nay said.

I was stunned and smiled, grateful for Nay Nay's patience and knowledge.

She takes me to the top of the community center. She says, "Since I was just a young woman, my husband and I, even Witu, would come up here to look over FFFHAMS and marvel at its beauty.

As I look, I can feel a sense of wonder and awe growing inside of me. From this vantage point, I am able to take in the full majesty of the FFFHAMS. This embodies the essence of wonder and beauty of humanity and earth.

The FFFHAMS is nestled in a lush valley, surrounded by towering mountains, with a river winding its way through the heart of the community, which is the giant food forest and lake. The scenery alone is enough to take my breath away, but as I look closer, I see the intricate, interconnected systems that make up this unique and thriving place.

From the Food forest they hunt and forage in and rainwater harvesting to the reliance on renewable energy sources, such as solar panels and wind turbines, the FFFHAMS is a true testament to the power of human ingenuity and innovation.

But what I truly marveled over was the sense of community that pervades every aspect of life here. The people of the FFFHAMS are deeply connected to one another and to the land, working together to create a self-sufficient and sustainable society. They have a strong sense of interdependence and mutual aid, and their relationships and networks of support are built through shared meals, festivals, and other social events. It had to be over thirty-thousand people living throughout these different communities.

And yet, despite all of this, the FFFHAMS remain humble and grounded, with a deep respect for the natural world and a commitment to environmental stewardship. It is a place of balance, where humans and nature coexist in harmony, and it fills me with a sense of awe and inspiration to see it with my own eyes.

As I stand there, looking out over the FFFHAMS, I am struck by a sense of wonder and gratitude. This place is a true gem, the garden... God's home. "Come, Lionel," a voice snaps me out of my awe. It's Nay Nay; she is holding her hand out. I take her hand. She leads me back outside and to a large gathering of people in a giant circle. It seemed to be all the adults. Maybe a few 17-year-olds. The older children were now watching the younger children.

I was welcomed with open arms by the people of the community, who invited me to sit down. Some took their places on chairs, while others sat on mats or at tables. We were all had a meal of delicious-smelling food, filled with fresh vegetables and fruit, with little meat to be seen. In the center of this circle was a roaring fire, casting shadows and light across the faces of those gathered around it.

As we ate and talked, a man stood up and asked if all the people from neighboring communities could go, for it was time to talk about Witu. I observed as everyone respectfully finished their meals, and the people from the other communities began to leave the gathering.

As the circle thinned, Witu emerged from the darkness, entering the circle and taking a seat cross-legged. She greeted everyone with a smile and showed her respect to the people gathered around the fire. It was clear that she was well-liked and respected by her community, and I felt grateful to be able to witness their way of life.

The meeting starts with a prayer.

Source, The All, Existence, The God, we come to you today as the FFFHAMS people of the south, a community with a rich and unique cultural heritage that dates back thousands of years. We are proud to be a part of a tradition that values our connection with the natural world and our ancestors. That believes in your bounty, my God.

We know you are The All and that all living beings are connected and interdependent. Let this be reflected in our daily lives, and we are grateful for the way it enriches our spiritual practices.

We come to you today to give thanks for the ancestors who have come before us and continue to exist in the spiritual realm and in our DNA. We believe that they offer us guidance, wisdom, and protection, and we honor them by performing rituals and keeping their memories alive.

We also thank you for the blessings of the natural world and the animals that share our community. We consider them to be citizens of our community, and we believe that they play an important role in maintaining balance in the ecosystem. We communicate with them and treat them with respect and dignity.

Thanks to you, our technology is sustainable and respectful of the environment, and we use our deep understanding of the natural world to create technology that supports biodiversity. We wish to emphasize community, cooperation, and interdependence, and we believe that everyone has something valuable to offer.

One God Above All, we come to you today to seek your guidance and blessings. We believe that through our spiritual practices, such as meditation and offerings, we can communicate with you and the spirits. We ask that you continue to guide us in our journey and help us to live in harmony with the world around us.

We are grateful for your love and grace, and we pray that you continue to bless us and our community. From you all is. I am because We are!

The people responded proudly, "We are because I am."

They gathered around a circle, discussing Witu's dilemma. Each person had five minutes to express their thoughts and opinions on the matter. The decision was critical since Witu had declined the offer made by the teenage Boy and his community. We had to agree if we would back Witu or not. If we didn't support her, there would be no competition, and she would be forced to settle for what was already offered to her, or fight a 25-minute battle sanctioned by both communities, or even move to a different community within FFFHAMS.

Finally, it was time for a vote, and the process was unique. We used two berries, one pink and one blue. If the majority of berries remaining in the bowl were pink, Witu would win, and if the majority were blue, she would not. Everyone voted by taking a berry from the bowl, without revealing their choice, and eating it.

When the bowl was passed to Witu, there was silence and anticipation. Then she smiled and began to eat the pink berries, crushed some in her hand, painted her face quickly as she stood, she proclaimed, "We go to war!" Everyone cheered as pink juice bled down her arms from her clenched fist.

As I sat among the community members, I asked Nay Nay about the games they played. She responded, detailing the three games they played, Strategic Arena, Gooker, and Bloodsport. Though the prospect of the final game made me anxious, I couldn't help but admire their dedication to these games. Witu and the Boy would be coaching while the communities competed on the field.

That night, I lay in bed, thoughts of the day's events swimming in my head. Belina's smile and Max's newfound confidence played on my mind, and I sighed as I rolled over, hoping for a good night's rest. The next morning, I awoke early to the sound of silence, the sun barely peeking over the horizon. I wiped my face, took a shower, and settled down in front of the sleeping Egg.

I continued to follow the community's preparations as the days wore on. I watched as they readied a space for a lioness to have her cubs and watched as they meditated in the peaceful morning air. The games came and went, and though Witu suffered two losses, she refused to yield and now prepared for the final event, the Bloodsport.

As I walked around the community, I couldn't help but feel fascinated by the families I encountered. Nay Nay had tasked me with observing their family dynamics to see how they all helped each other, not just the husbands, wives, and children, but even their brothers, sisters, grandmothers, and grandfathers.

I was no stranger to families, but these two families were unlike any I had ever seen before. Bune and Tu were a monogamous couple, and Sol, Ya, and Gie were a polygynous family. What struck me was the way they all worked together seamlessly, with each member having their unique role and contribution.

It was heartwarming to see even the youngest ones eager to help without any toys or incentives. They would stop what they were doing to assist, and the joy it brought them was evident. Even the parents made sure to teach the children how to help and gave them the confidence to do so. They never discouraged their children from helping, and if a task was too difficult, they would break it down into smaller parts that the child could manage.

The older the child, the more their responsibilities increased, and the frequency of requests decreased. With the guidance and patience of their parents, they learned how to be more effective helpers and became more confident in their abilities. The parents never made the tasks too easy, but they also didn't overburden the children. Working as a team was always emphasized, not working alone. I couldn't help but feel a sense of admiration for these families and the way they operated.

As I observed the families around me, I couldn't help but be amazed by their approach to parenting. Unlike the parents in my world, who often act as entertainers for their children, these parents encouraged their children to be involved in their lives and work. With fewer toys and distractions, the children grew more interested in their parent's activities and developed valuable life skills. Even the younger children were exposed to the adult world, with the older children given opportunities to plan their own activities and handle adult tasks.

But what struck me most was the parents' approach to motivation. They didn't outright reject their children's requests but instead worked with them to figure out a feasible way to fulfill their needs. The reward wasn't tied to specific tasks but to the child's overall helpfulness and the development of their behavior and emotional skills. Negotiating and nagging were not part of their parenting strategy; instead, the parents made requests, and if the children refused, they simply waited or walked away.

I was also impressed by the way the parents controlled their anger toward their children. They recognized that anger was unproductive and only built tension, causing a vicious cycle of anger between parent and child. Instead, they practiced calming techniques like taking a break or changing their perspective. Then, they calmly explained the child's mistakes and how it affected the world around them. By letting go of their anger, the parents could maintain productivity and communication with their children.

As I watched these families, I couldn't help but wonder what my own childhood would have been like if my parents had followed such an approach. But here, in this world, I was surrounded by parents who truly understood the importance of raising capable, empathetic, and responsible children.

The parents knew that children's emotional intelligence was often overestimated and that it was developed over time through practice and modeling. They were patient and kind, and their children were growing up to be well-rounded, helpful individuals. I was grateful for the opportunity to observe these families, and I left with a newfound appreciation for the power of parenting and family dynamics.

During my stay in this unique community, I experienced things I never thought possible. I hunted giant deer and ate meat from birds I had never known existed. I swam in beautiful ponds with colorful fish and witnessed Nay Nay deliver a baby and perform surgery with such ease and grace. I made friends of all kinds, but one, in particular, stood out to me.

As I spent time with my friend from another community, I noticed something different about him. He didn't use any words to describe it, but to me, it was clear that he was attracted to men. I was curious about how FFFHAMS, a community that valued freedom and respect, viewed homosexuality.

"Nay Nay," I began, "this place is quite different from what I'm used to. The way you all live in harmony with the land, it's truly remarkable. But, I have to ask, what is the stance on homosexuality here in FFFHAMS?"

Nay Nay's eyes sparkled with the wisdom of the ages as she replied, "Lionel, the FFFHAMS people have always believed in freedom and respect. If someone is attracted to the same gender, that is the same as a woman who doesn't forage - they are different. But the difference is not our weakness. As long as it doesn't interfere with our way, it is a strength. Creation, or what your people call evolution, can only take place if some things are different."

I nodded thoughtfully. "I have a friend who is gay, and I have no problem with it. I just thought since it's so rare here, that FFFHAMS might not allow it."

"We do not dictate who should be with who, Lionel. That is not for us to decide," Nay Nay explained. "It is about respect and following our ways. This man you speak of, he is the first in hundreds of years, but he won't be the last."

I was impressed with Nay Nay's words. "I see. It's just so different from what I'm used to. Back home, some people are not accepted for who they are."

"We do not oppress here in FFFHAMS, Lionel. We liberate. We believe in self-governance and collective decision-making, and we place a strong emphasis on community and cooperation. Everyone has something valuable to offer, regardless of what makes us different from one another." Nay Nay's voice was strong and resolute, and I knew I could trust in her wisdom.

Back home, people who were different were often not accepted. But here in FFFHAMS, everyone had something valuable to offer, regardless of their differences. The community was built on self-governance, collective decision-making, and a strong emphasis on community and cooperation. It was clear that they believed in liberation, not oppression.

I was taken aback by their perspective. FFFHAMS was an ancient community, yet they seemed socially and technologically far beyond anything I had ever experienced. It truly amazed me. One day, I saw Witu sneaking off to what looked like a secret door. I followed her, my curiosity getting the better of me.

As I stepped down into the underground space, I saw a see-through glass that let the sun's rays shine down on a Food Forest. The air was fresh and cool, and I could hear the sound of water trickling in the distance. The walls of the underground chamber were covered with lush greenery, and I could see fruit trees, berry bushes, and all manner of vegetables growing.

I walked down the aisle, admiring the beauty of the Food Forest. The plants were healthy and abundant, and I could see how the community had made the most of the space. The Food Forest was not only a source of nourishment for the people of FFFHAMS, but it was also a place of pride and community.

As I explored further, I discovered that the Food Forest was connected to a network of underground homes. These homes were carved into the earth and blended seamlessly into the landscape. I could see how they provided shelter and comfort while also preserving the natural beauty of the land.

I hear a woman's voice say, "It's for emergencies" I responded, "you all created this as well?"

Witu let out a sarcastic laugh as she looked over at me, "So, let me get this straight," she said with a smirk on her face. "You thought that 30,000 people with all the time in the world wouldn't create an underground backup FFFHAMS with a massive food forest capable of feeding 60,000 people? Don't you all have contingency plans for when The Devils from the skies hit Gaia?"

She paused, looking around at the towering trees and thriving crops. "Well, I'm here to tell you, my friend, that this is an impressive feat of engineering and sustainability. It's like a little underground world, complete with everything you could ever need."

Witu gestured to the interconnected tunnels and caverns that made up the community. "We've got the Earthships and Sleeping Eggs, with all the comforts of home. And, of course, the star of the show is this food forest," she continued, sweeping her hand over the massive greenhouse. "It's a self-sustaining ecosystem, where the waste produced by the plants and animals is recycled to provide nutrients for future growth. Plus, there are birds, deer, and fish providing the other animals and us with all the protein we need to survive as a unified ecosystem."

Witu let out a huff of laughter. "And let's not forget the backup solar grid, which will keep us powered in the event of a Devil ball impact that makes the surface uninhabitable. Because, you know, we wouldn't want to be without our lights in the middle of a disaster, would we?"

She turned to me, a playful glint in her eye. "So, what do you think? Impressed?"

"Yeah, I'm impressed. You knew I was following you?" "Lionel I led you here," Witu replied. I stood confused. Witu said, "I wanted to talk to you, just in case I don't make it in the fight tomorrow." I looked down and said, "Why are you doing this, Witu? It's not smart,"

Witu said, "Have you ever lost someone?" I thought of Ben, mom, and dad. I looked at her. She replied, "So you have." For you, some animal died becuase in your world, your people know not of the gods; they can't see the spirit in all that surrounds them. But for me, she was my best friend; her life was just getting good."

I stepped back from Witu and found a seat on a large rock, taking a deep breath to steady my nerves. As we spoke, I couldn't help but admire her strength and determination. "So what did you even demand?" I asked her.

Witu's gaze met mine, her eyes fierce with conviction. "My demand was simple," she replied. "Their community should join ours in swearing not to ever hunt elephants and to treat them as equals."

I shook my head at her stubbornness, feeling a sense of familiarity. "You remind me of someone," I told her.

Witu smirked at my words, teasingly asking, "I hope she's pretty?"

"She is," I replied, "but that's not the point. Witu, I'll be there at this fight, but I hope you'll consider pulling out."

Witu's eyes grew cold as she looked through my soul and said, "Never." I could see the determination etched on her face, and I knew then that nothing would dissuade her from her path. Her strength and courage were inspiring, and I felt a sense of respect for her that I had never felt for anyone before.

A few days go by, Nay Nay and I walk to the gym where this match would take place. It was at the neighboring community since they won both games. It was so interesting the two communities were so intermixed. They were all so friendly, and some were even family. I needed some air.

As I stood outside, taking a breather, Nay Nay joined me. The tension was palpable in the air, and I couldn't help but feel anxious about the upcoming match.

I turned to Nay Nay, hoping to take my mind off things. She sensed my nerves and I asked, "Have you ever marveled at the strength of the women in this community? Their lives are so intertwined with the very fabric of nature, each day a symphony of spirit and sustenance."

Nay Nay began to nod in with pride, a small smile playing at the corners of her mouth. "Lionel. The women of FFFHAMS are the backbone of our community, and their contributions are immeasurable. What did you learn of the men and women of this community."

I immediately responded, my words tumbling out in a rush. "The elder women are the guardians of the heritage, with wisdom garnered from a lifetime of care and devotion. They tend to the gardens and orchards, brewing remedies and passing down their knowledge, their very presence a comfort to all who know them."

Nay Nay listened attentively, her expression serene.

"The middle-aged women, juggling responsibilities with grace and ease. They nurture the children, prepare the meals, and keep the homes in order. But they also seek the solace of the natural world, connecting with the divine and communing with the spirits within."

I paused, taking a deep breath before continuing. "For the young women, their journey is just beginning. They lend their hands to household chores, soaking in the teachings that will sustain them in adulthood. They dance in the sun and bask in the light of the festivals, discovering the unique gifts they have to offer the world."

Nay Nay nodded. "And the teenage women, they stand on the cusp of a new dawn. They learn the skills that will sustain them, forging a path toward their own purpose. They are encouraged to dream, to explore, to blossom into the women they were meant to be."

Nay Nay responds calmly, "We are interdependent, cooperative, and in harmony with the world around us. And in this, we find true beauty."

I nod my head in agreement. I'm proud to have made friends with real men, "The men in this community, they are a sight to behold," I began. "An elderly man here is a sage, a wise one, whose years have earned him respect and a wealth of tales. His voice carries the weight of a lifetime of experience, and his words impart lessons that never fail. With reverence, the young ones listen to his teachings and seek his counsel on life's trials. And in spiritual rituals, he stands tall and dignified, a master of the culture's ancient trials. In his leisure time, he'll gather with friends, sharing stories, laughs, and smiles."

Nay Nay nodded in agreement, her eyes reflecting the same reverence that I felt for the elder men of the community.

"Middle-aged men are the reason why men are the skull of this community, a force of strength and will. From hunting to rituals, they play an active role, their presence felt on every hill. Leadership is bred in their spirit, as they guide the young and inspire all. And the knowledge they've gained, they impart with grace, ensuring their culture stands tall."

"The young men in this community," I continued, "they are the future, a new generation of heart and soul. With eagerness, they learn the ways of their land, the skills of hunting, foraging, and whole. Their spiritual training nurtures their spirit and helps them find their true goal. As they mature, they're encouraged to take part and carve their place in their community's soul."

Nay Nay's eyes sparkled with pride as I spoke of the young men.

"Teenage boys," I concluded, "they are at the crossroads of life, transitioning from childhood to manhood's role. With vitality, they embrace the land and learn, hunting, foraging, and becoming bold. In spiritual practices, they find their path, and in community life, they unfold. With potential and purpose, they stand tall, their future filled with promise untold."

Nay Nay smiled warmly, her eyes reflecting the same promise and hope that I felt for the young men of the community. "The lives of men in this community," she said, "are shaped by the land and the spiritual bold. Their knowledge and skills, they pass down a legacy that never grows old. In every stage of life, they find purpose, growth, and opportunities untold. With community at the forefront, they ensure their traditions never grow cold."

A man comes out; it was the man who was on the elephant when I originally came, while here I also got to know him as the great hunter, "It's time to support my daughter" For some reason, I wasn't surprised; that her father was the great hunter.

We sat down in comfortable seats and watched as Witu was locked in a circle. It just seemed so wrong. But I came to support my friend and her decision. I sat at the edge of my seat, watching in anxiety, wondering how could such a beautiful community, surrounded by the lush greenery of nature, have room for such ugliness?

As the first round of the fight began, the tension in the arena was palpable. The Teenage Boy strode confidently into the ring, his fists clenched and a warrior's look in his eyes. Witu, on the other hand, had a face of confidence, but I could see beneath the surface she was nervous and uncertain, as though she was about to face her worst nightmare.

As soon as the bell rang, The Teenage Boy pounced, taking Witu down to the ground with ease. He unleashed a barrage of punches and elbows, each one landing with bone-crunching force. Witu was completely overpowered, her attempts to defend herself useless against the brute force of her opponent. Blood flowed freely from her wounds, painting the canvas a sickening shade of red.

The second round was more of the same. The Teenage Boy took Witu down and dominated her, his strikes raining down upon her like hail in a storm. Witu's eye was sliced open, her face a mask of red pain and suffering. The crowd was on its feet, cheering and shouting her name, their excitement at the violence in the ring terrified me.

In the third round, The Teenage Boy took things to a new level of brutality. He took Witu down and kept her there, landing strike after strike, his fists a blur of motion. Witu's eye was swollen, her lips split and bleeding. Her body was battered and broken, but her spirit refused to be broken. Every time from the third through the fourth round when The Teenage Boy thought he had won, Witu rose to her feet, determined to fight on.

As the final round began, it seemed as though The Teenage Boy would finally claim victory. He took Witu down early and dominated her on the ground. But with just over two minutes left, Witu managed to catch The Teenage Boy in a triangle armbar submission, forcing him to tap out. The crowd erupted in cheers, but Witu was already on her feet, her face a mask of bloody triumph.

She looked at me and laughed, then made a silly face. Then she looked at her opponent lying defeated on the canvas in shame and picked him up. They embraced, and this made the crowd even louder. Witu screams blood on half of her face, "I am because we are," and the audience screams with the teenage Boy, "We are because I am."

In that moment, I realized that the true beauty of these communities was not just in their innovation and practices but in the strength and resilience of its people. Witu's victory was a testament to the power of the human spirit, a shining example of what can be achieved against all odds.

As Witu had wished, the Teenage Boy had honored his word and attempted to convince his community to swear off hunting elephants. Though they refused, he vowed not to eat the elephant and to work towards building a relationship with them. It was a small victory but one that filled Witu with hope.

Nay Nay, Witu, and I returned to Nay Nay's house, where the community was celebrating Witu's triumph. Nay Nay tended to her wounds, stitching her up as best she could. Despite her bruises and cuts, Witu looked more beautiful than ever.

As we sat together, I shared my thoughts on anti-fragility and how Witu embodied it. We spoke of the Matrix in my world, where everything was being consumed and intentionally made fragile. Witu added, "I mean, look at this place; it all makes sense in the end."

Perplexed, I asked, "What do you mean by that, Witu?"

Nay Nay interjected, "God hasn't told you?"

"Told me what?" I asked.

As Nay Nay began to explain, things started to get dark. The world around me began to fade, and I felt a sense of panic rising within me.

"Wait, no, no..." I protested.

Nay Nay silenced me with a gentle touch, whispering, "Shhhhh... It is time for the return of my husband and the return of you to your people."

Witu shed a tear, and I fell into the darkness.

Suddenly, I found myself in a dark room. The only light came from a figure sitting in a chair before me. It was God, and he had been expecting me.

"Why did you take me without warning?" I demanded, feeling frustrated and confused.

"You were there for the time you needed to be and did what needed to be done," He replied, His voice echoing through the void. He looked at me with curiosity, but his gaze was shattering.

I quickly humbled myself, realizing that I had spoken out of turn. "Sorry, my Lord, I was caught off guard. Please forgive me," I said, hoping to make amends.

"You are forgiven, Lionel," God said, His voice filled with understanding. "Listen closely; there are more important things at hand. You must stay vigilant and focus on your son."

"My son?" I asked, feeling a sense of confusion creeping in.

"Listen, Lionel. You have been gone for a week, but when you return, you will find that people have discovered FFFHAMS, and everyone will want to ask you questions. When faced with those who operate with ill intent, abstain from confrontation and instead embrace the opportunity to gather information through inquiry," He instructed.

I listened closely, feeling a sense of clarity beginning to form. "If a genuine inquiry is presented, respond with the most comprehensive response within your capacity. Should you lack the necessary information, make note of it and inform the inquirer that a deeper investigation will be conducted. Always view these interactions as opportunities for self-improvement, to enhance the public's understanding, and to further the advancement of knowledge."

He abruptly stops looking around as if someone else was in the room with us.

I struggled to comprehend His words, feeling lost and unsure. "God, I don't..." I started to say, but suddenly I was hurtling through the sky, my heart pounding in my chest.

I braced myself for impact as the ground rushed up to meet me, and I crashed through the roof of a hospital in North America, my mind reeling from the sudden shift in reality.

When I awoke, bleary-eyed and disoriented, I saw Belina's familiar face beaming down at me. "Lionel, we were worried sick!" she exclaimed, relief evident in her voice. "You've been out for a week. Everyone's talking about FFFHAMS, and they want to interview you about it."

I leapt to my feet, my mind still reeling from the incredible journey I had just experienced. Belina and Max watched as I began to recount my grand adventure through time of the wondrous FFFHAMS community I had lived amongst and all their unique ways and traditions.

As I spoke, I could see the wonder in their eyes and the excitement building within them. The memory of my incredible experience will stay with me always, and I know that Nay Nay and Witu along with the people of FFFHAMS will continue to hold a special place in my heart.

CHAPTER 12:

SACRIFICE

Weeks had passed since I returned to the present time and shared my incredible journey and experiences at FFFHAMS. Belina, Max, and I had been working tirelessly to set up the Food Forest and relocate all the animals. We had also constructed multiple 3D printers in the community center and started to dig our underground FFFHAMS. Despite the progress, I refused to allow journalists onto FFFHAMS, but I knew God wanted me to accept interviews.

As I prepared for a podcast interview with the biggest skeptic of them all, Dan Reder, Belina informed me that she couldn't come with me. She needed to pick up her "Krissy" from the airport. Apparently, it was a last-minute emergency. Belina promised to drop her off at the house and join me as soon as she could. Belina had always been my rock and helped me prepare for these meetings. I kissed her before she left, hoping that she would join me soon.

Max arrived shortly after, and after informing him that he had just missed Belina, I told him to be safe while I was gone. I boarded the plane with a little nervousness, knowing the worldwide reach of this platform. I wanted to do well by God and spread the message of FFFHAMS. As I entered the glass room for the interview, I realized that Belina still wasn't there to help me prepare. I felt the weight of the moment, and I yearned for her presence.

The interview was about to start, and my nervousness was mounting. But then, when I looked to my left, I saw Belina standing right outside the glass room. Her presence alone sent confidence through my body. It was as if, when she was around, I was complete.

The interview with Dan Reder continued on, and we talked about everything under the sun. I had to admit, it was invigorating to have someone challenge my ideas and beliefs, even if he was a skeptic. Dan leaned forward, raising his eyebrow with a skeptical look on his face. "You make it sound so easy, but the reality is that achieving self-sufficiency and sustainability is an enormous challenge. How can you guarantee that FFFHAMS will be able to produce enough food and resources for all its members? And what about the obstacles that will inevitably arise when trying to implement renewable energy and green infrastructure?"

I smiled confidently, pulling out a small notebook from my pocket. "I understand your concerns, Dan. But FFFHAMS has already developed a detailed plan for achieving self-sufficiency and sustainability. For example, the community can implement regenerative practices, such as permaculture, which not only produce ample food but also helps regenerate the land. Additionally, FFFHAMS can use renewable energy sources, such as solar panels and wind turbines, to create a reliable energy system. And if any obstacles do arise, the community can use collective decision-making to find the best solutions."

Dan raised an eyebrow. "But what about the challenges of implementing collective decision-making? Isn't that an inefficient way to make decisions? And what about the challenge of attracting and retaining committed members who are willing to live the FFFHAMS lifestyle?"

I nodded thoughtfully, jotting down notes in my notebook. "I can see where you're coming from, Dan. But collective decision-making has been successfully implemented in many indigenous and hunter-gatherer societies throughout history. And FFFHAMS believes that by leading by example and providing resources and support, it can attract and retain committed members who share its vision."

Dan leaned back in his chair, rubbing his chin thoughtfully. "I see your point. But I still worry about the practicality of achieving self-sufficiency and sustainability on such a large scale. It's one thing for a small group to live sustainably, but how can FFFHAMS do it for a large community?"

I smiled reassuringly, "I understand your concern, Dan. But FFFHAMS is not aiming for complete isolation from the outside world. The community seeks to reduce its dependence on outside resources slowly but surely and promote sustainable living practices. By doing so, FFFHAMS can create a more equitable, just, and environmentally responsible world. Not to mention that in the inevitable collapse of this civilization due to the lack of dependency, members of FFFHAMS will stand strong and be able to adapt to changing circumstances."

Dan nodded, looking more thoughtful than skeptical now. "I can see that FFFHAMS is taking a comprehensive approach to achieving its goals. I look forward to seeing how it all plays out. We have people calling in now, let's see how you answer their questions."

"How can we make sure that our community is sustainable and self-sufficient like FFFHAMS?" the caller asked.

"To ensure that your community is sustainable and self-sufficient, you can adopt regenerative practices, such as permaculture and agroforestry, and focus on renewable energy sources, such as solar panels and wind turbines. Additionally, you can work towards reducing waste, conserving resources, and promoting sustainability in all aspects of your community's operation. By living within your means, you can achieve greater self-sufficiency and create a resilient, sustainable community," I explained.

"Thank you for that response, Lionel. We have another caller on the line. Let's hear your question," Dan said.

"How can we ensure that our community has strong leadership and accountability while promoting collective decision-making?" the caller asked.

"To have strong leadership and accountability while promoting collective decision-making, you can establish the guardians. They are responsible for making sure FFFHAMS abstractly and physically is maintained. Additionally, never elect people to represent members. With the technology we have today, people are very much able to represent themselves. The people should be self-governed and meet every night to discuss the ups and downs of the community and life as a whole," I answered.

"Next caller. Go ahead; you're on the air," Dan said.

"What are some successful regenerative agriculture practices we can implement in our community?" the caller asked.

"Successful regenerative practices that you can implement in your community include permaculture, agroforestry, crop rotation, and rainwater harvesting. These practices can help promote soil health, conserve water, and increase yields. The key is to work with nature, not against it, and build a regenerative ecosystem that benefits the entire community. The Food Forest is, of course, absolutely essential," I replied.

The next caller, whose name was Alice, asked, "How can we protect our community from environmental hazards and ensure that we live in harmony with the natural world?"

I replied, "To protect your community from environmental hazards and live in harmony with the natural world, you can focus on green infrastructure, such as rain gardens and bioswales, and promote sustainable living practices that minimize environmental impact."

Another caller, named Malcolm, then asked, "How can we foster a strong sense of community and cooperation among our members?"

I responded, "To foster a strong sense of community and cooperation among your members, you can create communal living spaces and shared resources, such as kitchens and recreational areas, to encourage cooperation and mutual aid. You can also organize social events and festivals that bring the community together and build relationships. By creating a culture of cooperation, you can build a resilient, supportive community that benefits everyone involved. Remember, people should always be encouraged to hunt and gather together. They should also be encouraged to cook and play together."

As I listened to the next call, I heard a woman's voice on the other end. "What strategies can we use to attract and retain committed members in our community?" she asked.

I replied, "To attract and retain committed members, you can work to create a supportive and inclusive community culture that values diversity and individual choices. You can also provide resources and support to help individuals transition to a self-sufficient lifestyle and promote the benefits of sustainable living. Additionally, you can create a shared vision and mission for your community that resonates with prospective members and promotes a sense of purpose and meaning in their lives. It won't be that hard, honestly. We are offering people freedom from the enslavement of careerism and the life of driving to work and from work every day. We are offering their life back, their freedom."

The next caller, named Marcus, had a question about the community's values. "How can we ensure that our community values diversity and respects the choices and lifestyles of all its members?" he asked.

I answered, "To ensure that your community values diversity and respects the choices and lifestyles of all its members, you can create a culture of acceptance and tolerance that encourages open communication and understanding. You can also actively seek out and welcome individuals with diverse backgrounds and experiences to the community. What is really important is that no matter the religion, race, sexuality, or gender of a person, they will be accepted as long as they accept FFFHAMS. Everyone can make changes as long as it is within the principles and concept of FFFHAMS."

The next caller's name was Winnie, and she asked, "How can we balance the needs and desires of individual members with the collective goals of the community?"

I responded, "Balancing individual needs with the collective goals of the community is essential for maintaining a healthy and harmonious community. We can achieve this through a democratic decision-making process that ensures everyone has a voice and is heard. We can also have a conflict resolution process that is fair and respectful of individual needs. It is important to understand that individual needs can also align with the collective goals of the community. We want to create a community where individuals are fulfilled, and their needs are met while also contributing to the common good."

"How can we handle the financial aspects of starting and maintaining a community like FFFHAMS?" the caller named Maleek on the other end asked.

I leaned back in my chair and clasped my hands together. "The financial aspects of starting and maintaining a community like FFFHAMS can be challenging, but there are strategies we can use to overcome these challenges," I explained. "One approach is to pool your resources through group economics and crowdfunding to purchase land, equipment, and infrastructure. We can also develop a super passive business plan to support the community's economic activities as we grow. In our FFFHAMS specifically, everyone is given a year to learn a strategy of creating passive income, allowing the community and that individual to become financially anti-fragile. Additionally, we can look for grants and other funding opportunities that align with our mission and values."

The next caller's voice crackled through the speaker. "How can we ensure that our community is safe and secure?" she asked.

"Ensuring the safety and security of our community is a top priority," I replied. "We can achieve this through a community watch program and implementing security measures such as invisible alarm fencing and lighting. All FFFHAMS communities should have dogs who share a symbiotic relationship with the members of the community and instinctively protect them from danger. The best dog to adopt for this would be the Belgian Malinois, but any well-socialized guard dog breed can be a FFFHAMS dog. No animal is to be caged or leashed within the premises of FFFHAMS. All, including the dogs, should be free. The only exception being first generation babies of animals within FFFHAMS. We will also invest in emergency preparedness and first aid training. It's important to have clear rules and regulations that everyone agrees on to maintain the safety and security of the community. We also believe that creating strong relationships and open communication among community members is essential for maintaining a safe and secure environment."

As the questions continued, I couldn't help but feel impressed by the callers' curiosity and engagement. "Overall, starting a community like FFFHAMS requires careful planning, strong community building, and a commitment to sustainable living," I summarized. "By working together and leveraging group economics, we can create a thriving community that benefits everyone involved."

I took a deep breath, bracing myself for the next batch of questions. They weren't as friendly, but I remained humble and steadfast in my conviction that these hard questions would only make FFFHAMS stronger. They came in like a group of bullets, but I was ready to face them head-on.

I cleared my throat and responded to the callers, each with their own concerns about FFFHAMS. "In terms of safety," I began, "FFFHAMS strongly emphasizes building sustainable and resilient infrastructure, and the community is designed to withstand environmental hazards and other external threats. We drill for all possible threats." I paused for a moment to let the words sink in. "In addition, FFFHAMS values interdependence and collective support, which means that community members work together to ensure the safety and well-being of all individuals during times of crisis."

I turned to the next caller, "To address potential challenges of maintaining a self-sufficient lifestyle, FFFHAMS emphasizes sustainable practices, such as regenerative and renewable energy sources, to promote self-sufficiency and minimize waste. Additionally, the community values sharing and collaboration, which means that individuals work together to identify and address potential challenges to the community's self-sufficiency. The Food Forest is a non-negotiable; without it, you're not within FFFHAMS."

"FFFHAMS strongly emphasizes consensus-based decision-making," I said to the next caller, "which means that everyone in the community has a voice in the decision-making process. Additionally, FFFHAMS values interdependence and collective support, which means that community members work together to identify and address potential challenges to effective decision-making and governance."

I responded to the next caller, "FFFHAMS strongly emphasizes conflict resolution and mediation, which means that community members work together to identify and address potential conflicts and disputes. Additionally, FFFHAMS values interdependence and collective support, which means that community members work together to ensure the well-being of all individuals within the community."

I addressed the next caller's concerns, "To address potential health risks and the provision of medical care within the community, FFFHAMS strongly emphasizes preventive health practices, such as healthy eating (Using wild food grown in the Food Forest) and regular exercise (Hunting, Fishing, and Foraging), to minimize the risk of health issues within the community. Additionally, FFFHAMS values interdependence and collective support, which means that community members work together to ensure the well-being of all individuals within the community."

I took a deep breath and continued, "Major FFFHAMS or FFFHAMS on 500 acres plus would have a medical center to treat emergencies, but even the smallest FFFHAMS should have members who are educated in being a doctor or nurse. You will be responsible for making sure certain members receive their education in healthcare, rather mainstream or holistic; both would be the best. But all members should be educated in medicine and health within FFFHAMS. To clarify, If you do not have a major FFFHAMS, which is 500 acres plus, you are not required to have a medical center or a medical education facility. Only the first generation of FFHAMS should have to go outside of FFFHAMS for education. All following generation's medical education should be in house on the house, so to speak."

"FFFHAMS values interdependence and collective support," I concluded, "which means that community members work together to share resources and support one another. The community places a strong emphasis on sustainability and minimizing waste, which means that resources are distributed in a fair and efficient manner. Additionally, FFFHAMS may team up with other communities or organizations to leverage group economics and access resources more effectively."

As I listened to the questions of the callers, I felt a sense of pride in the vision of FFFHAMS. The next caller was eager to learn more, and I felt a renewed energy to share our message.

"Caller named Rishawn," I responded, "FFFHAMS values interdependence and collective support, which means that community members work together to support families and ensure the well-being of children within the community. Our approach to education is unique in that we believe learning is a lifelong process that takes place every moment of life. Children will be tested annually on their knowledge concerning FFFHAMS. We believe everything you need to know in order to be a functioning member of FFFHAMS is well beyond school standards, and yet it is more patient and less forceful. Children will mainly learn by watching and being given opportunities to participate. Most children within hunter-gathering societies may surprise you with how much they know in comparison to children their age in modern settings, relative, of course, to culture."

The caller seemed impressed with our approach, and I felt a sense of satisfaction in knowing that we were making a difference in people's lives.

"Rishawn continues, "That's fascinating, Lionel. It sounds like FFFHAMS really values interdependence and community building. I'm curious, how does FFFHAMS plan to address potential conflicts and disputes within the community, particularly in the absence of a clear legal system?"

I responded, "FFFHAMS strongly emphasizes conflict resolution and mediation, which means that community members work together to identify and address potential conflicts and disputes. Additionally, FFFHAMS values interdependence and collective support, which means that community members work together to ensure the well-being of all individuals within the community. We have guardians who are responsible for overseeing the community's operations and decision-making. They are responsible for maintaining FFFHAMS abstractly and physically, as well as maintaining peace, mediating conflicts, and managing crisis situations. Though the guardians volunteer, they are also selected based on their skills, experience, and commitment to the community, and they are held accountable by the community through a democratic process."

One of the callers named TT says, " That sounds great, Lionel. How can we ensure that our community values diversity and respects the choices and lifestyles of all its members?"

I was a little frustrated at the questions but responded, "I believe I might have covered this before, but to ensure that your community values diversity and respects the choices and lifestyles of all its members, you can create a culture of acceptance and tolerance that encourages open communication and understanding. You can also actively seek out and welcome individuals with diverse backgrounds and experiences to the community. What is really important is that no matter the religion, race, sexuality, or gender of a person, they must be accepted as long as they accept FFFHAMS. They can only make changes within the principles and concept of FFFHAMS.

TT continued, " I understand; sorry if you already answered that question. Is it true you're not allowing contraception in FFFHAMS and if so, don't you think you're hurting the women in your community and taking away their rights."

She was really trying to paint a picture; I took a deep breath with a smile and told her what one of my friends from FFFHAMS told me, " Yes, in FFFHAMS, there is no contraception. In our world, we cherish children and believe they are a blessing. We don't see the need to limit the number of children we have. In our society, we are hunter-gatherers. We work together as a community to provide for each other. Children are very valuable to us and contribute to the work and well-being of our community." I added, "Women within western society and generally within civilization were oppressed and their children used against them like chains. Used to keep them from owning things, used to keep them uneducated, and used to keep them from providing for themselves. This is not civilization, this is FFFHAMS.

You must also understand women's bodies are less likely to develop cancer when having children at a natural rate. Women who breastfeed their children are less far likely to develop breast cancer becuase the child provides the correct hormonal levels the body is used to. Because the women in our communities breastfeed until the child is two to three years old, she may only get pregnant once every three years.

Unlike within agricultural societies where moms may feed their babies the milk of cows and goats, causing not only an imbalance in their hormonal levels but the ability to have more children than their bodies can handle. Our ways may be different, but that doesn't mean one is better than the other. We have learned to live in balance with nature and value the sanctity of life. But, to add to that, major FFFHAMS communities will be required to have STI tests available so that people can freely get tested.

The next caller, named Tom, asks, "How can we ensure that FFFHAMS is not just an isolated echo chamber and that we remain engaged with the wider world and its challenges?"

I take a moment and say, "FFFHAMS is not an isolationist community, and we recognize that we are part of a larger global community. We are always seeking to build connections and relationships with other communities, and we are active in sharing our ideas and practices with others. We also recognize that there are many pressing issues facing the world, such as climate change, social inequality, and political instability, and we are engaging with these issues through FFFHAMS, which we believe is the ultimate solution to these problems.

Another caller named Samyia says, "What can we learn from the failures of other utopian communities in history, such as Jonestown and the Branch Davidians?"

I confidently say, Good question. While we acknowledge the failures of "utopian" communities in history, FFFHAMS is not based on the same principles or practices as those "communities." We make no claims to be utopia; we only assert that we are in line with what humans evolved for and that we are a better solution to human life's problems in comparison to modern civilization. We are not a cult or a religious organization, and we do not promote or condone any form of violence or extremism. FFFHAMS is based on a set of values and practices that promote sustainability, community, and interdependence, and we are committed to ensuring that our community is a safe and welcoming place for all who wish to join us. We also recognize that we are not perfect, and we are always open to feedback and constructive criticism in order to improve and grow as a community. I must also add there is no one leader in FFFHAMS; there is no prophet, no messiah who governs FFFHAMS. Only the people, and if anyone within a FFFHAMS community elects himself as such, or if the people elect him as such, it can no longer be considered FFFHAMS.

I was relieved to hear that the interview was over after the last caller, and Belina gave me a thumbs up. I smiled, thinking that was the end, but then Dan Reder said, "Actually, there is one more caller."

I sighed with a smile and said, "Yes" A female voice said, "Mr. Lionel? My jaw dropped at the familiarity of the voice, "Sekhmet?"

The line went quiet for a second, and the awkward silence was unsettling. "I was just calling to tell you it wasn't your fault; you're not responsible for the death of Ben."

Before I could say anything, Dan Reder cut the line due to an agreement Belina had with all interviewers not to talk about any of my "legal problems." We wrapped up the interview and flew back home.

As we left that night, flying back home, I couldn't stop thinking about Samantha and why she would say that. Belina could tell it was bothering me and told me, "No worries, Lee. We will figure all of this out. I got your back."

I asked, "Did you introduce Max to your niece?"

"I don't think Max was there when I arrived. I just dropped her off quickly and told her to stay on the property. I showed the dogs to her, and they saw she was no threat. Then I pulled off to make it to you on time," she quickly responded.

"And I appreciate you for it, Belina. You truly are a goddess sent from the stars. You are my better half," I said.

"No, Lee. You're mine," Belina responded, putting her head on my shoulder.

Exhausted and with the moon shining above us, we are in the car finally back in Georgia. Belina was asleep beside me, looking like the queen of the stars with her mouth open and all. As we pulled up to the massive property, I had a bad feeling. Belina woke up, we both exchanged a glance, and I asked, "You feel that?" She nodded slowly, up and down. Belina pulled out her phone to call her niece, but there was no reception. We could see the barn house in the distance, and half of it was falling apart. "Krissy," Belina said with a terrified voice. I hit the accelerator and sped towards the house.

As we got out of the car, we could see Krissy's legs sticking out from beneath all the wood and debris. Max was on the floor, unconscious but breathing. There was dug-up earth all around us. I quickly brought Max to the deck while Belina was crying and frantically moving all the wood off her niece. "No, no, no, my Krissy, no!" she kept saying. I helped to move the objects off of her, and finally, we got everything off. Krissy's body lay there seemingly lifeless, but there was a pulse. The poor girl was all scratched up and beaten down, and she must have had broken bones all over her body. Krissy held her in her arms, and finally, the ambulance arrived. Belina said, "Grab Max," and I ran over to get him. We put both of them in the vehicle, and I followed the ambulance to the hospital while Belina rode with them both.

Not long after, they told us that Max was fine and was just resting, not even a cut on his body. The report on Krissy wasn't ready, and they said she could be in a coma. Belina was panicking and trying to call her best friend while I was trying to figure out what had happened. Belina came into Max's room to tell me, "She won't answer!" I held her and reassured her, saying, "It's going to be alright," while rubbing her back. Then, the doctors knocked on the door, and Belina said, "Come in." The doctors came in and revealed that it was a miracle, Krissy would be fine and should make a full recovery. She should be waking up in a day or two. Belina cried in relief, and I held her in my arms, telling her, "See, God is watching over us."

The hospital allowed us to take both Max and Krissy home. The doctor said, "She never had any broken bones," which I found to be strange since Krissy was all scratched up and beaten down. We drove back to the house, and Belina was texting someone while I was lost in thought. When we arrived, we put Max in his room and Krissy in our bedroom.

I sat in Max's room, wondering how I could be around a kid this long and not know his parents' address or number. It was beyond reckless, and I needed to get in contact with Max's parents. It was so late at night, and they were probably worried sick. Max began to wake up, and I asked, "Max, are you okay?" He responded, "I don't remember... What's going on, Mr. Lee?"

"Max, you were hurt and knocked unconscious. I know you don't want to, but I need you to give me your parent's phone number. I just want to tell them you're okay," I explained. Max looked down and went silent. "Max, I need to talk to your parents. This is not okay!" I said, raising my voice. Belina heard me getting angry and came into the room. She gave Max some green tea and told him to drink and rest up. She patted my shoulder as a sign to leave the room.

Before closing the door, I said, "I just care about you, don't want to lose ya, kid." I closed the door and turned to Belina, whispering aggressively, "Belina! Four years! Four years! Why don't we know his parents? That isn't strange to you?" Belina whispered back, "Calm down, my love. He might hear you." I replied, "Don't do that, Belina! Don't act like I'm acting crazy. His parents are worrying right now. I know what that's like," as a tear rolled down my face. Belina grabbed my face gently and said, "I know, I'm already on it; I...."

Max pushed the door open, and I could see he had been listening to our conversation. He was shaking his head and looking down. "Just as I thought I found...." His tears began to flow, and he pointed at me with all his rage, and with these words, he broke my heart, "You said you loved me! I thought you two would never... You said we were a team!" I reached out to him and, at the same time, saw the image of my son, Ben. Belina pleaded, "Max," which reminded me of the time we split. Max looked at Belina with tears in his eyes and ran out of the house toward the food forest. Belina followed.

I stood frozen in my tracks, my heart heavy with grief and despair. Tears streamed down my face as memories of my past mistakes flooded my mind. Just then, my phone began to ring, but I ignored it, consumed by my sorrow. However, the person on the other end was persistent, and I finally answered with an angry, "WHAT!"

It was Samantha, and as soon as she spoke, my ears perked up. "I have been trying to tell people for years what happened on the ship that night," she said, "and due to all the legal stuff, my mother and father never allowed me to call you."

My heart began to race as she revealed, "Mr. Lionel, I know who killed your son!" I could barely speak, my voice shaking with emotion. "I thought it was some freak accident," I managed to say.

Samantha explained that she had seen a viral photo of FFFHAMS on the internet and noticed someone in the picture with me. "Is his name Max?" she asked. I confirmed that it was, but I couldn't understand what Max had to do with my son's death.

Samantha began to sob, revealing that Max had transformed into something on that fateful night and had destroyed everything, including my son Ben. My world crumbled around me as she told me that Max had killed them all.

Suddenly, I saw the forest burst into flames of red, orange, and yellow, with a massive blue explosion illuminating the sky. I dropped my phone and screamed, "Belina!" and ran out of the house and into the fiery inferno.

My heart raced with fear as I called out for Belina and Max, but all I could see was a world consumed by flames, with animals screaming and burning alive. I finally spotted Max, and what I saw left me speechless. A giant red snake, larger than Nay Nay's elephant, was coiled around him while Max was uncontrollably vomiting flames. His eyes were white as snow, and he appeared to be in agony.

I saw Belina lying on the ground, unconscious, and I scooped her up in my arms, carrying her back to the house. As I opened the door, I was shocked to see God standing there. I placed Belina at his feet, and he looked at me with piercing eyes, commanding me to grab my sharpest blade and meet him with Max at the community center.

I ran back into the fiery forest, thinking about all we had worked for in the past four years, destroyed in an instant. I found Max lying on the ground, unconscious, with no sign of the snake. I lifted him over my shoulder and ran to the community center, where I placed him at the center of the floor, as God had instructed.

It was silent as I looked at my knife, unsure of what to do next. Suddenly, God appeared again and spoke in a booming voice, "Did you not hear what the girl said? That boy on the ground caused the death of your son."

"So it's true…." I said.

"Yes, it is," God replied.

"This must be some sort of mistake," I said.

"Kill it…" God, his expression cold and distant.

It was terrifying, and I had never seen him like this before. I looked up at him, trying to make sense of everything, to see a face of disappointment.

"God, you can't be serious…." I said.

"You still don't see it, Lionel," God said.

"See what?" I asked, still confused.

"That boy, that thing in front of you is Entropy itself. He is the reason from the time he was born that everything around him fell apart. Your son, the forest, Belina's niece, this is all nothing compared to what he will do! His evil will never end until his heart is dead!" God said, his voice filled with anger.

"My Lord, he is just a boy," I said, trying to reason with him.

God became like a storm of thunder and lightning, swirling around me and echoing with questions and judgment.

"Were you not the one who said that he was willing to give anything, to sacrifice whatever it takes…" God asked.

"Yes, my Lord," I replied nervously.

"Did you swear to move when I say?" God demanded.

"Of course!" I replied.

"You swore it to me!" God said.

"I swear…" I said, my voice trembling.

"The blood of God and the blood of man, where God steps, is here I stand. No one shall separate the skin of man and the flesh of God. I am God's fist, I am God's tongue, and if from God's mouth comes a sword…." God said, his voice rising.

"I will kill what must die!" I said, tears falling from my eyes.

"THEN DO IT! I HOLD YOU TO YOUR WORD TO GOD!" God thundered.

"He is like a son…." I said, trying to reason with God.

"He killed your son!" God thundered.

I felt a pang of grief in my heart at the mention of my son. But still, I said, "He is like a best friend."

"Then take mercy on his soul before he must witness what he will become!" God said, his voice echoing with anger.

I kicked the knife away in rebellion, refusing to kill Max.

"I won't," I said firmly.

"Pick it up!" God demanded.

I hesitated, unsure of what to do next. The weight of God's words was too heavy, and I felt lost in my thoughts.

He forms in front of me as a man with dark skin and a white robe. His face didn't look as it normally looked, but he still looked angry. His eyes looked like he could destroy me with one blink. For the first time, he was horrifying.

He was so terrifying that I slowly walked over and grabbed the knife. I walk over to the boy and say, "But… But My Lord…"

He grows large, looming over me, and says, "IF YOU DON'T KILL IT!" in a loud, deep voice, he screams, THEN YOU! WILL! LOSE EVERYTHING!"

I drop to my knees, staring at the large knife in my two hands, large enough to reflect my shameful face….

I quiver, then hold the knife tight, feeling the warmth of a tear as it rolls down my face. I raised the knife in the air over the boy's body, letting out a scream of rage and terror. Thinking about everything this boy had put me through then…

I think back to being on the porch with Max, building the Earthship, playing ball; I think back to not only the bad but the good; Max built the majority of this place on his own…

"I will not," I said firmly, my heart heavy with the weight of my decision.

"Why?" God asked.

"He may be entropy manifest, but I love him, and I need him. We need him. He is necessary," I said, trying to explain.

I dropped the knife and held Max tighter than I'd ever held anything while I wept. It was as if I could feel all the pain of the world at that moment. All the pain and all the love.

God looked at me with what I could only call a hint of pride, for lack of a better word. It almost looked as if he wanted to smile. Then he gently faded away.

CHAPTER 13:

MAX'S JOURNEY TO BELONG: PART 2

I ran, and I ran, and I ran. For days, I ran, hiding in the bare, dry forest. The cold handcuffs and chains pressed against my skin like snow. I do this every night, as I thought about Kris and Sam, I hoped I wouldn't hurt anyone. Kris's angry eyes seemed to be behind every tree, waiting for me. Her eyes visited my dreams almost as much as those eyes of terror and disbelief Sam kept in that moment of dread. I saw those eyes, those faces, every time I closed my eyes at night.

As I held tight to my black cat. I thought of my mother and father's embrace, but I knew in my heart now I could never return. Every time the sun came up, my black cat would find me, giving me the keys in the morning to unlock the handcuffs. He always trails close by. It was more than just trailing; it was guiding me and keeping me safe. He found the handcuffs I used and brought me clothing, blankets, everything. He was pretty awesome.

I looked up at the Delaware Memorial Bridge and knew I was far from home. New Jersey felt like a distant world. "This is a good thing," I thought. "I can start over." I didn't see how God expected me to reach Georgia anytime soon. Our feet carried us, and it seemed like there was no end. Until the cat led me to a portal. It was like a hole in the fabric of space and time. It was purple on the inside, with a swirl of black, purple, and silver on the outside.

I reached my shaking hand toward the mysterious hole, placing my faith in this black cat. But then, a voice said, "Nothing but misery in that black hole." I turned to see a white Asiatic-looking man. He stood there confidently with a grey suit and a briefcase. Next to him was a strange butler kind of guy. He looked nice but very intimidating. The man was eating a greasy Philly cheesesteak. The grease dripped down but never touched his suit or his fingers. He was so clean, and he ate them so fast while his "butler" kept handing him more. It was disgusting.

He stopped eating and said, "I am just a man, and this gentleman next to me, his name is Belinda. Drake Belinda."

I looked at Belinda, and he made me feel uneasy.

My cat began to meow loudly.

"I don't have time to talk. Nice to meet you," I said, trying to end the encounter before it began.

"I just want to know if you met someone who some may call God," the man said, ignoring my dismissal.

"How do you know about God?" I asked, curious despite my unease.

"Kid, I'm God's favorite creation," the man replied, his mouth full of cheesesteak.

"You are?" I asked skeptically.

"Yes, God has chosen me to spread civilization across the stars. That is my purpose," the man said, smacking loudly.

"I don't think God would tell you to do something like that," I said, feeling a chill run down my spine.

"Listen, tell me if I'm wrong. You're afraid of something 'dark' inside of you?" the man asked, his eyes locked onto mine.

"How did you know?" I asked, my heart pounding in my chest.

"Kid, I know everything," the man said, taking another bite of his cheesesteak.

"I don't think you do…." I replied, taking a step back.

"There is no need to fear me; we are the same. I am here to save you, and only I can," the man said, reaching his hand out toward me.

"I don't know you, and you don't know the gods, I can tell," I said, feeling a sense of dread wash over me.

"Kid, the gods are not what you think; most aren't even conscious. Almost none of them are rational. They just flow and do. They don't care if we live or die; only the one true God does, the God that has chosen me as his most precocious creation," the man said, his voice growing louder and more intense.

"I'm not going with you!" I shouted as he grew impatient and grabbed my arm. But the cat scratched him, and he let out a scream. "Drake! Do something!" His assistant's face turned into that of a dragon, and my black cat turned into a giant lion with all black fur and an all-black mane, letting out a terrifying roar. I had never seen something so majestic and beautiful. He looked back at me with his deep yellow eyes, signaling me to run. So I did. I jumped through the portal.

I fell onto the other side and immediately looked back, terrified that the man was going to get me and that my feline friend was dead. But the portal was gone. I just fell back into the leaves and dirt in the forest, looking at the sky and wondering where God was in all this horror. I finally got up and began to walk where my heart led me. I saw a man and a woman by a house in the distance. I thought to myself, "This must be the tribe God has sent me to." I began to run toward the woman, excited, thinking, "They'll know who I am. God would have told them to expect me."

When I ran up to the woman, I quickly realized she had no idea who I was. I said, "Surely God told you." She responded, "Told me what?" But she seemed so familiar as if I'd met her before. She was talking, but I was in complete awe of this woman and how she felt like home. Behind her, there was a man coming out of the wooden house. He looked angry, and so yet again, I found myself running.

I ran behind a tree. The man saw me and said that he was sorry. I came from behind the tree, and this started my journey with my tribe, the people I was meant to be with.

The next morning, the black cat came out of the woods and gave me the key. I was so relieved to see him safe and unharmed. Though knowing he was secretly a giant lion bigger than a city bus, it felt weird. Every night, I stayed in the woods and actually used the skills I learned from Sankofa to create a small home for myself. I made a wooden cage to lock myself in around my bed. She also taught me how to make a fire, which was great because summer was ending, and the nights were getting colder. I wanted to protect Belina and Mr. Lee from me at all costs. As I built this cage I called home, I remembered thinking of Ben and how we felt like we knew each other in another life or something. I thought about how he must have suffered when he drowned beneath the sea. I cried, thinking, "This time is different."

Belina was always checking on me, always asking how I was, and so quick to go on walks with me and talk about life. I remember we were talking about her family and how she wasn't close to them. She said, "I have sort of a family back home. My best friend and her daughter are truly my only real family. My mother passed right before I could tell her something." "What were you going to tell her?" I asked. "Well, Lee and I had a big argument about a baby we were going to have. I didn't want to keep the baby, and I told him. But in hindsight, I should have gone to my mother first and told her I was pregnant. She passed right after Lee left and would have guided me better."

"Well, I gave up my baby, and somewhere out there in some world, that child is looking for me, wondering why I let him go." I told her, "Your baby will always love you. How could they not?

You're such a great mother." I truly wished in my mind that day that she was my mother.

Years went by, and I had never been so happy. I constantly thought about my parents, but they could never understand this mission I was on. Everything was going great until one day, while we were finishing up the Earthship, Mr. Lee said something strange that reminded me of my friend Ben. It terrified me and took me back to that terrible yacht, that terrible night. Then, out of nowhere, Mr. Lee fell into a week-long coma.

Eventually, the awaited day came, and Mr. Lee woke up from his deep sleep. Belina cried; she was so happy, and I was grateful to have Mr. Lee back in my life. He was different, but in a good way, and he told us about the adventure God put him on. We were absolutely amazed and inspired by his stories of Nay Nay and Witu. Everything was perfect.

Not too long after, maybe a couple of weeks, one night, I fell asleep waiting for Belina to get back, and Mr. Lee left for a podcast interview on some guy's show. I heard the dogs barking and woke up. I walked out of my bedroom, and there was a girl outside. As I looked through the blinds, I could see she wasn't far from my age. She had brown skin and long curly hair. She had a strange kind of beauty to her, like a building or a painting. I figured she was probably one of those people looking to see FFFHAMS. I then thought to myself, "These dogs don't guard anything." I walked out the front door. "Hey! This is Mr. Lee's property! It isn't open to the people yet. It ain't ready." She just stood there, her eyes wide like an owl's. I nervously said, "Are you okay?"

"You," she said, her head tilted to the side like a bird. "Kris?" I responded. Her hair began to rise, turning white, and the objects all around us started to float. "I haven't seen my father in over four years! Why are you here? To steal away Aun B too?" "Aun B?" I said, extremely confused. The ground began to form around her sneakers, and her eyes grew cold. I watched as the dogs ran away. I screamed, "Kris, I'm so sorry! Please for-." The earth moved as if there was a giant hand reaching through the surface between the space of Kris and me. Before I had a chance to say anything, I was in the air, held by some sort of invisible power. She was squeezing me. I could feel each bone cracking under the pressure. "Kris, please forgive m-" She made it tighter, and then I felt the otherworldly feeling of my ribs cracking and bones slipping out of place.

I screamed an agonizing scream, one like which no one had heard. I struggled to pull myself together. I just saw Kris's eyes glowing, they were like fire, and the anger from her was unbound. I couldn't move my head, only my eyes, and I looked desperately at the road in hopes Mr. Lee would come to my rescue, but the road was clear. Then, I began to regret running from home. I thought of my mother's smile as my life was being crushed out of me. I looked to the sky, and I could see the moon; it was now night. A deep feeling of worry filled my body, and it was written all over my face.

Kris said, "I see you looking and hoping someone will save you. No one is coming this time, demon!"

But I wasn't worried about me anymore; I was worried about her. Behind her was the Food Forest, and I could see deep red, dark eyes glow in the darkness of the forest. I try to warn her, but every time I say a word, she squeezes tighter shattering bones.

As the giant red snake slithered out of the food forest, I found myself fading to black. But before I could lose consciousness completely, I heard a voice in my head. "Wait," I said, struggling to hold on as the creature caused havoc around me. "I need...to...open my eyes!"

Just in time, I managed to open my eyes and saw Kris hurtling towards the house. The building collapsed as she hit it, and the giant red snake loomed over her, ready to finish the job. Its skin glistened like that of a king cobra, with alluring colors all over. It raised its head, and I knew it was about to deliver the last strike.

"Leave her! Leeeeeave her alone!" I screamed at the top of my lungs. The snake turned to face me, its terrible eyes fixed on mine. It then swiftly slithered back into the forest, leaving me fading to black once more.

When I woke up, I found myself in the house with Mr. Lee talking to me. I was confused and disoriented and could barely understand what he was saying. Gradually, though, I began to realize that he was asking to talk to my parents. I looked away, and he grew angry.

But then Belina came into the room and gave me some green tea. They leave the room to go talk, and then Mr. Lee, in his own way, tells me he loves me. "They just don't get it," I think to myself, "I can never tell them the truth; they wouldn't understand."

I hear them arguing, it reminds me of my parents, and so I go over to the door to listen... Mr. Lee whispers loudly, "Belina! Four years! Four years! Why don't we know his parents? That isn't strange to you?" Belina whispered back, "Calm down, my love." Mr. Lee replied, "Don't do that, Belina! Don't act like I'm acting crazy. His parents are worrying right now."

At that very moment, I had a flashback to my parents.

"We already went to a therapist like you said we should," I heard my mother say. "All they did was medicate him, and it didn't even work! My father responded, "I say we find his real parents, Clare."

My eyes opened wide as I listened, struggling to understand. "I'm not listening to this," my mother replied, beginning to walk away. "We took care of him, but maybe they have some answers, Clarissa!"

My heart raced as I slammed the door open, catching my mother by surprise. "Max," she said, her voice sad and resigned. "You...you both lied to me..." Tears streamed down my face.

"You're not my mother!" I shouted at her, my voice filled with pain and anger.

But my mother only leaned against the wall and cried while my father tried to calm me down. "Max, calm down, son," he said, holding his arms open for a hug. But I ran into my room and slammed the door shut, locking it tight.

"Max, open the door; let us talk to you, son!" my father shouted from the other side. But my mother begged him to let me breathe.

I slipped on my headphones, blocking out the sound of the world around me. Turned o my video game and escaped that moment. The memory of the familiar click of the game console brought me back to the present day.

"My tribe," as I called them, had turned against me. Belina and Mr. Lee, who I had thought were my closest of family, were plotting to hand me over to my parents. It wasn't that my parents even wanted me - they had made that much clear. But the very idea that the people I trusted most could even consider doing this to me filled me with a wave of boiling anger.

I raged, slamming the door open with all the force of my pent-up frustration. "Just as I thought I found..." I trailed off, tears welling up in my eyes. I pointed a shaking finger at Mr. Lee, my voice shaking with emotion. "You said you loved me! I thought you two would never... You said we were a team!"

Belina's pleas cut through my rage, her voice soft and desperate. "Max," she said, and the sound of my name on her lips was like a knife twisting in my heart. It reminded me of my mother, and the memory only made my anger burn brighter.

With tears streaming down my face, I looked her in the eyes and then turned away. I ran from the house, my feet pounding against the ground as I headed for the food forest.

I took off into the food forest, my legs pumping beneath me, a sense of weightlessness filling me with each step. But as I ran, a searing pain began to take hold of my chest. It felt like cold flames burning me from the inside out, and I knew it wouldn't be long before I had to stop.

I tripped over a tree root, tumbling head over heels until I hit the ground with a jarring thud. I rolled over, my vision blurred with tears, and looked up at the sky. The moon still hung there, a bright orb of white light mocking me with its placid glow.

"I refuse to be alone!" I screamed at the moon, my voice breaking with emotion. Tears streamed down my face, burning like hot oil as they made their way down my cheeks. The pain in my chest grew, a searing agony that made it hard to breathe.

Suddenly, I heard Belina's voice calling my name. I turned to see her running towards me, arms outstretched. She looked defeated, her face etched with lines of worry.

"Max, come back!" she shouted.

I shook my head, the pain in my chest making it hard to speak. "No!" I roared out, my voice barely recognizable.

Suddenly, a loud rumble filled the air. I turned to see a giant red snake slithering from behind me, its head large enough to swallow a bus. Its eyes glowed with a malevolent light, and I knew instantly that she was in danger.

Belina recoiled in terror, her face contorting with fear. "Those eyes," she whispered before collapsing in a heap on the ground.

I tried to run, but something was lodged in my throat. It felt like acid, burning its way through my flesh. I retched and vomited, my body convulsing with pain as flames and lava poured from my mouth. I watched in horror as my body began to levitate off the ground, the snake slithering around me in a sinister dance.

Everything began to fade to black once more, and I knew that I was lost.

I found myself back in that dark void, the only thing visible before me being the Lion and the snake locked in battle. The black Lion and the red snake were grappling with each other, each trying to devour the other. I watched as they tussled, their movements fluid and powerful, like two gods fighting over the fate of the world.

"I will not let you have them," the Lion growled, his voice a deep rumble that shook the air around us.

"One is already mine," the snake hissed, its eyes glowing with an otherworldly light.

The Lion stepped on the snake, crushing its body beneath his massive paw. But the snake wasn't finished yet, and it managed to bite the Lion's paw, causing the Lion to roar in pain.

This went on for what felt like hours, the two creatures locked in a deadly dance. But finally, I could take it no longer. I approached the giant beasts, my heart pounding with fear and anticipation.

"Are the two of you fighting over me?" I asked, my voice shaking with emotion.

They stopped their struggle and turned to look at me with their dominating eyes, each one a force to be reckoned with. I realized, in that moment, that they were both me. The Lion represented my best qualities, while the snake symbolized my darker side.

"I have destroyed things, and I have built things," I said, my voice ringing with conviction. "That was me. Both of you are me, and I am both of you. We must come together."

The snake didn't want to obey, but it had no choice. I was its master, and it had to do as I commanded. The Lion and the snake merged together, their forms becoming one. I watched in amazement as they coalesced into a single entity, a creature that was both dark and light, good and evil.

As I slowly opened my eyes, I found myself in the arms of Mr. Lee. He was crying, his tears a testament to the pain he had caused me. I looked into his eyes and said, "Mr. Lee, I forgive you." He looked at me, his face twisted with confusion, and then he let me go.

"Max, you're glowing," he said, his voice filled with wonder.

I walked out into the food forest, the fires still burning fiercely. But instead of feeling afraid, I felt a sense of calm wash over me. I began to walk towards the flames, my steps steady and sure. Mr. Lee grabbed my arm, trying to stop me, but I turned and told him it was okay.

As I walked into the middle of the forest, the flames parted before me as if in deference to my presence. I felt a great light welling up within me, and I began to float off the ground, my body weightless and free.

A bright light exploded from within me, a white blast that scattered around the world. The forest fires were extinguished, and the burning trees and plants were replaced by thriving greenery. Even the animals that had perished in the flames were restored to life, their forms stronger and more vibrant than before.

But as the light faded, I felt myself falling back to the ground. Everything went black.

When I opened my eyes again, I was in my bedroom. My mother and father were there, along with Belina and Mr. Lee. Mr. Lee looked like he had been crying, and my parents were smiling through their tears. My mother hugged me tightly, and it was the greatest hug in the world. My father embraced me next, holding me close as if he was afraid to let go.

"We love you," he said, his voice choked with emotion. "I thought that you were..." He trailed off, unable to continue, but his embrace only grew tighter.

After, we hugged and cried for some time. My mother and father left the room, and she said, "I'll give you all some time alone" Belina grabbed my hand and said, "There is something I have to tell you."

CHAPTER 14:

BELINA'S SONG PART 2

My voice quavered as I recounted my painful story to Max. "I just got done telling this to Lee. You see, after our terrible argument in college, I went to the clinic the next day. But something inside me was telling me, 'No!' It was terrifying because I knew I couldn't take care of a child," I said, my eyes filling with tears.

Despite my fears, I made the difficult decision not to go through with the abortion. I began taking classes online so that no one would know I was pregnant. I left her home and found a decent job, determined to make a life for myself and my child.

"But I knew deep down that I couldn't keep the baby," I continued, my voice filled with regret. "I couldn't give him the life he deserved. So I made the heartbreaking decision to give him up for adoption."

"It was a journey that would haunt me for years to come. I didn't want to hear the disappointment of my mother or the rest of my family. I knew they would judge me and call me names. You know, Max, that I regretted not telling my mother before her passing," Lee grabbed my hand. "But looking back, I know I made the right decision for my son."

"Something felt off, so I went to the doctor and said, "Doctor, I've been experiencing some strange symptoms during my pregnancy, and I'm not sure what's causing them. I've been feeling extremely fatigued, and it seems to be more severe than what I was expecting during my first trimester. I've also been gaining weight very quickly, even though I've been trying to maintain a healthy diet. My appetite has increased significantly, and I'm experiencing more intense cravings. I've been feeling nauseous and vomiting frequently, and it seems to be worse than the average morning sickness. I'm also feeling a lot of fetal movements, which is surprising since I'm only a few months along. I've also noticed that my belly is growing larger than I expected, and I have a noticeable 'baby bump' already."

The doctor explained that I could schedule an appointment to check on things but that there was probably nothing to worry about. "Just a large baby," he said.

But I knew there was something special about my baby. I could feel it. So I went back to the doctor and explained that I was having uterus pains. He told me it was normal, but I couldn't shake the feeling that something wasn't right.

As the months went by, my belly grew larger and larger. But when I finally had it checked out, the doctor confirmed that my baby was healthy. And that's when I knew that my instincts were right all along - my baby was no ordinary child.

I still knew deep down that I couldn't take care of the baby. As much as I wanted to, I wouldn't dare call Lee. So, I made the difficult decision to call my best friend Clarissa and her fiancé at the time, Herald. They had been trying for a year to have a child but hadn't been successful.

When I told Clarissa about my situation, she didn't hesitate for a moment. "I'll take your baby, Belina," she said without a second thought. "I've always wanted to be a mother, and I know I'll love him just as if he were my own."

And just like that, I knew that my son would be in good hands with Clarissa and Herald.

From the first day here, on FFFHAMS, I just knew we were connected somehow, but when Lionel pointed out how you looked exactly like my ancestor, I knew at that moment you were the child I had given up, and somehow you made your way back to me. For years I debated on calling my long-lost friend your mother; I thought to myself, "He is my son, after all, and he came to me looking for his family" until I was at the hospital worried about you and Krissy.

After finishing the story, the emotions ran high. Lee was filled with remorse and regret, tears streaming down his face as he apologized to his son. Max, confused and overwhelmed by the sudden turn of events, looked at us both with a mix of confusion and bewilderment.

But despite it all, Max knew that we were his true family. "Belina and Mr. Lee, I always knew," he said, his voice quivering with emotion. "I felt that you were both out there somewhere in this world. I couldn't prove it, but I knew the people to who I belonged were out there. And the fact that you are my parents and that God brought us together is a testament to our love and what I knew all along - I must keep us together at all cost."

We all embraced, our tears mingling together as we held each other close. And in that moment, I knew that no matter what challenges lay ahead, we would always be a family.

The next morning, I woke up feeling a sense of joy and purpose, knowing that Clarissa and Herald were staying with us on FFFHAMS. We sat together at the table, eating a scrumptious breakfast that we had foraged from outside. The plate was a rainbow of colors, filled with eggs, peppers, spinach, fish, and an array of fruits. We laughed and caught them up on everything that had happened. Tears were shed, and we shared a deep bond of love and support.

However, my thoughts turned to Kris, who was still asleep in the other room. I worried about her mother, who was not answering the phone. Suddenly, Herald's phone rang. He answered it and said, "What dog?" before excusing himself from the table. Clarissa and I began to pick up the dishes, hoping that everything was okay.

Today was a momentous day as we welcomed people from all around the world to FFFHAMS. People of different races, ages, religions, and nations came to learn our ways, to be free from the Matrix's grasp. I was not afraid, for we were antifragile, and we represented the future, the next step in human evolution. We had discovered how to return humanity back to its prime, back to its glory.

I stood up, feeling an immense sense of responsibility, and spoke to the crowd. "Fear not, children of God, for the children of man have never known a darker day. But the sun is bright for us, the children of God. We are the future, and together, we will overcome any obstacle. We will rise up and thrive, for we are one."

Max welcomed the newcomers, and they all gathered in front of the first food forest of FFFHAMS. Standing in front of them, Max began to speak, his voice strong and clear, "First, always remember that you do not need me. I am not your messiah; I am not your savior. Only God knows the future. I am just a man on a mission. If you are here, it's because the universe and your ancestors want me to give you this message. There is a place for you - a living, breathing meditation. A place where prayer meets the day, where the gods live with man. Here, you will not kneel, for we know not of a place where it is necessary to be on your knees. You will have a relationship with humans, animals, and trees. You will see the face of God in your water, and you will be free."

Max paused, looking over the crowd, before continuing, "I could give you this place, but you don't need me. There is a map to this place in your anatomy. Learn from us, and spread this message.

Remember, I am because we are." The crowd responded with a resounding, "We are because I am!"

Lionel stepped forward and took the group on a tour, reminding them to leave all plastics, outside of their clothes, and phones outside. No plastics were permitted on FFFHAMS.

As Lionel led the group, Max walked into the food forest that had burned down. He spoke, "Eclipse!" and a giant serpent with the body of a snake, covered in plates and fur, with the face of a lion, came down from the trees. Max hugged the serpent, saying, "I think they're ready for us."

EPILOGUE

Back on the beach on the Jersey shore

God is on a beach. He is looking around; what is he looking for? He continues to look around until he finally sees you…

To you, who are reading this for the first time, I speak to you through one of many possible realities. You, who are meant to hear this, whether reading or listening, do not make wishes you do not dare to climb toward. Do not be founded in the darkness of man's thoughts. Instead, be here with me, in the truest forest within the hearts and minds of the soul. You know who I am, just as well as you know the sky and the Earth. You are here for a reason. You are here because what must be done. The selected few to spread the genes and cultures, for the way of man has never stood the test of time, but the way of God is time itself. Humanity is in grave danger, and you must act.

You must return to the garden, to the bounty of God. Many will not listen, and many will perish. But many will listen, and many will thrive. This is the way of creation, and the choice is yours. Go now and restore humanity and Earth back to its former glory.

God looks toward the beach and sees four naked people walking out of the water. Each step they take, they take toward God. They finally walk out of the water, and there are two females and two males. One of them says, "Where are Max and Sam?"

THE BACK MATTER

You made it to the end of this part of the story, which means now, with the knowledge you have, like me, you have a responsibility to act on that knowledge. We all do. https://www.thephilosophyoforder.com is where you will find people like us dedicated to creating FFFHAMS and making this a reality for future generations. We have already started, and we have a discord for all those who need help getting started or just need a group to team up with. For more information, go to my youtube channel, God Told Me, and subscribe to the TikTok profile, the philosophy of order, and the Instagram, the philosophy of order. Make sure you follow.

To help FFFHAMS spread worldwide through donations, purchase the audiobook on audible using a free trial and maintain your membership for over two months. This will cause audible to pay us a commission. These help much more than most know, and I can guarantee this donation goes to spreading FFFHAMS as far and wide as possible. Remember, you don't have to follow me on social media or donate a dime; you have the power to do all of this on your own.

ACKNOWLEDGMENTS

First, I must acknowledge my wife, who helped me edit this. Instead of paying $15,000 to hire editors. I utilized AI programs like Grammarly as my proofreader, developmental editor, etc., helping with my rough draft. I believe this will help writers who, like myself, didn't have a publisher or the money for editing. I would write the rough draft, allow these programs to be my editors, rewrite it again, and then present it to my wife, who would read over it to ensure it was coherent. She had a good eye for identifying flaws. She will probably find even more after the initial release.

She has been more than supportive of my mission, and because she places so much faith in me, I am truly able to rise to heights most men could not. I want to also acknowledge my children, who inspire me to do what I need to do now, so I may do what I want to do later. Next, I must acknowledge my mother and father. My mother told me since I was a small boy to write stories and follow what God has told me. Only when I truly began to listen to these words did my life change for the best. My father always encouraged my intellectual habits of questioning everything. Because of him, I remained strong through my college years of uncertainty. I must also thank my grandmother. It is in her home I wrote this book, and she has allowed us to be in her home that was previously empty while we build up the finances needed to build FFFHAMS and write this book. Finally, I thank God for everything and my Higher Self for guidance. Thank you to my ancestors for remaining by my side.

Shoutouts: The following people provided me with the information to remember my mission, which is the core information in this book.

Malcolm X
Marcus Garvey
Elijah Muhammad
Fred Hampton
Dr. Flint
Dr. Muzerawa
Dr. Kwame
Dr. Leaman
William Lane Craig
Nassim Taleb
Christopher Ryan
Michaeleen Doucleff
Daniel Quinn
Alan Watts
Aseer The Duke of Tiers

Made in the USA
Las Vegas, NV
09 December 2023

82450222R00164